F 1619 .T83 1988

Tyler, S. Lyman 1920-

Two worlds : the Indian
encounter with the European

DATE DUE

DEC 1 0 1992		
DEC 1 0 1992		

DEMCO 38-297

SO-BAQ-580

Two Worlds

TWO WORLDS

The Indian Encounter with the European

1492–1509

S. Lyman Tyler

University of Utah Press
Salt Lake City
1988

18017878

12-89

Selections from pages 34–60 and pages 86–159 from
HISTORY OF THE INDIES by Bartolome de las Casas.
Translated and edited by Andree Collard
Copyright © 1971 by Andree Collard
Reprinted by permission of Harper & Row, Publishers, Inc.

Library of Congress Cataloging-in-Publication Data

Tyler, S. Lyman (Samuel Lyman), 1920–
    Two worlds : the Indian encounter with the European,
1492–1509 / by S. Lyman Tyler.
        p.   cm.
    Bibliography: p.
    Includes index.
    ISBN 0-87480-297-0
    1. Indians of the West Indies—First contact with Occidental
civilization. 2. Indians of the West Indies—Public opinion—History.
3. Public opinion—Europe—History. 4. West Indies—History—
16th century.   I. Title.
F1619.T83 1988
972.9'00497—dc 19   88-15054
                                                      CIP

To
Bessie

Contents

Preface

I am grateful to the William H. Donner Foundation of New York and to the National Endowment for the Humanities for supporting background research and translation by personnel of the American West Center in conjunction with Indian studies programs.

At the University of Utah, my colleagues in the American West Center and the history department have assisted in many ways, as have deans and vice-presidents. Reference and administrative personnel in research libraries and museums in the United States, elsewhere in the Americas, and in Europe provide indispensable help with all research for books on the history of the Indians of the Americas. I appreciate their assistance.

Two Worlds

Introduction

October 12, 1992, will mark the five hundredth anniversary of the meeting of a group of Arawak-speaking people (the Indian world) and the Christopher Columbus party (the European world) on an island in the Bahamas. The international observance of this quincentenary will take various forms. As my contribution, I have described the earliest contacts, on the basis of firsthand observations, as recorded by the participants themselves. There is admittedly still controversy concerning the exact route taken by Columbus through the islands of the Caribbean, but I will not contribute to the dispute here. Instead, I will report arrivals, observations, and departures as noted by early observers. The bulk of this volume will thus present texts from the period, carefully selected and arranged to portray the Indians as the Europeans themselves came to see them. My account will proceed chronologically, following the spread of European contact. This approach gives the reader a dynamic view of the inhabitants of the Indian world and the changes they underwent as a result of European contact during the seventeen-year period from 1492 to 1509.

My major purpose, then, is to view the Indian through the eyes of contemporary observers, so that the Indian appears as he was seen at particular times and in particular places. Second, I hope to enable the reader to visualize the Spaniard as he was portrayed by contemporaries in the Caribbean islands, so that the reader can understand the observer and can place his description of the Indian in the proper perspective.

I am also interested in the role of the Spanish sovereigns, particularly of Queen Isabela, who continually reminded her administrative officers of her concern for her Indian vassals. Isabela left a codicil to her will at the time of her death in 1504, which I include as an appendix, entreating her husband, King Ferdinand, and instructing her heirs and future rulers to ensure that the Indians were treated well. In this way, she took responsibility for the incipient Indian programs and policies, sometimes benevolent, with respect to the orders and laws issued by the sovereigns, sometimes cruel, as these laws were interpreted and applied by local administrators.

CAST OF CHARACTERS

The primary figure in this saga of discovery and encounter is, of course, Christopher Columbus himself. He will be referred to as Columbus or the Admiral. His younger brothers and sons are also notable personages. The elder of his younger brothers, Bartolomé Columbus, will be called Don Bartolomé or the Adelantado, a title granted by the Crown to one who governed a frontier area or a recently conquered province. The younger brother, Diego Columbus, will be referred to as Don Diego. Christopher Columbus's two sons were named Diego and Ferdinand. Diego, the first son, inherited some of his father's titles including that of admiral. Accordingly, he is sometimes known as the Second Admiral. He also became governor of Española in 1509. I will be careful to differentiate Diego the son from Diego the brother. Ferdinand, the second son, accompanied his father on the fourth and last voyage of discovery, from 1502 to 1504, and kept a personal record of it. He later collected books and manuscripts of the period and established an important library. His own book, *The Life of the Admiral Christopher Columbus*, is an essential source on the great explorer.[1]

Outside the Columbus family, the most important character is Fray Bartolomé de las Casas. His lengthy contact with the Indians, his lifelong interest in their affairs, and his many significant writings on the period make him a witness of great value. I will always call him Las Casas or Fray Bartolomé, if I do not use his full name, to distinguish him from Bartolomé Columbus.

Three Indians are particularly notable: Guacanagarí, a young *cacique*, or native ruler, who befriended Columbus at the time of the loss of his flagship *Santa María*; the lady Anacaona, the *cacica* who befriended the Spaniards; and especially Diego Colón, an Indian captured by Columbus to serve as an interpreter; he was taken to Spain after the first voyage and returned to the Indies on the second voyage, where he became a great asset to the Admiral in his subsequent contacts with Indian leaders.

Numerous other personages, both native and European, crossed the stage of history during this seventeen-year period. Since their names and identities pose no special difficulties, I will introduce them individually as they appear on the scene.

GEOGRAPHY AND NOMENCLATURE

Five hundred years ago, political entities in both the Old World and the New of course had names and identities different from those we know today. Even Spain itself was not as we know it. Ferdinand ruled the kingdom of Aragón, and Isabela, the kingdom of Castile. Spain was approaching unity as a result of the marriage of the two sovereigns, but Castile and Aragón were not technically unified. For the sake of clarity, however, I will call these kingdoms Spain and their people Spaniards. The terms "the Crown," "the Sovereigns," "the Catholic Kings," and "Their Majesties" designate Ferdinand and Isabela as joint rulers.

In the Caribbean, I will generally call the islands visited by Columbus and others by the names in common use during the period, Spanish and/or Indian. Throughout this book I will call the large island of Hispaniola, presently Haiti and the Dominican Republic, by its Spanish name, Española, which I have preferred to the Latin, since, once again, it is the appellation that the discoverers themselves used. Following European practices, Indian leaders or rulers were called kings and queens, and their territories, kingdoms. The native Arawaks used the term *cacique* to identify their leaders, and the territory under the cacique's leadership was called a *cacicazgo*. The Spaniards adopted these terms and carried them to regions beyond the Caribbean.

BASIC SOURCES

Columbus's own journal is, of course, a fundamental source for the period. Since the original has been lost, the abstract made by Fray Bartolomé de las Casas is a primary document for modern research. The titles given to this abstract are *Diario de Colón*, or *Journal of Columbus*, and *El Diario de a Bordo*, or *The Journal from Aboard Ship*. This Las Casas abstract was first made available in print in the first volume of Martín Fernández de Navarrete's *Collection of Voyages and Discoveries that the Spaniards made by Sea since the end of the Fifteenth Century, etc., in the Indies*, which was complete in five volumes and was published in Madrid from 1825 to 1837.[2]

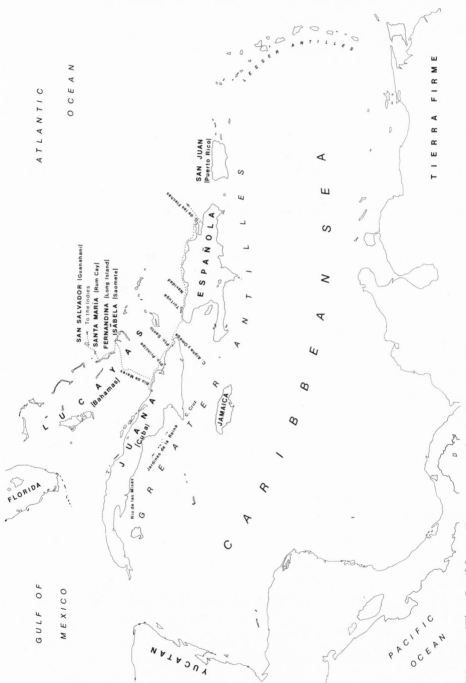

Map 1. The Caribbean Entrance to the Indian World.

Draftsperson: Winston P. Erickson

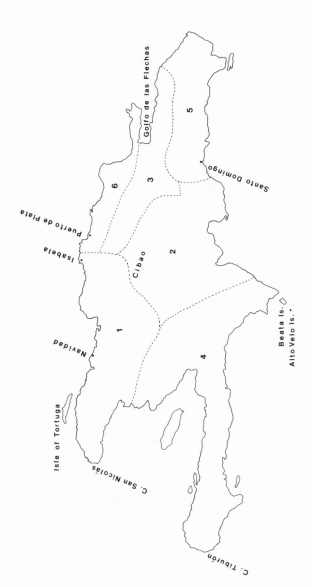

ESPAÑOLA

1. Marien: Cacique Guacanagarí
2. Maguana: Cacique Caonabó
3. Magua: Cacique Guarionex
4. Xaragua: Cacique Behechio
5. Higuey: Cacique Cotubanamá
6. Ciguayo: Cacique Mayobanex

Draftsperson: Winston P. Erickson

Map 2. Caciques and Cacicazgos on Española.

The first English translation was made by Samuel Kettell "from a manuscript recently discovered in Spain." I have used as authorities for the voyages of Columbus the following: Samuel Eliot Morison, ed., *Journals and Other Documents on the Life and Voyages of Christopher Columbus*; *The Journal of Christopher Columbus*; and the two-volume *Diario de Colón*, which includes a facsmile of the abstract in the hand of Fray Bartolomé de las Casas and a line-by-line printing of the facsimile, with a critical introduction by Carlos Sanz.[3] Morison calls Sanz's edition the best text but notes that it was completed too late for Morison's own use.[4] I have made my own translation, based on the Sanz text, beginning with the journal entry for Thursday, October 11, 1492, and ending with Wednesday, October 24. This portion includes the words of Columbus from October 12 through October 24. There is little difference between my translation and that of Morison. The last of the basic sources included here is *The Life of the Admiral Christopher Columbus by His Son Ferdinand.*[5]

A NOTE ON THE TRANSLATION

There are certain inherent difficulties in preparing English translations of contemporary Spanish writers for the period 1492–1509. I have tried to make the translations as readable and as easily understood as possible, considering the stylistic complexity of the original material. I have tended to be formal and even old-fashioned at times in the choice of wording, in order to retain the flavor of the original text and period, but in the interest of continuity and completeness of thought, I have sometimes preferred shorter sentences to long, involved ones, and I have altered the rhetoric and have supplied words to clarify the text when its meaning was implicit or incompletely expressed. Some words or expressions that do not have appropriate equivalents in English and are therefore not easily translatable have been left in the original Spanish or Arawak. In these cases, I have placed translations and/or explanations in the text or in a note at the first appearance of the expression. Parentheses and square brackets in the original sources indicate that material was added at different times; square brackets with initials identify my editorial additions.

I thank Charles W. Wonder for the original translation of material from Spanish to English. He holds an M.A. in languages from the University of Utah, 1936, and was language officer, U.S. Navy, World War II; chief, Division of Language Services, U.S. Department of State, 1951–1956; administrative officer, U.S. Foreign Service, 1957–1963; and, after retirement, an administrator in various capacities, and translator for the American West Center at the University of Utah. Ted J. Warner, professor of history at Brigham Young University, graciously reviewed part of the material translated from Fray Bartolomé's *History of the Indies*.

1

Two Worlds

Scholars believe that thousands of years have passed since modern man reached all parts of Europe, Africa, and Asia and moved with game animals from northeast Asia across the Bering land bridge, Beringia, to North America. The oldest traditions of indigenous Americans have not preserved an account of this journey in recognizable form. The aboriginal commentator might say, "This was so long ago that time runneth out."

Men and animals probably continued to leave northeastern Asia as long as the Bering land bridge remained open. It may have been, at times, more than a thousand miles wide, and these hunters may not even have known that they were passing from one continent to another.

There came a time, according to the theory, when the glaciers melted, the waters of the Bering and Chukchi seas rose, water covered Beringia, and the Bering Strait became, in the finite minds of human beings, a permanent reality. Thus two separate worlds emerged, and the indigenous Americans would live in isolation from the inhabitants of Europe, Africa, and Asia for such a long time that the peoples of one world would develop separately from those of the other.

There is evidence that, at intervals probably involving hundreds of years, vessels capable of surviving long periods at sea may have reached the Americas. Whatever the intervals, we believe that peoples in the Americas or Europe-Africa-Asia had no ongoing awareness that human or animal life existed in that "other world" until after the Columbian discoveries began in 1492.

Moreover, the numbers involved in these infrequent contacts are generally agreed to have been so few that additions to the indigenous American population by approaches other than the Bering route would likely have amounted to no more than a trickle; thus the American Indian physical type is relatively uniform.

THE DISCOVERY OF LIFE IN OTHER WORLDS

On March 1, 1961, a group of eminent scientists met to discuss the possible results of the discovery of life in other worlds, specifically in outer space.

Samuel Bronfman set the stage for the discussion by observing, "The age of exploration that flowered half a millennium ago . . . has its counterpart today as we emerge into a new age that promises to overshadow anything heretofore accomplished in man's long and venturesome existence."

A physical chemist, a social psychologist, an astronomer, and a radio astronomer subsequently presented their views, which Arnold J. Toynbee, a historian, afterward summarized, observing that they had agreed on two important things: first, "that it is improbable that in our solar system there is life on any other planet that is comparable to life on this planet," and second, "that it is very probable that there is life comparable, or more than comparable, to life on this planet on planets attached to other solar systems."

Toynbee then suggested that it is probably "rather fortunate for us" that "those other living beings are safely parked in other solar systems" where "they cannot arrive bodily on this planet of ours." Returning to Bronfman's original observation, he asked the panelists to consider whether we had not already experienced something similar to the discovery of intelligent life on another planet. "Think of life in another world which was suddenly and abruptly and disastrously discovered by the pre-Columbian inhabitants of the Americas when the Old World burst upon them. Think of the disastrous effect on their life of that impact, how they were conquered, massacred, raided, robbed—their whole life was broken up. It is fortunate that there is no intelligent life, as far as we can guess, within near enough range of this planet to do that to us."[1]

The Dominican Fray Francisco de Vitoria reflected these concerns in a discussion during the 1530s of the "aborigines of the New World, commonly called Indians, who came forty years ago into the power of the Spaniards, not having been previously known to our world." "For, at first sight," Vitoria said, "when we see that the whole of the business has been carried on by men who are alike well-informed and upright, we may believe that everything has been done properly and justly. But then, when we hear of so many massacres, so many plunderings of otherwise innocent men, so many princes evicted from their possessions and stripped of their rule, there is certainly ground for doubting whether this is rightly or wrongly done."[2]

In this volume I will attempt to present the native peoples of the Bahamas and the Caribbean islands, the first encountered in the Indian world, as they were observed during the years of the Columbian discoveries, from 1492 to 1509. I will seek to show how the invasion of their territory by Spanish representatives of the European world affected their personal lives and their way of life.

FRAY BARTOLOME DE LAS CASAS

As noted in the Introduction, Christopher Columbus kept a daily journal during his first voyage to the Americas. Fray Bartolomé de las Casas made an abstract from a copy of that original journal, and subsequently, both the journal itself and the copy from which Las Casas worked disappeared. Where modern scholarship is concerned, then, the Las Casas abstract most closely approximates the original account that Columbus made of his first voyage. Fray Bartolomé is, by the same token, a vital witness for the period through his contribution to the preservation of the Columbian record and also through his numerous personal writings.

Fray Bartolomé's involvement in this era of discovery dates from the very beginning. As a youth of eighteen years, he saw Columbus and his Indians on the streets of Seville after they had returned from the first voyage. He saw his father and uncle depart with Columbus on the second voyage, and he entered the Indian world himself in 1502 when he went to Española with Governor Nicolás de Ovando. His direct personal experience with the New World thus began only a decade after the discovery, when many of the participants, both Indian and Spanish, were still alive. Fray Bartolomé continued to be involved with Indian affairs for the remainder of his long life. He had access to members of the Columbus family and their papers, and he knew personally and used as informants Indians who served as interpreters and were otherwise employed by the Columbus retinue from the beginning. His magnum opus was the *History of the Indies*, based on these contacts, on related documentation, and on his personal experiences in the Caribbean.[3]

Unfortunately, Fray Bartolomé has not always received the respect he is now accorded. One part of his experience with the Indian world took the form of his *Brevissima relación de la destrucción de las Indias*. This work was completed in manuscript in 1542. It was transmitted to some and was seen in manuscript by others. It was published in Seville in 1552 and was later translated and distributed widely. Even in the early period, some scholars believed there was no question that Spaniards had indeed brought about the destruction of the Indian world as Fray Bartolomé had charged in his *Relación*. Others, however, doubted his account, and still others believed that the numbers he used were exaggerated. The writings of Fray Bartolomé de las Casas were thus considered undependable for some four hundred years.

More recently, however, and particularly in publications that have appeared since 1966, in commemoration of the four hundredth anniversary of his death, scholars are recognizing the extent to which we depend on Fray Bartolomé for a record of the Spanish invasion of the Indian world, in the period from 1492 to 1520.[4] Population studies of the last quarter century suggest that even his numbers may be more correct than has been generally assumed. Of particular interest in the present context is the conclusion of Sherburne F. Cook and Woodrow Borah, "The Aboriginal Population of Hispaniola," in *Essays in Population History* (Berkeley: 1971, 1:376–410), that Fray Bartolomé may have been conservative in his population estimates for Española. Whereas his estimate was 2 million to 3 million Indians, the Cook and Borah estimate is 7 million or 8 million. Another commentator, Juan Pérez de Tudela Bueso, in his "Estudio Critico Preliminar," which prefaces the Las Casas *Historia*, refers to Fray Bartolomé as "a man of considerable knowledge" and one having "great mental capacities."[5] Tudela supports particular statements made by Las Casas, saying, in effect, that "because of his temperament, habit, and religious dignity, he is incapable of uttering a falsehood."[6]

In addition, one must remember that the conclusions reached by Fray Bartolomé had many years to season before they were finalized. He was writing, gathering additional material, and rewriting his *Historia de las Indias* and *Apologética historia* for some thirty-five years, or from about 1527 to 1562.[7] He made his last revisions when he was between eighty-five and ninety years of age, prior to his death in 1566 at the age of ninety-two. After years of contemplation, he made the final decisions concerning the presentation of his life work as he waited to meet his God. The venerable Fray Bartolomé was a religious man at a time when religion was taken very seriously. In this book I contend that he sincerely tried to present the cause of the Indian accurately as he understood it.

In sum, despite earlier doubts about some of his writings, Fray Bartolomé emerges as a perspicacious observer and as a man of his own time. As such, he offers us a window on both the Spanish and Indian worlds. Tudela concludes that Fray Bartolomé's *Historia* is "the fundamental source of information concerning the beginning of Spanish colonization"[8] and, further, that (in summation) "the Las Casas episode is one of the most necessary things to know about in understanding the history of the Spanish spirit."[9]

FRAY BARTOLOME'S HISTORIA

As we have seen, Fray Bartolomé had a long and active interest in the Indians. His father, Pedro, returned to Seville from the Americas in 1498 and brought with him a young Taino Indian. This Indian was retained in the Las Casas household for about two years, until the Sovereigns ordered such Indians freed and sent back to Española. In February 1502, both father and son embarked in the fleet commanded by Fray Nicolás de Ovando, the third administrator sent to govern Española. Bartolomé de las Casas went to the Indies as Fray Bartolomé, for he had received the religious order authorizing him to serve as a Doctrinero, the title given to the official who was later responsible for the *Doctrina*, or Indian parish.

For more than sixty years, Fray Bartolomé was closely associated with matters affecting the Indians. He received a *repartimiento* on Española, which gave him land and the right to use Indian labor. He later participated in the conquest of Cuba as chaplain to Pánfilo de Narváez. He crossed the ocean many times on behalf of the Indians and spent the last years of his life in Spain, representing Indian interests before the Crown and the Council of the Indies. In 1516, he was appointed "Protector of the Indians" and was later unofficially designated the "Apostle of the Indians" as a result of his tireless efforts on their behalf. Fray Bartolomé's reasons for writing concerning the Indians and the Indies are set forth at length in the prologue to his *Historia de las Indias*.

HISTORIA DE LAS INDIAS, *PROLOGUE*

I am moved to write this book only by the very great and extreme need in all the Spanish kingdoms for trustworthy information and enlightenment about this Indian world, information which I have observed to be lacking throughout Spain for many years.

In the absence of such information, how much damage, how many calamities, disruptions, and devastations of kingdoms have there been? How many souls have perished in the Indies over the years, and how unjustly? How many unforgivable sins have been committed? How much blindness and torpidity of conscience has there been? How much deplorable harm has been caused and is now being caused to the kingdoms of Castile by all that I have referred to? I am very certain that these things may never be enumerated, pondered, judged, or lamented as they should be, until the final and dreadful day of righteous, rigorous, and divine judgment.

I see that some have written about things in the Indies. . . . instead of ploughing the field of serious subjects with the plough of Christian discretion and prudence, they planted the dry, wild, and fruitless seed of their human and temporal sentiment. Therefore a fatal discord of scandalous and erroneous knowledge and perverse conscience has developed and grown among very many people to such an extent that for this reason the Catholic faith itself, the ancient Christian customs of the Universal Church, and the greater part of the human race have suffered irreparable harm.

The cause of these troubles lies in the ignorance of the principal purpose of Divine Providence in the discovery of these people and lands. This purpose is simply that, as we are mortals, all temporal concerns must be subordinated, ordered, and directed to the conversion and salvation of these souls. It also lies in the ignorance of the dignity of a rational being [the Indian/SLT], who has been so unprotected and destitute of divine care that he is no more singularly respected than the entire community of other inferior creatures.

It has hardly been possible that so many or countless kinds of men in extensive regions would act contrary to the ways of nature, that is to say, with a lack of understanding and ability to govern their lives. For nature works always, or nearly always, and for the most part, for the most and best and for perfection, in all kinds of inferior things that are created, hardly ever or rarely failing in this respect.

Moreover, as will be seen throughout this history, it is evident that the Indians have much better judgment and maintain much better public order and government than many other nations which are overwhelmingly proud of themselves and which hold Indians in contempt.

They have ignored another necessary and Catholic principle, that is, that there is not, nor has there ever been, a generation, race, town, or language group in all mankind (according to Holy Scripture, Saint Dionysius in Chapter 9 of "De caeleste hierarchia", and Saint Augustine in Epistle 99 of Evodius) from which, especially after the Incarnation and Passion of the Redeemed, it may be impossible to come upon and assemble that great multitude which no one can enumerate and which Saint John saw (Chapter 7 of the Apocalypse), that multitude which is the number of predestined that Saint Paul calls by another name—Mystical Body of Jesus Christ and the Church, or Perfect Man.

Consequently, the Divine Providence must have also naturally predestined these people, making them fit for the doctrine and the divine grace, and getting them ready for the time of their calling and conversion, as it has done, and as we believe it will do to all the other peoples who may have been outside the Holy Church during the course of the first advent. . . .

It has also been a mistake to lack knowledge of ancient histories, not only divine and ecclesiastical, but also many secular histories, because if people were to read them they would know that there has been no generation or people in the past, either before or after the Flood, who, however governed and discreet they may be, did not at their beginning have many wild faults and irrationalities, living without public order and abounding in very serious and unnatural crimes that follow as a consequence of idolatry. Many others, who are now very well governed and Christian, lived without houses, without cities, and like savage animals before they were converted to the faith.

And since uncultivated land produces only thistles and thorns, but is capable of producing domestic, useful, and necessary fruit by being cultivated, in the same way and manner, all the men of the world, however barbarian and brutal they may be, may acquire the use of reason and of things they are capable of learning about.

And thus, through instruction and doctrine, it is consequential and necessary that there may not be any people in the world, however barbarian and inhuman they are, nor may there be found any nation, which by being taught and indoctrinated in a way befitting the natural condition of men, especially through the doctrine of faith, may not yield very productive men. . . .

Thus it appears that, although the men were all uncivilized at the beginning, and like uncultivated land, were fierce and wild, because of the natural discretion and ability that is innate in their souls as God created them to be rational, if they are converted and persuaded by reason, love and good work, which is the proper method by which rational beings are to be moved and attracted to the exercise of virtue, there is no nation, nor can there be, however barbarian, fierce, and depraved in customs, that cannot be attracted and converted: to complete political morality; to the humanity of men who are gentle, politically moral and rational; and especially to the Catholic faith and Christian religion. It is certain that evangelical doctrine has much greater efficacy to convert souls than any human labor and procedure, as it is a gift conceded from above.

As an example of what has been said, we could point out many nations, but it will suffice to single out the nation of Spain. Well known to those who are conversant with our histories and other histories is the barbarian simpleness and fierceness of the Spanish people, especially those of Andalusia and certain other provinces of Spain, as things were when the first Greeks came to settle in Monviedro, and when Alceus, a captain of pirates, and the Phoenicians, came to settle in Cádiz. They were all very astute people, in comparison with whom the natives were like animals. Consider the stupidity and simpleness of the Andalusians! Who could deceive them? Also, by the grace of God, in matters of faith, what nation could be ahead of Spain?

It should be much easier for those who are mostly ruled and governed by reason in many matters concerning social life and human communication, to be induced and persuaded to develop the true and perfect virtues that make up the Christian religion. For the Christian religion is the only religion that purifies and cleans all of the impurities and barbarity from the uncivilized nations. This applies in large part to all of these our Indies.

Lack of knowledge about things and people and their ancient customs has caused many to be astonished and to regard it as very new and irregular to discover those Indian people who for so many centuries have been allowed to walk in the wrongful ways of human corruption, like all other people of the universal world, as Saint Paul and Saint Barnabas said in the book Acts of the

Apostles, Chapter 14: "Who in times past suffered all nations to walk in their own ways." Those who are ignorant are astonished, I say, to sometimes find many natural and moral defects, as though we were all very perfect naturally and very holy in matters of spirit and Christianity.

Secondly, with regard to those who are surprised to see persons who are imperfect and not so readily perfect as desired, if they are not ignorant, it might occur to them the very great difficulties that all people had in their conversions: labors, sweat, anguish, contradictions, incredible persecutions, schisms, and controversies. Even among the Christians themselves, the Apostles and disciples of Christ suffered in preaching and promulgating the Gospel, and in bringing people to the Christian religion at all times and in all places. So did all true preachers, because God wished and ordered it so. Clear evidence of all this is given by the irrationality and vices throughout Spain, and the difficulty in converting, for Saint James converted or won no more than seven or nine in all of Spain for the militia of Jesus Christ.

As we have said, because of this lack of knowledge of the things noted above, it will be evident to anyone who wishes to look into it, that great and incomparably harmful errors about the natural inhabitants of this world have been written in many and diverse articles by both learned and unlearned men. Among them, some have made the spiritual object of this entire matter reversed and have inverted it by making it the means; and the means which is made up of temporal and profane things that even according to the gentile philosophers must always be subordinated to virtue, is established as the principal object of this Christian exercise.

The philosopher Aristotle deploring this in Book 6 of his "Ethics", says it is a very bad mistake because it is opposed to the optimum and the excellent, which nature and reason establish as the object in all things. He says, *"Ideo error circa finem est pessimus"*. From this very bad inversion or reversing, it has soon and necessarily followed that all these nations have been viewed with contempt, and the people have been considered as animals incapable of doctrine and virtue. They have been considered only to the extent that they have been of use to the Spaniards, just like bread and wine and similar things that are useful to men only when they are consumed.

Greatly contributing to this contempt and annihilation has been the fact that all of these people [the Indians/SLT] are *toto genere* by nature very gentle, modest, poor, defenseless or without arms, simple, and above all, long-suffering and patient. For these reasons, our Spaniards have taken, and are still taking today, the full opportunity to deal with them in any way they wish, and to treat them all in the same way, without regard to sex, age, status, or dignity. This will be evident in this history. Hence, it has become the practice to have no scruples or fear of depriving and divesting the native kings and lords of their dominions, status, and importance. God, nature, and the common right of man made them lords and kings, confirmed and authorized by divine law.

In ignoring the rules and provisions of natural, divine, and human law, one must consider the three different kinds of infidels: those who unjustly usurp our kingdoms and lands; others who harass, molest, and oppose us, not only disquieting us and trying to disturb and destroy the temporal state of our republic, but also our spiritual state, trying as a main objective to ruin and pull down as much as possible our holy faith, Christian religion, and the entire Catholic church; and others [the Indians/SLT] who never usurped us, never have been obligated to us, never disturbed or offended us, never knew about our Christian religion, never knew of its existence or of our existence in the world, and who live in their own native lands [the Indies/SLT] in kingdoms that are very different from ours.

Wherever and whenever infidels such as these appear or are found in the entire universe, regardless of how many and whatever serious and very serious sins of idolatry and of any other nefarious practice that they might have, we can only do the loving, peaceful, and Christian things that we owe to them, charitably, as we ourselves would wish to be attracted, that is, bring or attract them to the holy faith by sweetness and by gentle, humble, and evangelical preaching in the form established and ordered by Christ, Our Lord and Master, for His Church. All the Indians of these our Indies belong to this third kind of infidels.

To this end, and to no other, the Apostolic See, being lawfully able to act by the authority of Christ, established the kings of Castile and Leon as sovereign and universal princes of all this vast Indian world. The native kings and lords were to remain in their own immediate dominions, each one in his own kingdom and land and with the same subjects he had before. The kings and lords were to recognize the most serene Lord Kings of Castile and Leon as superior kings and universal princes, because this was advisable and necessary for the purpose of dissemination, extension, and preservation of faith and Christian religion throughout the Indies. Recognition was not to be with or by any other title.

With regard to this universal domain, many have fallen into another pernicious and grievous error, one that is inexpiably harmful, by expressing the opinion and insensibly believing that it is impossible for the said universal domain to be compatible with the immediate domains of the native lords of the Indians. We have clearly demonstrated this in a special treatise on the subject which we wrote through divine grace.[10]

Having thought, therefore, and having many times considered the defects and errors that are expressed above, and the inexcusable and harmful difficulties that have followed as a consequence and continue each day, and because law, according to what the jurists say, is born and has its origin in the true reporting of facts, I decided to apply myself to writing about the most important things, and also public and famous occurrences, not only past occurrences, but very many that continue to occur. Some of these things I have seen happen with my own eyes within a period of more than sixty years, having been present in various places, kingdoms, provinces and lands of the Indies.

Just as one cannot deny that the sun is bright when there are no clouds in the sky at midday, in the same way no one can reasonably refuse to concede that the calamities occurring now in 1552 are the same as those that occurred in the past. And if I refer to some occurrences that I did not see with my own eyes, or that I saw and do not remember very well, or that I heard about in various ways, I shall always conjecture on the basis of the very long experience that I have had with all the other occurrences that I have known about, in arriving at what seems to me to come closest to the truth. I was inspired to assume this responsibility and to undertake this rather sizable work, along with my many other occupations, for the motives that follow. The first and principal motive is for the honor and glory of God, for the manifestation of His profound and inscrutable judgments, for the execution of His very upright and infallible divine justice, and for the good of His Universal Church.

The second motive is for the common, spiritual, and temporal benefit that may result for all these numerous people, if by chance they are not annihilated first, and before this complete history is written.

The third motive is not to satisfy, or to please, or to flatter kings, but rather to defend the royal honor and fame of the renowned rulers of Castile, because otherwise, people who come to know about the irreparable harm and damage that has occurred in these vast regions, provinces, and kingdoms, and who know how and why these things happened and about other occasions, might not know what the Catholic rulers, past and present, always commanded to be provided, what they provided, and what they strove for, and also people might believe or suspect or consider that these things must have occurred due to a lack of royal concern or justice in the kingdoms.

The fourth motive is for the good and benefit of all Spain, because if Spain knows what is good and bad in the Indies, I believe that Spain will know what is good and bad in all of Spain.

The fifth motive is to afford clarity and certainty to the readers about many things in the beginning when this world stage was discovered, the knowledge of which will probably be much appreciated by those who read about it. I offer complete assurance that I am the only living man who can refer in such detail to these things as they happened. There are also many other things that few have written about. Or, they may have written about them without the sincere fidelity they should observe, perhaps because they did not comprehend those things, or because they did not see them, or because they were too imprudent, or because they received their information from people who were corrupt; and therefore, many intolerable defects may be found today in their writings.

The sixth motive is to liberate my Spanish nation from the very serious and pernicious error and deceit in which it is now living, and has lived until now, considering these oceanic peoples not to be human beings, considering them to be brute beasts incapable of virtue and doctrine, corrupting the good in them and increasing the bad in them that has resulted from their having been uncivilized and neglected for so many centuries. And to give them a hand in some way, so that they will not always continue to be abased as they are and thrown down into the abyss.

The seventh motive is to temper the arrogance and excessive vainglory of many, and to expose the injustice of more than a few, who glory in vicious deeds and detestable corruption as if they would be able to herd like animals, heroic men of very illustrious deeds. This is so that, for the benefit of those in the future, the bad may be recognized and distinguished from the good, and great sins and highly abominable vices may be recognized and distinguished from virtues. No one should be surprised at or attribute to harshness or folly the fact that I may rebuke and detest mistakes of the Spaniards, because, according to what Polybius says in his "History of the Romans", Book I: "He who becomes a historian must sometimes exalt enemies with high praise, if this is merited by the excellence of what they did; and other times he must severely upbraid or rebuke friends when their errors deserve to be condemned and rebuked."

The eighth and last motive is to show, by a different road than others have taken, the grandeur and great number of admirable and prodigious things that have been accomplished, and that we believe were never accomplished in centuries now forgotten. Everything, however, is directed to the end that: through knowledge of virtuous things, if there were any, and if the world lasts very long, those who survive may be inspired to imitate them; and also, through knowledge of offensive things, divine punishments, and the disastrous fate of those who commit offenses, those who survive may fear doing wrong. For as Diodorus said above, it is a beautiful thing to learn, from mistakes of those in the past, how we should order our lives, according to the way many have ordered their lives. . . .

In accounts of things that happened in these Indies, especially those things pertaining to the first discoveries, and things that happened in Española and in other neighboring islands, no one among those who wrote in Castilian and Latin, up until 1527 when I began to write, saw the things he wrote about. Nor was there hardly any man present in the Indies who was able to write about them. Everything people have said was caught by hearsay, as in the refrain "de luengas vias". Although they have not lived in these lands as long as they say, some of them make a lot of noise. In fact, therefore, they have not learned any more about the Indies, nor should any more credit be given to them, than if they had only heard about it while being absent, in Valladolid or Seville.

Among them, with regard to the first happenings, no one should be trusted more than Pedro Mártir [Peter Martyr/SLT], "Décadas" in Latin, although he was in Castile during that period, because what he wrote about the first happenings was obtained: by the diligence of the Admiral himself, the first discoverer, with whom he spoke many times; from those who were in the Admiral's company; and also from others who were on the first voyages. The "Décadas" of Mártir contain many falsehoods with regard to other things pertaining to the discussion about these Indies and their progress.

Américo Vespucci gives testimony as to what he saw on the two voyages that he made to our Indies, although he appears to have omitted some circumstances, either knowingly or because he overlooked them. Some attribute to him what should be attributed to others. Others should not be defrauded this way, as we shall explain at the appropriate time.

All the others who have written in Latin should be disregarded, because they were distant from the places, language, and nation, so they have had many errors and various absurdities in their accounts. And although it has been many years since I began to write this history, but because I have been unable to finish it due to my great travels and occupations, some writers in the meantime appear to have written for that reason and have put general public interest ahead of their histories. They may possibly pardon me if I reveal their defects, because they set about writing by declaring things that they did not understand.

Since about the year 1500 [actually 1502/SLT], I have observed and wandered through these Indies for about sixty-three years [actually he spent the last nineteen years, 1547–1566, of his life in Spain/SLT], and I do have knowledge of what I have written about. May God receive infinite thanks for having granted me such a long life. My writing embraces: not only the profane and secular occurrences of my time, but also the ecclesiastical happenings, sometimes including moral considerations; the quality, nature, and properties of these regions, kingdoms, and lands and what they are composed of, along with the customs, religion, rites, ceremonies, and condition of their native peoples, comparing other nations with them in those respects; and matters of cosmography and geography when it seems necessary to comment on them. Knowledge of these things is known to be advantageous to many, and especially to princes, as agreed by the ancient men of learning. Therefore, this chronicle will probably be able to create less dislike and more desire on the part of the readers to pursue it. . . .

Everything that has been said until now pertains to the formal cause, or form, and the material cause, or content, of this book. The formal cause will probably be realized in the form of six parts or six books, which may contain nearly sixty years of history. [He was only able to complete three books, for the period 1492 to 1520/SLT.] Each book may relate events for ten years, except for the first book which may relate events for eight years, because we had no knowledge about these Indies until 1492. If the Divine Providence were to decide to extend my life, anything new that happens will have to be reported if it is worthwhile to history.

The author, or efficient cause, of this history, after God, is Don Fray Bartolomé de las Casas or Casaus [in the history he frequently refers to himself in the history as "the clergyman"/SLT], Friar of the Dominican Order, and Bishop of Ciudad Real on the Plains of Chiapa, which is known as Zacatlán by the Indians and which is one of the provinces or kingdoms now included in New Spain. By divine mercy, I am perhaps the oldest person alive who has spent so much time and who has had so much experience in these West Indies, unless by chance there are one or two others. Thanks to God. The history begins.

CHRISTOPHER COLUMBUS AND THE "ENTERPRISE OF THE INDIES"

Before his transatlantic voyages, Christopher Columbus had gained experience as a seafarer on the Mediterranean, with a window on the local trade from his base in Genoa. Later, from a Portuguese base, he made voyages to the Guinea Coast of Africa, where he observed that trade goods were being used to acquire slaves, as was customary at the time. Spain had acquired exclusive title to the Canary Islands by the Treaty of Alcaçovas, signed by Spain and Portugal in 1479, and Columbus was also aware that the Guanches, native people of those islands, were being taken to Spain for sale as slaves.

Christopher Columbus had apparently developed plans for his "Enterprise of the Indies" by 1483, and they were presented to John II, king of Portugal, in 1484.[11] The king referred Columbus to a maritime advisory committee, recently appointed, which heard him and dismissed him as a person with an active imagination, someone not to be taken seriously.

About mid-1485, Columbus and his young son Diego departed for Spain. He had persuaded his brother Bartolomé of the feasibility of reaching the islands and mainland of Asia by sailing west, and Bartolomé also left Portugal to present his brother's proposition to the kings of England and France. After placing young Diego in the Franciscan monastery of La Rábida, near Palos, Christopher gained an audience with Queen Isabela and presented his ideas for the western voyage. The Queen appointed a special commission to consider the "Enterprise of the Indies" and to recommend acceptance or rejection of it.

For the next six years Columbus waited upon the commission and the Crown, met with them in various cities for discussions, was turned down, and was then asked to return for subsequent hearings. In Book I, chapters 31 and 32, of his *History of the Indies*, Fray Bartolomé de las Casas describes the last agonizing period, which ended with the drawing up of the capitulation, or agreement, that approved the requests of Columbus and set in motion the Columbian discoveries.

HISTORIA DE LAS INDIAS,
BOOK I, CHAPTER 31: NEGOTIATIONS

In the previous chapter, we have spoken of the method used by the Sovereigns in deciding whether to favor the enterprise of Christopher Columbus. We learned this from a person who was among the early residents of this island [Española/SLT]. I have not doubted him, no one else would doubt his credibility.

In this chapter, I wish to tell of another approach, which has been verified by others, as a result of which the proposition was again considered and the Monarchs may have again been willing to listen to him; but it was also defeated, and it left Columbus with more disappointment and greater bitterness. Part of this negotiation can be inferred from some words in letters that I have seen, letters that were from Christopher Columbus to the Sovereigns, and especially from evidence obtained by the king's solicitor, after Admiral Diego Columbus, [son of, and/SLT] first successor to the first Admiral, made claim to the King for his status and privileges.

Although there may seem to have been little similarity with the first negotiations, these negotiations which did not succeed should not be condemned, because although the matter may not have been pursued, it may possibly have been that the Duke of Medina-celi agreed to the enterprise at first, and then later, the enterprise was prevented by some difficulties or unaccountable things that happened.

Finally, of the first and second approaches, and the third approach which will be discussed in the next chapter, the reader may decide which seems to have been the best, or he may sum up all three of them as one approach if it seems that they had any similarity. Or, it may be that Christopher Columbus, having taken leave of the Duke of Medina Sidonia and of the Duke of Medina-celi, left displeased with the disapproval that he had suffered at court, as has been said by those who said that he went to the village of Palos with his son, Diego Columbus, who was a child.

I believe this. And, it may be that he went to the Franciscan monastery of La Rábida, which is near that village, with the intention of going to the village of Huelva with his brother-in-law, whom they say was married to a sister of his wife, and from there going to France to submit his proposal to the king. And if he were not welcome there, he would be going to the king of England, also to learn about his brother, Bartolomé Columbus, from whom he had received no news up to that time.

A Father appeared whose name was Fray Juan Pérez, who was the guardian of the monastery. He began to speak with him about the matters of the court, because he knew he had come from there. Christopher Columbus gave him a lengthy account concerning: everything that had happened to him with the Sovereigns and the dukes; the little credit they had given him; the little respect they had for such a great enterprise; how they all considered it to be futile and frivolous; and how most of those at court disfavored him. After some reflection, the Father decided to become fully informed about the subject and about the reasons that Columbus advanced. And, because sometimes Christopher Columbus referred to subjects and used words concerning the heavens and astronomy, things that he [Fray Juan Pérez/SLT] did not understand, he called for a doctor or physician, whose name was Garci Hernández, who was his friend, and who, as a philosopher, understood more about such subjects than he did.

After all three of them talked and deliberated together, the physician, Garci Hernández, was very pleased, and consequently, so was the Father Guardian. They say that he was either the confessor of the most serene Queen, or had been. With this assurance, he most immediately begged Christopher Columbus not to depart, because he had decided to write to the Queen about the proposition, and to stay there in the monastery of La Rábida until the reply came.

Christopher Columbus was pleased to do this. One consideration was that he had already spent six or seven years presenting his proposal at court, and he wanted to serve the Sovereigns, because he had heard of their good will and reputation for virtue and mercy in many places. He could see that he had not been received by Their Highnesses, not through their fault, but through the fault of those who were advising them and who did not understand the subject. He had affection for the Kingdom of Castile, where he had his children whom he loved very much.

Another consideration was to avoid the hardships and delays of moving again to France, according to what he says in a letter that he wrote to the Monarchs. I believe the letter was from this island of Española, and in it, he says: "To serve Your Highnesses, I chose not to deal with France, England, or Portugal.

Your Highnesses have seen the letters from the princes of those countries, as they were hand delivered to you by Doctor Villalano." Thus it appears that all three kings had invited and called him, although at different times, wishing to be informed, and that they had agreed to the enterprise.

Therefore, returning to the subject, they got a man named Sebastián Rodríguez, a pilot from Lepe, to deliver the guardian's letter to the Queen. According to the letter, it seems that the court was in the village of Santa Fé, for the Sovereigns were occupied with the war in Granada, and the war was nearly over. The Queen replied to the Father, Fray Juan Pérez, expressing very much her gratitude to him for his advice and good intention and for his devoted service. She implored and ordered: that he come to court before Her Highness immediately upon receipt of her letter; and that, until Her Highness wrote to Christopher Columbus, he should leave him with the hope of a favorable reply to his proposal.

When the father, Fray Juan Pérez, saw the letter from the Queen, he departed secretly at midnight. He kissed the hands of the Queen, and Her Highness discussed the matter with him at length. They say that at last, she decided to give the three vessels to Columbus, and the other things that he wanted. [The physician, Garci Hernández, who had put this matter aside, must not have known what happened at court, but when he saw the guardian did not return to Palos until the matter was settled, he reached the conclusion that it had been settled.]

Following this, the Queen wrote to Christopher Columbus, and she sent 20,000 maravedís [a maravedí is a Spanish coin of little value/SLT] in florins for him so that he could leave. Diego Prieto, a resident of the village of Palos, brought the maravedís and gave them to the physician, Garci Hernández, so that he would give them to Columbus. Upon receipt of this dispatch, Christopher Columbus, and the guardian, and a few persons who favored Columbus, went to court. They appealed to the Queen to again consider the proposal.

Again there was much activity, and many persons met together. There were reports from philosophers, astrologers and cosmographers (if, however, there were any in Castile who were excellent at that time), and from mariners and pilots. Unanimously, they all said that it was all madness and nonsense, and, according to what the Admiral himself referred to and testified in his letters to the Sovereigns, they frequently ridiculed and laughed at it.

Acceptance of the proposal was made more difficult, because of all that Christopher Columbus was asking for as remuneration for his troubles, services, and proficiency, such as: status, being an admiral, viceroy, permanent governor, etc. Actually, these things were considered to be very grand and superior at that time, as they were, and this is how they might be considered today. But it was a great error at that time, and it might be so today, not to realize that it was simply a matter of his asking for rewards (as we said previously, speaking of the king of Portugal). It reached the point of their not believing or respecting anything that Christopher Columbus proposed, resulting in his complete dismissal. The Sovereigns ordered that he be told to leave.

It is believed that the main person who was the reason for this final dismissal was the previously mentioned Prior Prado, and those who followed him, and that it was for no reason other than that they did not comprehend or understand anything else. Dismissed by the Queen, Columbus took leave of those who supported him there. He took the road to Córdoba with his mind made up to go to France and to proceed as previously stated.

Here, one can clearly note the great constancy, and strength of spirit, and no less, the wisdom of Christopher Columbus, and also the certainty that he had of his discovery, as has been stated before. Although he was afflicted and held back with such great constraint by so much refusal and opposition, perhaps losing faith in the favors he was asking, contenting himself with less, and although it seems he would have to be satisfied with anything, the Sovereigns might be moved to give him what was necessary for his voyage, and he might be given the other things that should be given to him. He did not choose to yield in any respect, but he chose to persevere in his request.

At last despite all these difficulties, they acceded to his request. Thus he achieved a capitulaltion, as though he already had locked in a chest what he was offering and what he discovered, as we have stated before.

HISTORIA DE LAS INDIAS,
BOOK I, CHAPTER 32: APPROVAL

Dismissed this second time, by order of the Sovereigns, Christopher Columbus departed from the city of Granada without being given any hope, such as he had been given before, to the effect that sometime the matter might be considered again. Instead, he departed in complete sadness and disfavor, as everyone probably knows. According to what Christopher Columbus himself says in the prologue to the journal of his first voyage, the Sovereigns had already entered Granada on the second of January with great triumph, glory to God, and happiness of the Christian people. I would say that Christopher Columbus left Granada in that same month of January to proceed with his travel to France.

Among those persons who favored him at court and wished that his project would be decided on and would move forward was Luis de Santángel, Keeper of the Privy Purse, whom we mentioned above. He was greatly and excessively distressed and sad because of this second final refusal without any hope, as though it was very important to him and only a little less important than his life. He saw that Christopher Columbus had been dismissed, and he was unable to permit the damage and loss to the Sovereigns that he thought would follow as a consequence: by losing the great wealth and riches that Christopher Columbus was promising, if the promises turned out to be true, and some other Christian king were to have them, and by the lessening of their royal authority, which was so highly regarded in the world, as a result of their not wishing to risk such a small expenditure for such an unlimited enterprise, by trusting in God and in the protection or respect that the Sovereigns knew they had through their faith in Him, and through his desire to serve them.

Confidently, he went to the Queen and spoke to her in this manner: "Señora, the desire that I have always had to serve My Lord The King and Your Highness has compelled me to appear before Your Highness, and to speak to you about a matter that is none of my affair. Nor do I fail to realize that it goes beyond the rules or limits of my position. But with the confidence that I have always had in the clemency of Your Highness and in your royal generosity, and that you will seriously consider what I say, I have decided to make known to you what I feel in my heart. Others, who also faithfully love Your Highnesses and who wish for your prosperity as I your least important servant do, perhaps feel this way much more so than I do. I am saying, Señora, that I have often considered the very noble and firm spirit with which God adorned Your Highnesses in order that you might undertake great things and most excellent works, and I have been very surprised that you have not agreed to an enterprise such as this Columbus has proposed to you.

"So little would be lost, even if it were in vain, and so much might be achieved in the service of God and for the welfare of His church, with considerable growth in the royal estate of Your

Highnesses and in the prosperity of all your kingdoms. Truthfully, Most Serene Señora, this enterprise is of such a nature that there would be obvious dangers to the authority of Your Highnesses, and damages to your kingdoms, if what Your Highness considered to be difficult or impossible is offered to another king, giving him very good reasons for it, and if he accepts it and becomes prosperous, as Columbus has indicated. If this were to happen, may God not allow it, Your Highnesses would be terribly sorry for all your lives. You would be blamed by your friends and servants. Your enemies would have cause to insult and ridicule you, and all of them would venture to state that Your Highnesses were getting your due punishment. In the minds of those who profoundly consider this matter, there is little doubt as to how the royal successors to Your Highnesses might feel and perhaps might suffer.

"This Columbus is a wise and prudent man with a very sound mind. It seems that he presents very good principles, some of which are accepted by the learned men to whom Your Highnesses have referred him, although they reject others. But we see: that they do not know how to respond to him with regard to many things; that he gives reason and replies with regard to all of their opposition; that he is risking his own life; that what he is asking for at the present time is very little; and that he does not want favors and remuneration except for what he himself discovers. I beg Your Highness that you not judge this enterprise to be so impossible that it cannot succeed with much glory and honor to your royal name, growth of your state, and prosperity of your subjects.

"As for the fact some allege that Your Highnesses would be regarded somewhat unfavorably for having undertaken such a doubtful thing if the enterprise does not succeed as we wish, and as this Columbus promises, I am of a very opposite opinion. I am certain that this enterprise will add many degrees of perfection to the praise and reputation that Your Highnesses have, as most magnificent and courageous Sovereigns who are endeavoring to learn, at their own expense, the great secrets that the world holds.

"You will not be the first sovereigns who have undertaken similar achievements, such as have been undertaken by Ptolemy, Alexander, and other great and powerful monarchs; and granted that they did not succeed in all that they tried to do, they were acclaimed by all the world for their great courage and their little regard for expense. Moreover, Señora, all that he is asking for at this time is a million, and to say that Your Highness is deserting him by failing to give him such a small amount would really sound very bad. In no way is it necessary for Your Highness to give up such a great enterprise, even if it were much more questionable."

Then, the Catholic Queen, knowing the disposition and great zeal that Luis de Santángel had in her service, said that she was very pleased with his wishes and with the opinion that he was giving her, and that she would be glad to pursue it, but that she would defer it at that time until she had a little quiet and rest, because now she was realizing how needy they [the Sovereigns/SLT] were, with those wars that had been so lengthy. The Queen said, "But, Santángel, if you still feel that that man can no longer put up with such a delay, I shall be glad if the money that he wants for the armada is borrowed with my personal jewelry as a pledge, and if then he will proceed with the enterprise."

Luis de Santángel knelt before her and kissed her hands, being very grateful to her for the decision she made, by choosing to accept a proposal that was so much doubted and opposed by all the others. He added: "Most Serene Señora, there is no need to pledge the jewels of Your Highness for this. It will be a very small service that I render to Your Highness and to my Lord, the King, by lending the million myself, but Your Highness must send for Columbus, whom I believe has already gone."

Then the Queen ordered a court bailiff to go posthaste after Christopher Columbus, to tell him to return, and to bring him back. He found him two leagues from Granada at the bridge called Pinos. Christopher Columbus returned with the bailiff, and he was happily welcomed by Santángel.

When the Queen learned that he had returned, she immediately ordered the secretary, Juan de Coloma, to prepare the capitulation in all haste, and to prepare all the dispatches that Christopher Columbus requested and said were necessary for his entire voyage and discovery.

It is not right to continue from here without taking into consideration the order and law that God has placed in His world, as I believe I have mentioned previously. How difficult is the achievement of the good and important things that God tries to do! How much anxiety, opposition, anguish, rejection, and grief does God wish to inflict upon those that He chooses to be the instrument and means of achievement of these things! How much favor and help from God is needed by those who have to manage these things! How much perseverance, constancy, suffering, patience, and strength of virtue, must be had by those who dedicate themselves to serve God in prominent and great undertakings until they achieve them! Temporal things are concluded with no less hardship and grief, even though this matter may be considered to be both spiritual and temporal and highly acceptable to God.

And therefore, I believe that Christopher Columbus was principally moved by God, by spiritual and eternal values, and by the salvation of the predestined. Who could have endured seven years of exile, with so much anguish, disregard, reproach, sadness, poverty, cold and hunger (just as he says in a letter that he suffered in Santa Fé) as Christopher Columbus had suffered, in obtaining this support, help, and favor?

This is nothing compared with what he must endure and suffer later during his entire life, when he arrives at prosperity, and a greater station in life. It will be seen in the account of this first Book, God be willing, that all the days of his life were full of dangers, surprises, hardships—the like of which have never been heard: bitterness, persecution, pain, and a continuous martyrdom. No one can have confidence in personal advancements, in deeds and services that he may have rendered to the Sovereigns, in grants that he may have received from them, or in riches and treasures that he finds.

One must also consider that kings are men like other men, and that they are all in the hands of the highest and true King, God, who is omnipotent, and by whom they rule on earth. His heart turns them as He wishes, when, how, where, and for whom He pleases. Despite the number of learned men and persons of so much and such high authority who were near the Sovereigns, who hindered them, and who advised them against agreeing to such an enterprise, the Sovereigns conceded to it and provided for it, being persuaded by a man who was not a man of learning.

He was only a man of good will, who knew, in a Christian way and in a prudent manner, how to persuade and effectively influence the Queen. The "Historia" by the Portuguese, Joao de Barros, speaking about this, says that Cardinal Don Pedro González de Mendoza was the main party responsible for the Queen's agreement. It may well have been that, as I believe, he was previously and sometimes very much in favor, and that finally the above-mentioned Santángel may have finally settled the matter.

Thirdly, neither shall we go on from here without considering that Castile was so poor at that time in gold and silver and money, that the Sovereigns did not have a million maravedís to carry out such a great enterprise, without having to pledge the jewels that the illustrious Queen had for her royal adornment.

Finally, this courageous and enormous venture, because of its importance and greatness, had to begin with a million maravedís lent by a servant of the Sovereigns, who was not very rich. Eyes have not seen, ears have not heard, the mind has never conceived, nor has man been able to dream of any other treasures comparable to the treasures that have come to Castile from the Indies to this day, and have been used by the Sovereigns of Castile.

There is something else to note at this point. According to some letters from Christopher Columbus to the Sovereigns, letters which I have had in my possession, which were written in his own handwriting, and which were from this island of Española, a cleric by the name of Fray Antonio de Marchena was the one who very much helped the Queen to be persuaded and to agree to the request. No mention is made of his order, to where or when.

Columbus says: "Your Highnesses already know that I spent seven years at your court repeating the same request. Never in all this time was there any pilot, mariner, philosopher, or person of any other branch of knowledge, who did not say that my enterprise was wrong. Next to support from God Eternal, I never found support from anyone, except from Fray Antonio de Marchena, etc."

Further on, he again says that there was no one who did not make fun of him, except for that Father, Fray Antonio de Marchena (same as above, etc.). I could never find out what order he belonged to, although I believe that it was the Franciscan Order, because I knew Christopher Columbus was always attached to that order after he became Admiral. Nor could I find out when or where, or how he helped him, or what access Fray Antonio de Marchena might have had to the Sovereigns.

OFFICIAL DOCUMENTS OF AGREEMENT

When arrangements for his voyage of discovery had been completed with King Ferdinand of Aragón and Queen Isabela of Castile and León, Columbus intended to sail westward to the landfall in the islands or mainland of Asia. Thus the official documents drawn were "The Articles of Agreement, 17 April 1492,"[12] which specified the financial understanding, and the "Conditional Grant of Titles and Honors, 30 April 1492,"[13] which specified the kinds of recognition that would be given to Columbus and his heirs if his voyage were successful, both as to discoveries and to material rewards, as a result of this commercial venture.

2

The European Invasion of the Indian World: Columbus's Own Account

The world on the eve of the Columbian discoveries had been the scene of great activity and expansion on both sides of the Atlantic. The seafaring peoples of the Iberian peninsula had been working their way southward down the west coast of Africa and had pacified and occupied the Canary, Cape Verde, and Madeira islands. The indigenous peoples of the Indian world had also been moving and displacing one another. From the mainland of South America, new inhabitants had entered the Caribbean, displacing the Ciboney: the Arawaks had occupied the Bahaman Islands and the Greater Antilles, and the Caribs had occupied the lesser Antilles and a portion of Puerto Rico. The Aztecs had moved southward into the Valley of Mexico, where they eventually absorbed the culture of the Toltecs and militarily dominated the region. The Incas had developed the administrative, diplomatic, and military system which enabled them to gain preeminence in the Andean area from Quito, Ecuador, to the Maule River in Chile.

The era of discovery in the Old World was marked by controversy and uncertainty. One area of dispute of great importance to explorers concerned the size of the earth. Many Portuguese and Spanish scholars believed that the earth was approximately the size we know it to be today. Accordingly they were convinced that the ocean between Europe and Asia was so vast that ships and crews could not survive the voyage: thus the ships of the period could not reach Asia by sailing west. Another school of thought, which Columbus espoused, held that the earth was some 30 percent smaller than it actually was. This theory was strongly influenced by Ptolemy's world map and also by recent information about Asia that had been provided by the journeys and exploration of Marco Polo. If the Asian mainland and its islands extended as far to the east as Marco Polo had led Europeans to believe, then the distance between Western Europe and Asia was manageable by sailing ships. Of course, neither school of thought knew of the existence of the two Americas or of the Pacific Ocean as a separate body of water lying between the unknown continent and Asia. As a result when Columbus made landfalls in the Bahamas, Cuba, and Española, he was convinced that he had reached the islands off Asia; according to his concept of the size of the earth, these places were exactly where he expected "the Indies" to be.

This chapter will follow the encounters of Columbus and his men during their first two weeks in "the Indies", beginning with the journal entry for October 11 and the sighting of land from the ships during the night of October 11 and 12. Although Las Casas, in his summary, uses the words "Indians" and "Indies" from the very beginning, Columbus himself calls the island people "natives" until October 17. Only at that point does Columbus identify those he has taken captive to carry back to Spain as "Indians" and the islands themselves as "the Indies."

The text here is my own translation, based on the Sanz edition (1962) of the Las Casas abstract, a text not available to Vigneras (1960) or Morison (1963). Only the first few pages given here are in the words of Fray Bartolomé, and this portion of the text uses the third person to refer to Columbus and his party. For the remainder of this extract, Fray Bartolomé quotes directly from the Columbus journal. The narrative thus changes midway to the first person and is enclosed in quotation marks. For clarity of exposition, the English version has been divided into paragraphs. My editorial notes are bracketed and initialed. There is no journal entry dated October 12. Perhaps with the excitement of sighting land on the night of October 11 and the landing itself the next morning, the two days seemed like one and the same until the entry was made for October 13.

ABSTRACT OF THE JOURNAL OF COLUMBUS

Thursday, 11 October. He sailed to the west-south-west. They encountered much sea, greater than they had experienced the entire voyage. They saw petrels and a green reed near the ship.[1]

Those aboard the caravel Pinta saw a cane and a stick, and they also took on board a little stick fashioned, as it appeared, with iron, a piece of cane, another plant that grows on land, and a small board.

Those on board the caravel Niña also saw other signs of land and a little branch loaded with dog-roses. With these signs they all relaxed and rejoiced. On this day, by sunset, they went 27 leagues.

After sunset, he sailed on his original course to the west. They must have made about 12 miles every hours, and up to two hours after midnight they must have gone 90 miles, which are 22½ leagues.[2]

The caravel *Pinta*, sailing more swiftly and being ahead of the Admiral [who was aboard the ship *Santa Maria*/SLT], found land and gave the signals that the Admiral had ordered.

A sailor called Rodrigo de Triana first saw this land, although at ten at night, the Admiral, standing on the sterncastle, saw a light. It was so obscure that he did not want to affirm that it was land, but he called Pedro Guitiérrez, the King's butler or steward, and told him that there seemed to be a light and to look for it. Guitiérrez did look and he saw it.

The Admiral also told Ridrigo Sánchez de Segovia, whom the King and Queen had sent in the fleet as inspector or comptroller [*veedor*]. He saw nothing because he was not in a place from where he could see the light.

After the Admiral had spoken, it was seen once or twice, and it was like a little wax candle being lifted up and rising. To a few, this seemed to be a sign of land, but the Admiral was certain he was near land. Therefore, when they had said the *Salve*, which all sailors were accustomed to say and sing in their own way, and all were assembled, the Admiral asked and advised them to maintain a good watch from the forecastle and to look with care for land.

He said that he would immediately give a silk doublet to the one who might first tell him that he saw land. This would be besides the other reward the Sovereigns had promised, which was ten thousand maravedís as an annuity to the one who first saw land.

At two hours after midnight, land appeared, from which they must have been two leagues distant. They lowered all sails and set the squaresail, which is the mainsail without bonnets, and they lay to, waiting for daylight on Friday [October 12, 1492/SLT], when they arrived at a small island of the Bahamas which, in the language of the Indians, was called Guanahaní [and which has been identified as San Salvador/Watlings Island/SLT].

Soon they saw naked people, and the Admiral went ashore in the armed boat. Also Martín Alonso Pinzón and Vicente Yáñez, his brother, who was captain of the *Niña*.

The Admiral unfurled the royal standard, and the captains displayed two banners of the green cross, which the Admiral flew on all the vessels as a signal. The banners had an F and Y [for Fernando and Ysabel/SLT], with his or her crown above each letter, one at one side [of the cross] and the other at the other.

Once ashore, they saw very green trees, many streams, and fruits of various kinds. The Admiral called the two captains, the others who came ashore, Rodrigo de Escobedo, purser of the entire fleet, and Rodrigo Sánchez de Segovia, and he said that they should bear testimony and witness that in their presence he was taking, as in fact he took, possession of the said island for the King and for the Queen, their Lord and Lady, making the declarations that were required, as is set forth at length in the attestations that were made there in writing.

The "Exact Words" of Columbus

Soon many people of the island gathered there. Following are the exact words of the Admiral, in his book of his first navigation and discovery of these Indies: He says, "So that they might be very friendly toward us, and because I knew that they were a people who would better be freed and converted to our Holy Faith by love than by force, I gave to some of them red caps, and glass beads which they hung on their necks, and many other things of little value. So then they were very pleased, and they continued to be so much our friends that it was a marvel.

"Later, they came swimming to the ships' boats where we were. They brought to us: parrots, balls of cotton thread, [wooden] spears, and many other things. They exchanged them for other things that we gave them, such as little glass beads and hawks' bells. Finally, they took everything and gave everything they had, in good will. It seemed to me they were very poor people in everything.

"They all go naked as their mothers gave birth to them. So do the women, although I only saw one young girl. Those that I saw were youths, none of them more than thirty years of age.

"They are very well built, with handsome bodies and very good faces. The hair above their eyebrows is coarse, somewhat like that of a horse's tail, and short, except for some hair that they wear long behind and never cut.

"Some paint themselves a blackish color, but they are of the color of the Canary Islanders [the indigenous Guanches/SLT], neither black nor white. Some paint themselves white, some red, and some paint themselves with what they find. Some paint their faces, some their entire body, some only the eyes, and some only the nose.

"They do not bear arms [such as the Spaniards have/SLT] nor are they acquainted with them. I showed them some swords, and they grasped them by the blade and cut themselves, through ignorance. They have no iron. Their spears are [wooden] rods without iron. Some have a fish tooth at the end, and others have other things [to give them a sharp point].

"They are generally of good stature, fine appearance, and well built. I saw some who had scars from wounds on their bodies, and I made signs to find out about them. They showed me that people from other nearby islands [the Caribs/SLT] came there and tried to capture them and that they defended themselves. And I believed and still believe that people come here from the mainland to take them as captives [Columbus shows that he thinks these are islands off the Asian mainland/SLT.]

"They ought to be good servants and of good mentality, for I see that they very soon say everything that is said to them. I believe that they would easily become Christians, because it seemed to me that they belonged to no creed.

"If it please Our Lord, at the time of my departure I shall bring six of them from here to Your Highness [*sic*], in order that they may learn to speak [our language]. I saw no animal of any kind in this island, except parrots." All are words of the Admiral.

Saturday, 13 October. "At dawn, many of these men, all youths, as I have said, came to the beach. They are all of good stature, very handsome people. Their hair is not curly, but straight and coarse like horsehair.[3] Their foreheads and heads are very broad, more than any other race I have seen before. Their eyes are not small and are very attractive. None of them are black, but they are of the color of the Canary Islanders, nor should anything different be expected, because this island lies on the same line [latitude/SLT] from east to west, as the island of Ferro in the Canary Islands. The legs of all of them, without exception are very straight. They have no paunch, and they are very well built.[4]

"They came to the ship in [dugout] canoes which are made from a tree trunk into a long boat, all in one piece.[5] They are surprisingly well made, considering the country, and they are so big that 40 to 45 men came in some of them. Others were smaller, some in which only a single man came. They rowed with an oar that was like a baker's peel and it works very well. If they capsize, they all immediately start swimming, they set it upright, and they bail it out with calabashes that they carry.

"They brought balls of spun cotton, parrots, light spears, and other little things that it would be tedious to write about, and they gave everything for anything that might be given to them.

"I was attentive and tried hard to find out if there was any gold. I saw that some of them were wearing a small piece hanging from a hole that they have in their nose. By signs I was enabled to understand that, going to the south or going around the island to the south, there was a king who had great vessels of it, and that he possessed very much [gold].

"I tried to persuade them to go there, but later saw that they had no desire to go. I decided to wait until tomorrow afternoon, and then depart to the southwest, where according to many of them who informed me, there would be land to the south, southwest, and northwest. They said that the people from the northwest had come to fight them many times, then [had gone on] to the southwest to search for gold and precious stones."

San Salvador, or Guanahani

"This island is very large and very level, with very green trees, many streams, and a very big lake in the middle. It is without any mountain, entirely green, and it is a pleasure to behold it.

"These people are very meek, and because of their desire to have some of our things, and thinking that nothing will be given to them unless they give something, they take what they can [get] and soon swim away. They give everything they have for anything that is given to them, and they even bartered for pieces of crockery and broken glass cups.

"I even saw 16 balls of cotton given for three *ceotis* of Portugal, which is [equivalent to] a *blanca* of Castile [a coin worth less than a cent/SLT]. And those balls would have comprised more than one *arroba* [25 pounds/SLT] of spun cotton. I would have objected to this and not allowed anyone to take anything, except that I had ordered that everything there in abundance be taken for Your Highnesses.

"It [the cotton] is grown here in this island. In this short time I could not be sure of anything more. The gold they wear in their noses also comes from here. But, to lose no time, I wish to go and see if I can get to the island of Cipango [Japan/SLT]. Now, as it was nighttime, all went ashore in their canoes."

Sunday, 14 October. "When day was breaking, I ordered that the ship's batel and the caravel's barges be ready,[6] and I went along the coast of the island in a north-north-easterly direction in order to see what was on the other side, which was the eastern side, and also to see the settlements, and then I saw two or three settlements, and all the people who came to the beach called to us and gave thanks to God. Some brought water to us. Others brought some things to eat. Others, when they saw that I might not come ashore, swam out to us, and we understood that they were asking us if we had come from the sky.

"One old man got into the batel, and others in loud voices called to all the men and women: 'Come to see the men who came from the sky.' Bring them things to eat and drink.' Many came, including many women. They all carried something, giving thanks to God and throwing themselves to the ground. They raised their hands to the sky, and then loudly called to us to come ashore.

"I was fearful at the sight of an extensive ridge of rocks [or reef] that encircles that entire island. Inside, it is deep and would be a harbor for as many ships as there are in all Christendom. But the entrance to it is very narrow. It is true that within this enclosure there are some shoals, but the sea moves no more than within a well.

"In order to see all this part, I went on this morning, so that I might give an account of everything to Your Highnesses, and also find out where a fort might be built. I saw a piece of land that is shaped like an island, although it is not, and there were six houses on it. In two days it could be cut off as an island, but I do not consider this to be necessary, because these people have very little knowledge of arms, as Your Highnesses will see from the seven whom I arranged to be taken in order that they might be brought to learn our language and then returned, unless Your Highnesses should order that they all be brought to Castile, or held captive on the same island. With fifty men, all could be subdued and could be made to do all that is desired. Then, next to this small island are the most beautiful groves of trees I have seen. They are so green and have leaves like those of Castile in the months of April and May, and there is much water.

"I looked at that entire harbor, and then I returned to the ship and made sail. I saw so many islands that I could not decide which one I should go to first. Those men whom I had taken told me by signs that there were so very many that they were numberless, and they referred to more than a hundred by name. Finally, I looked for the biggest, decided to go to it, and did.

"It is probably five leagues from San Salvador [the name Columbus gave to the island the natives called Guanahaní, and which has been identified as Watlings Island in the Bahamas/SLT], and some of the other islands are more distant, some less. They are all very level, without mountains, and very fertile. They are all inhabited, and the people make war against each other,[8] but they are very simple, and have very handsome bodies."

Santa María de la Concepción

Monday, 15 October. "I had lain to this night for fear of coming to shore to anchor before morning, not knowing whether the coast was clear of reefs. I made sail at dawn. Because the island was more than five leagues distant, probably seven, and because the tide held me back, it was probably midday when I arrived at the island mentioned.

"I noted that the coast of the island off San Salvador runs five leagues from north to south. The other coast I followed, running from east to west, must be more than ten leagues. From the island, I saw another bigger island to the west. I set sail to travel the whole day until night, because otherwise I would not have been able to reach the western cape, to which I gave the name of the island of Santa María de la Concepción [Rum Cay, SLT].

"Just as the sun was about to set I was anchoring near the cape to find out if there was any gold there, because those whom I had taken captive on the island of San Salvador told me that they wore very big bracelets of gold on their legs and arms. I really believed that everything they told me was a trick to escape. However, it was my wish not to pass up any island without taking possession. Even so, if one is taken, all can be considered taken.

"I anchored and stayed until today, Tuesday, when at dawn I went to the beach with the armed boats and walked from the shore. There were many people, also naked and in the same condition as those of the other island of San Salvador. They let us walk around the island and gave us what we asked for.

"I did not wish to stay, because the wind was shifting to the southeast, as I departed for the ship. A big canoe came alongside the caravel Niña, and one of the men of the island of San Salvador, who was on board, jumped into the sea and went away in it. On the night before, about midnight, another man had gone. [We? (text garbled)] pursued the canoe, which went so fast that no boat could ever overtake it, although we pressed her closely. However, it reached the land, and they left it. Some of the men of my company went after them, and they all fled like chickens.

"The canoe they left we brought on board the caravel Niña, where already from another cape came another small canoe with a man who was coming to trade a ball of cotton. Because he did not wish to come aboard the caravel, some of the sailors jumped into the sea and seized him. Being on the poop deck of the ship, I saw everything.

"I sent for him and I gave him a red cap, and some small beads of green glass which I put on his arm, and two hawks' bells which I attached to his ears, and I ordered that his canoe, which was also on the ship's boat, be returned to him, and then I sent him ashore. Then I set sail to go to the other big island, which I saw to the west, and I also ordered that the other canoe, which the caravel Niña was towing astern, be cast off. Later, I saw it ashore, at the time of the arrival of the other man to whom I had given the aforementioned things. I had not wanted to take the ball of cotton, although he wanted to give it to me. All the others gathered around him, and he considered it to be a great surprise, and it very much appeared to him that we were good people, that the other man who had fled had done some harm to us, and that this was why we had him with us. And this is the reason I favored him, and gave him those things, so that he might hold us in such esteem that at another time, when Your Highnesses again send [people] here, they may not make bad company. All that I gave him was not worth even four maravedís."

Fernandina

"And so I departed about ten o'clock, with a southeast wind veering to the south, to go to this other island, which is very big. All these men that I am bringing from the island of San Salvador make signs that this is where there is much gold, and that the people wear it as bracelets on the arms and on their legs, and in their ears and noses and on their necks. From the island of Santa María, it is nine leagues west to this other island.

"This entire side of the island runs northwest to southeast. It seems that the coast on this side is probably more than 28 leagues. It is very level, without any mountains, just like San Salvador and Santa María. There are no rocks on any of the beaches, but all of them have some rocky ridges [reefs] under water near the shore, where it is necessary to be watchful when deciding whether to anchor very close to the shore, even though the water is always very clear and you see the bottom.

"Among all these islands, two lombard shots [one thousand to two thousand yards/SLT] away from the shore it is so deep that you cannot find the bottom. These islands are very green and fertile, the air is very pleasant, and there may be many things that I do not know about, and I do not want to stop searching and going to many islands to find gold. Inasmuch as these people give these signs that they wear gold on their arms and legs, and it is gold, because I showed them some pieces that I have, I cannot fail, with God's help, to find out where it comes from.

"Standing in mid-channel between these two islands—that is, Santa María and this big island, which I am naming Fernandina [Long Island/SLT]—I came upon a man alone in the canoe on his way from the island of Santa María to Fernandina. He was carrying a piece of bread about as big as a fist, a calabash of water, a bit of bright red earth made into a powder and then kneaded [probably for body paint/SLT], and some dry leaves [probably tobacco/SLT] which must be something much appreciated among those people, because they had already brought some to me in San Salvador as a present.

"He was carrying a little basket of his own, and in it he had a string of little glass beads and two blancas [Spanish coins worth less than a cent/SLT]. From the blancas, I knew that he came from the island of San Salvador, that he had gone to the island of Santa María and that he was going to Fernandina.

"He approached the ship. I had him come aboard, as he requested, had his canoe put on board the ship, and arranged for everything he was carrying to be guarded. I ordered that he be given bread and honey to eat and something to drink.

"In this way, I shall take him to Fernandina, and I shall give him everything that is his, so that he may give a good account of us, and so that, pleasing the Lord, when Your Highnesses send others here they may be honored, and they may give to us of all they have."

Tuesday, 16 October, and Wednesday. "I departed from the island of Santa María de la Concepción, probably about midday, for the island Fernandina, which seems to extend very far to the west, and I sailed all that day in a calm sea.

"I was unable to get there in time to see the bottom so that I could anchor where it was clear. In this situation, one must be very careful in order not to lose the anchors. And so, I stood by all this night until daybreak, when I came to the village where I anchored.

"Here had come that man whom I had met yesterday in that canoe in mid-channel. He had given such a good account of us, that there was no lack of canoes alongside the ship all this night. They brought us water and what they had.

"I ordered that something be given to every one of them, that is, some little beads, 10 or 12 glass beads on a string, some brass jingles, like those that are worth one maravedí each in Castile, and some lace points, all of which they greatly appreciated. Also, I ordered that they be given molasses to eat, when they came aboard the ship.

"Later, at the hour of *tercia* [ecclesiastical tierce, about nine in the morning], I sent the small ship's boat [batel] ashore for water. They very willingly showed my people where the water was, they themselves carried the filled casks to the boat, and they were very happy to please us.

"This island is very large, and I have decided to sail around it, because, as I understand, there is a mine of gold in or near it. This island is off the island of Santa María eight leagues, nearly on a parallel to the west. This cape, to which I came, and this entire coast runs northwest and south-southwest [*sic*], and I saw at least 20 leagues of it, but it did not end there.

Now, as I am writing this, I have set sail with the south wind to try to sail around the entire island and endeavor to locate Samaot [Saomete; Columbus's spelling of the name of this island varies/SLT], which is the island or the city where the gold is. All these men who are coming aboard this ship say this, and the people from the islands of San Salvador and Santa María also said this.

"These people are similar to the people of those islands. They have the same language and the same customs, except that these people appear to me to be somewhat more domestic and more subtle in their dealings, because I note that when they have brought cotton and other little things here to the ship, they know better how to settle on the payment than the others do. Also in this island, I saw cotton cloth made into cloaks. The people are better looking. The women wear a small piece of cotton in front of their body which scarcely covers their genitals.

"It is a very green island, level, and very fertile. I have no doubt that they plant and harvest corn [*panizo*] all year, and all other things as well. I saw many trees that are very different from ours. Many of them had many kinds of branches, and they were all from one trunk. One small branch is one kind, another is another kind, and they are so different, that the diversity of one kind and another is the greatest wonder of the world. For example, one branch had leaves like cane, another like those of a mastic tree, and so, in one single tree there were five or six kinds of leaves, and they were all different. One might say that grafting brings this about, but they are not grafted. They are in the woods, and these people do not take care of them [possibly this was a tree with various parasitic plants growing on it/SLT].

"I do not know of any creed they have, and I believe that they would become Christians very quickly, because they have very good understanding. The fish here are so different from ours that it is astonishing. Some are like dories, they have the most delicate colors of the world, blue, yellow, red, and all colors, and others are colored in a thousand different ways. Their colors are so delicate that there is no man who would not marvel and take great satisfaction in seeing them. Also there are whales.

"I saw no land animals of any kind except parrots and lizards. A boy told me that he saw a big snake. I saw no sheep, goats, or any other animal. Although I was here for only a very short while, half a day, if there were any animals, I could not have failed to see some. I shall write about the journey around this island after I have sailed around it."

Wednesday, 17 October. "At midday I departed from the village where I was anchored, and where I took on water, to sail around this island Fernandina. The wind was southwest and south. I wanted to follow the coast of this island from where I was to the southeast, because there the coast runs north-northwest to south-southeast.

"I intended to follow the course to the south and southeast, because there, according to all the Indians I have on board, and the other one who made signs to me, is the island they call Samoet, where the gold is. Then, Martín Alonso Pinzón, captain of the caravel *Pinta*, where I had sent three of these Indians, came to me and told me that one of the Indians had very definitely given him to understand that he would sail around the island much more swiftly by going north-northwest. I saw that the wind was not helping me on the course that I wanted to take, and that it was favorable in the other direction, so I set sail to the north-northwest.

"When the ship came close to the cape of the island, two leagues away, I discovered a very wonderful harbor with one mouth, although one can say two mouths, because there is an island in the middle. Both mouths are very narrow. Within the harbor, it would be wide enough for one hundred ships, if it were deep and clear and deep at the entrance. I thought it well to inspect it carefully and take soundings, and so I anchored outside and went into the harbor with all the vessels' boats, and we saw that there was no depth. And because when I saw it I thought that it was the mouth of some river, I had ordered that casks be taken along to get water. On shore, I found eight or ten men who soon approached us and showed us the village nearby, where I sent the men for water, some with arms and some with casks, and so they got it.

"Because they were a little distance away, I was detained for two hours. During this time, I walked through those trees, which were more beautiful than anything else I have ever seen, and I saw as much verdure as there is in Andalusia in the month of May. All the trees are as different from ours as day is from night, and so are the fruits, and the plants, and the rocks and everything. It is true that some trees were of the same nature as other trees that are in Castile. However, there was a very great difference, and there were so many other trees that were different, that no one can say what they are or compare them to others in Castile.

"The people were all like the other people already mentioned. They were in the same condition, naked, and of the same stature, and they gave what they had for anything that was given to them. Here I saw some young men from the ships trade some pieces of broken crockery and glass with them for spears.

"The other men who went for water told me how they had been in their houses, that the houses were well swept and very clean inside, and that their beds [hammocks] and coverings are like nets of cotton. The houses are all like tents. They are very high, and have good chimneys.[9] Among the many villages I saw, I did not see any that had more than twelve or fifteen houses.

"Here it was seen that the married women were wearing clouts of cotton. Young women did not wear these, except some who were now eighteen years of age. There were dogs, mastiffs and small dogs.[10] There they found a man who wore in his nose a piece of gold which was about like half of a castellano [Spanish coin/SLT] and they saw letters on it. I reproached them for not trading for it and giving him what he was asking, and they replied to me that he did not [offer?] to trade.

"After getting the water, I returned to the ship, set sail, and sailed to the northwest until I had explored all that part of the island along the coast that runs east to west. Then these Indians said that this island was smaller than the island Samoet, and that it would be well to turn back, to be there sooner.

"Then the wind fell calm, and it began to blow from the west-northwest, which was contrary to the way we had come. So I turned about and sailed all this night to the east-southeast, sometimes to due east and sometimes to the southeast. This was so that

I could keep clear of the land, because it was very cloudy and the weather very oppressive. There was little wind, and therefore I was unable to approach land to anchor.

"It rained very hard this night, from midnight nearly until daylight, and there still are rainclouds. We are at the southeast cape of the island, where I hope to anchor until the weather clears, in order to see the other islands where I must go.

"And so, all these days, since I have been in these 'Indies,' it has rained more or less. May Your Highnesses believe that this land is the best, the most fertile, temperate, and level and the most pleasing that there is in the world."

Thursday, 18 October. "After the weather cleared, I followed the wind. I went around the island as far as I could go, and I anchored when the weather was no longer satisfactory for sailing. But I did not go ashore, and I set sail at dawn."

Isabela or Saomete

Friday, 19 October. "I weighed anchor at dawn, sent the caravel Pinta to the east-southeast, sent the caravel Niña to the south-southeast, and with the ship, I went to the southeast. I had given orders that they follow those courses until midday, and that then they both change courses and join me. Then, before we had gone as much as three hours, we saw an island to the east, and we headed there. All three vessels arrived there before midday at the north point, where there is a small island [Bird Rock/SLT] and a rocky reef extending beyond it to the north, and another between it and the big island. These men from San Salvador that I have aboard called this big island Saomete, and I gave it the name of Isabela [Crooked Island/SLT].

"The wind was from the north, and, from where I had left Fernandina, the small island was east. Then, from the small island, the coast ran twelve leagues westward [*sic*] to a cape, which I called Cabo Hermoso, and it is on the west side.[11] It is indeed beautiful, round, and has very deep water, with no shoals offshore. On approaching, it is rocky and not so good, but further inside, the beach is sandy, as is nearly the entire coast. I anchored here this Friday night until morning.

"All this coast, and the part of the island that I saw, are nearly all beach. The island is the most beautiful thing I have seen. If the other islands are beautiful, this one is more beautiful.[12] It has many trees, and they are very green and very big. This land is higher than that of the other islands that have been discovered.

On it, there is a small hill, which cannot be called a mountain, and this is another thing that beautifies the rest.

"It seems there are many bodies of water there in the middle of the island. From here to the northeast, the coast makes a big bend, there are many dense groves of trees, and they are very large. I wanted to go there and cast anchor, in order to go ashore and look at so much beauty, but the water was shallow, and I could not anchor except a long way from shore.

"The wind was very good for me to come to this cape, where I am now anchored, and which I have named Cabo Hermoso, because it is so. Therefore, I did not anchor within that bend. Also, I saw this cape further on, and it was so green and so beautiful, just like all the other things and lands of these islands, that I do not know where to go first. Nor do my eyes grow tired of looking at such beautiful green growth that is so different from ours.

"I even believe that there are many plants and many trees in these islands that are worth a lot in Spain for dyes and for medicinal drugs. I do not know any more about these things, and I am sorry. When I arrived at this cape, the smell of flowers or trees of the land was so pleasant and delicate, that it was the sweetest thing in the world.

"Tomorrow, before I leave here, I shall go ashore to see what is here on the cape. The village is further inland, where, according to these men [the Indians] I have on board, lives the king who has much gold. Tomorrow, I want to go far enough to find the village and see or speak with this king who, according to the signs these men make, rules over all these neighboring islands, is clothed, and wears much gold. However, I do not have much faith in their talk, because I do not understand them well, and I know they have so little gold that, however little this king may have, it seems a lot to them.

"I believe that this cape that I call Cabo Hermoso is an island separated from Saometo, and that there is still another small island in between. I do not intend to find out so much in detail, because I could not do that in fifty years. I want to see and discover the most that I can in order to return to Your Highnesses, please the Lord, in April. Certainly, if I find where there is gold, or there are spices, in abundance, I shall stay until I have all I can get. Therefore, I am doing nothing else but to try to find it."

Saturday, 20 October. "Today, at sunrise, I weighed anchor from where I was with the ship, and anchored at this island of Saometo at the southwest cape to which I gave the name Cabo de la Laguna. I was at the island of Isabela in order to sail to the northeast and east from the southeastern and southern part of it, where I understood from these men that I have on board, the village and its king were located.

"I found that it was all so shallow, that I could neither enter in that area or sail in it. I saw that following the southwesterly route would be a very long way, and therefore I decided to turn back, to the route whereby I had come from the north-northeast to the west, and to sail around this island from there. The wind was so much ahead, that I was never able to keep to the land along the coast, except at night. And, because it is dangerous to anchor in these islands, except in daytime when one can see where to drop the anchor, all being patches, one clear, another not, I lay by all this Sunday night.

"The caravels anchored, because they found themselves near the shore early, and they thought, from the signals they were accustomed to, that I would anchor, but I did not wish to."

Sunday, 21 October. "At ten o'clock I arrived here at this cape of the small island and anchored, and the caravels did likewise.

"After having eaten, I went ashore, where there was no village other than one house, in which I found no one. I believe that the occupants had fled in fear, because all their furnishings were there. I did not allow anyone to touch anything, but I set out with these captains and men to see the island.

"If the other islands already seen are very beautiful and green and fertile, this island is much more so, and it has large groves of trees, and they are very green. There are some large lagoons here, and the woods around them are marvelous. Here and on the entire island, everything is green and the grass is like it is in April in Andalusía. And, with the singing of the little birds, it seems that a man would never want to leave here.

"Flocks of parrots darken the sun. There are so many kinds of large and small birds, and they are so different from our birds, that it is amazing. And then, there are a thousand kinds of trees. They all have their kinds of fruit, and they all have a wonderful fragrance. I am the sorriest man in the world not to know about them, for I am sure they are all something of value, and I am bringing specimens of them, and also specimens of the plants.

"Walking around one of these lagoons, I saw a snake, which we killed, and I am bringing the skin to Your Highnesses. When the snake saw us, it slid into the lagoon, and we followed it under the water, because it was not very deep, until we killed it with spears. It is seven palms in length, and I believe there are many similar to it in these lagoons.[13]

"Here I became acquainted with aloes [probably actually an agave plant/SLT], and I have decided to take ten quintals of it on board ship tomorrow, because they tell me that it is worth a lot. Also, while going in search of very good water, we came to a village nearby, half a league from where I am at anchor, and when the people of the village heard us, they all fled, left the houses, and hid their clothing and whatever they had in the woods. I did not allow anything to be taken, not even the value of a pin.

"Then, some of their men approached us, and one of them came right to us. I gave him some hawks' bells and some glass beads, and he was very satisfied and very happy. So that the friendship might further increase, and some request might be made of them, I asked him for water. After I went aboard ship, they came to the beach with their calabashes full, and they were very pleased to give it to us. I ordered that they be given another string of glass beads, and they said that tomorrow they would come. I wanted to fill all the casks on the ships with water here. Then, if time permits, I shall leave to go round this island until I may speak with this king and find out if I can get from him the gold that I hear he has."

Cipango or Cuba

"After that, I shall leave for another, much bigger island, which I believe must be Cipango [Japan/SLT],[14] according to the signs given to me by these Indians whom I am carrying on board. They call it Colba [Cuba/SLT], and they say that there are many very large ships and merchants.[15]

"Beyond this island is another island they call Bohío [Española/SLT], which they also say is very big. As for the other islands that are in between, we shall see when we pass, and if I find a collection of gold or spices, I shall decide what I have to do.

"I am still determined to go to the mainland and to the city of Quisay [Quinsai, presently Hangchow or Hangzhou/SLT], to present the letters of Your Highnesses to the Great Khan, to beg a reply, and to return with it."

Monday, 22 October. "All this night and today I was here waiting to see if the king here, or other persons, would bring gold or anything else substantial. Many of these people came, like the others of the other islands, naked in the same manner, and painted in the same manner, some of them white, some of them red, some of them blackish, and some of them painted in many ways. They brought spears and some balls of cotton to barter, which they exchanged here with some sailors for pieces of glass, broken cups, and earthenware.

"Some of them brought pieces of gold hanging from their noses, which they willingly gave for a hawk's bell, of the kind [made] for the foot of a sparrow-hawk, and for small glass beads. More than that is so little that it is nothing. The truth is that, however little a thing is given to them, they also considered our coming to be a great wonder, and they believed 'that we had come from the sky'.

"We took water for the vessels from a lagoon that is here near the so-called cape of the island. In this lagoon, Martín Alonso Pinzón, captain of the *Pinta*, killed a snake [Las Casas said this was an iguana/SLT], just like the other one of yesterday that was seven palms long. I had them gather as much of the aloes as could be found."

Tuesday, 23 October. "I would like to leave today for the island of Cuba, which I believe should be Cipango, according to the indications these people give of its greatness and riches. I shall not stay here any longer, or [try to go] around this island to go to the village, in order to have speech with this king or lord, as I had decided to do. I shall not stay long, because I see that there is no mine of gold here, going around these islands requires many kinds of wind, and the wind does not blow here as people would like it to.

"Since I must go where there may be a big affair, I say that it is right not to delay, but to go ahead and pass through much land until striking very profitable country. However, it is my understanding that this island may be very profitable in spices. But I do not know [about this island], which causes me the greatest sorrow in the world.

"I see a thousand kinds of trees, and they each have their own kinds of fruit. They are green now, as they are in Spain in the months of May and June. There are a thousand kinds of plants, the same with flowers. Of everything, only these aloes were recognized, much of which today I ordered brought aboard ship to bring to Your Highnesses.

"I have not set sail, nor am I setting sail, for Cuba, because there is no wind, only dead calm. It is raining hard, and it rained hard yesterday, without being at all cold. Instead, the days have been hot and the nights mild, as in May in Spain and in Andalusía."

Wednesday, 24 October. "This is night at midnight, I weighed anchors from the island of Isabela, Cabo del Isleo, which is on the northern side where I was lying, to go to the island of Cuba, which, I heard from these people, was very big with much activity, and where there was gold, spices, big ships, and merchants.

"They showed me that I would reach it by going west-southwest. I am keeping to this course, because I believe that this is indeed it, in view of the signs that have been given to me by all of the Indians of these islands, and by those whom I am carrying on board the vessels, for I do not understand their language. It is the island of Cipango [Japan], about which marvelous things are told. On the globes that I have seen, and on the delineations of the world map, it is in this area.

"I sailed to the west-southwest until daybreak, and as dawn was approaching, the wind fell calm and it rained. Thus it was during nearly all the night. I remained, therefore, with little wind until it was past midday, and then the wind blew again very gently, and I set all the sails of my ship: the mainsail and two bonnets, the foresail, the spritsail, the mizzen, and the topsail, with the batel astern.[16] Thus, I followed the course until nightfall, and then there was Cabo Verde, which is at the western part of the southern end of the island Fernandina, and it was seven leagues distant from me.

"The wind was blowing strongly now, and I did not know how far it was to the so-called island of Cuba. I wanted to avoid trying to find out at night, because [the water around] all these islands is very deep, and there is no bottom around them, except at a distance of two lombard shots [one thousand to two thousand yards/SLT]. It is all patchy here, sometimes rocky and sometimes a sand bar, and for this reason it is impossible to anchor safely except by eyesight. Therefore, I decided to lower all the sails except the foresail, and proceed with it only.

"After a short time, the wind increased considerably, I was in doubt about much of the way, it was very much overcast, and it was raining. I ordered the foresail to be lowered, and we did not go even two leagues this night."

3

The Discovery of Cuba, Called Juana or Cipango

The first few weeks in the Bahamas brought many encounters between Columbus's party and the most peaceful and gentle of the Arawak peoples of the Caribbean. Concerning the aboriginal condition of these islands and their inhabitants, geographer Carl Sauer concludes: "The tropical idyll of the accounts of Columbus and Peter Martyr was largely true. The people suffered no want. They took care of their plantings, were dexterous at fishing and bold canoeists and swimmers. They designed attractive houses and kept them clean. They found aesthetic expression in woodworking. They had leisure to enjoy diversion in ballgames, dances, and music. They lived in peace and amity."[1]

Columbus's repeated mention in his journal of the ingenuous and open nature of these peoples can be taken as indicating how deeply they impressed him. He says much the same thing after the first voyage in a letter written to Luis Santángel, who had interceded for him with the Queen: "They [the Indians/SLT] are . . . so free with all they possess, that no one would believe it without having seen it. Of anything they have, if you ask them for it, they never say no; rather they invite the person to share it, and show as much love as if they were giving their hearts; and whether the thing be of value or of small price, at once they are content with whatever little thing of whatever kind may be given to them."[2] Yet his was a mission with a purpose, and as we have seen, when he reached the shore of Guanahaní (San Salvador) in an armed boat, Columbus did not hesitate to take possession of the island in the name of the Sovereigns of Castile and Aragón. That the matter of possession was to extend to the natives themselves was soon manifested by the detention of certain individuals aboard ship. The periodic capture and escape of the island people is noted repeatedly throughout the record of the first voyage until the explorers finally returned with their booty, both human and material, to show the Sovereigns and their countrymen in Spain.

When Columbus did not find the anticipated quantities of gold and spices in the lands he discovered, he was anxious to identify other possibilities for financial reward that would justify the investment the Sovereigns had made in ships, men, and supplies. Three such possibilities presented themselves: first, the land itself, which Columbus reported to be beautiful wherever he went and capable of yielding a rich reward; second, the indigenous people, who could be brought to Spain for service or put to productive use in their native land; and finally, the gold and promise of pearls and spices, concerning which Columbus sought information wherever he went.

Columbus's exploration and search for wealth were, of course, greatly facilitated by the peace-loving and very hospitable island peoples. Any visitor to a native village would be welcomed to the dwelling of the local cacique. There, he would be feasted and offered the comforts of the household. It was even customary to offer women of the village for the pleasure of the honored guest.[3] Morison calls attention to the first "liberty" enjoyed by the crews of the vessels: "All day Saturday, October 13, the caravels lay at anchor on Long Bay [San Salvador/SLT] with a swarm of canoes passing back and forth, while the Spaniards in turn took shore leave, wandered into the natives' huts, did a little private trading for the curios that all seamen love, and doubtless ascertained that the girls of Guanahaní were much like others they had known."[4] These pleasant island peoples were obliging in other ways as well. Columbus found them able-bodied, willing to perform tasks when the occasion required, and anxious to please their visitors "from the sky." In many ways, then, the friendly Arawaks had unwittingly entered on a course that would lead to their own doom at the hands of these visitors from another world.

DISCOVERY—AND A PUZZLE

It is not difficult to imagine the puzzlement and frustration which Columbus must have felt as he moved from island to island about the Caribbean. For one thing, there was the problem of communication. However obliging the island peoples were, attempts to exchange information by sign and gesture must have been discouraging to Europeans and natives alike. For another thing, there was the matter of geography. Night after night, after dropping anchor at another new island, Columbus was forced to write in his journal some account like the following: "The people were all like the other people, already mentioned. They were in the same condition, naked, and of the same stature, and they gave what they had for anything that was given to them." Where were the sophisticated people that Marco Polo had found in his travels? Where were the great buildings and cities, the rich apparel, the quantities of gold, precious jewels, and spices? And where were the merchants who were prepared to trade for all these riches? In his mind, Columbus was certain that he had theoretically traveled the necessary distance to reach the Indies. He tried by making signs to raise questions concerning directions to particular places, by means of which he hoped to find the people and precious objects he sought. He relied mainly for this purpose on the natives taken aboard ship. Not really understanding his questions but eager to be of service, his captive Indians tried to direct him to what he continually asked for, but it was never enough.

Although disappointed at each move among the smaller islands, Columbus had great hopes for what the natives called Colba or Cuba. Presumably, by this time, the captive Indians whom the Spaniards had carried aboard ship, as expressed in the Las Casas abstract, "understood something and showed themselves well pleased with the Christians." From the rudimentary communication which this circumstance would have made possible, Columbus had learned that this island was of great size and richness. Because of the "gold, spices, big ships, and merchants" which he believed could be found there, he had formed the opinion that this land of Cuba, which he also called Juana, was Marco Polo's Cipango, our Japan. As Columbus recorded in his journal of October 24: "I am keeping to this course, *because I believe that this is indeed it*, in view of the signs that have been given to me by all of the Indians of these islands, and by those whom I am carrying on board the ships, for I do not understand their language. *It is the Island of Cipango*, about which marvelous things are told. On the globes that I have seen, and on the delineations of the world map, *it is in this area*" [emphasis added/SLT].

Accordingly, when the party reached Cuba a few days later, the three vessels proceeded along the north shore until they came to a large stream, which Columbus called the Río de Mares. Here the first encounters with the Cuban Arawaks took place, as is shown in the following excerpts of Columbus's journal. The account at this point is mainly from the Las Casas abstract, but the Admiral's exact wording appears here and there and was enclosed in quotation marks by Las Casas.

ADAPTED FROM THE
ABSTRACT OF THE JOURNAL OF COLUMBUS

Monday, 29 October. . . . They found many images in the shape of women here and a number of heads that were like masks, very well fashioned. It was not apparent whether these were used as ornaments or objects of worship. Here were small fowl about the houses, originally wild but now tame, as also curious collections of nets, hooks, and other gear for fishing, but the Spaniards, as they were ordered, touched nothing. . . .

Columbus said of the houses in this Cuban settlement: they were of a large size, constructed in the shape of a tent, and each collection of them appeared like a camp, without any order of streets but scattered here and there. The interiors were found very clean and neat, well furnished and set in order. They were all built of fine palm branches.

Thursday, 1 November. At sunrise the Admiral sent the boats ashore to visit the houses they saw there. They found the inhabitants had all fled, but after some time they espied a man. The Admiral then dispatched one of his Indians on shore, who called out to this man from a distance and bade him not be fearful as the Spaniards were friendly people . . . and had made many presents of their goods among the inhabitants of the islands. . . .

More than sixteen canoes came to the vessels bringing the usual trade goods, which the Admiral ordered should not be taken from them, as he wished them to understand that he was in search of nothing but gold. . . . Columbus saw no gold among them, but said he had observed an Indian with a bit of wrought silver at his nostrils, which he conceived to be an indication of the existence of that metal in the country.

These people [the Cubans, SLT] were found to be of the same race and manners as those already observed, without any religion that could be discovered. They had never seen the Indians they kept on board the ships engage in any sort of devotion of their own, but they would, upon being directed, make the sign of the cross and repeat the *Salve* and *Ave Maria* with the hands extended towards heaven.

The language is the same throughout these islands, and the people friends to one another, which the Admiral says he believes to be the case in all the neighboring parts, and that they are at war with the Great Khan, whom they call Cauila, and his country Basan. These people of Cuba go naked like the rest. . . . It is certain, says the Admiral "that this is the mainland, and that I am, says he, before Zayto and Quinsay, a hundred leagues more or less distant from one or the other," . . .

Ambassadors Sent to the Great Khan

Friday, 2 November. The Admiral resolved to send two of the Spaniards into the country. He selected for this purpose Rodrigo de Jerez, of Ayamonte, and Luis de Torres who had lived with the Adelantado of Murcia, and knew Hebrew, Chaldaic, and some Arabic; he had been formerly a jew. To these he joined two of the natives, one of those he had brought from Guanahaní, and another coming from the houses near the Río de Mares.

Tuesday, 6 November. Last night, says the Admiral, the two men whom I sent into the country returned, and related as follows. After having travelled a dozen leagues they came to a town containing about fifty dwellings, where there were probably a thousand inhabitants, every dwelling containing a great number; they were built in the manner of large tents. The inhabitants received them after their fashion with great ceremony; the men and women flocked to behold them, and they were lodged in their best dwellings.

They signified their admiration and reverence for the strangers by touching them, kissing their hands and feet, and making signs of wonder. They imagined them come from the sky, and signified as much to them. They were feasted with such food as the natives had to offer.

Upon their arrival at the town they were led by the arms of the principal men of the place to the chief dwelling, where they gave them seats, and the Indians sat upon the ground in a circle around them. The Indians who accompanied the Spaniards explained to the natives the manner in which their new guests lived, and gave them a favorable account of their character.

The men then left the place, and the women entered and seated themselves around them in the same manner, kissing their hands and feet and examining whether they were flesh and bone like themselves. They entreated them to remain there as long as five days.

Use of "Tabacos"

The Spaniards upon their journey met with great multitudes of people, men and women with firebrands in their hands and herbs to smoke, after their custom.

[In his *History of the Indies* (Book I, Chapter 46), Las Casas related this circumstance in more detail: "On their journey, these two Christians saw many people in their villages, men and women. The men all had firebrands in their hands and certain plants from which they got smoke. The plants are dry and are put on a certain leaf, which is also dry. It is like [the barrel of] a musket made of paper, like those the boys make at Easter time. It is lighted on one end, and they suck or draw or inhale that smoke from the other. As a result of this, they become drowsy and almost drunk. These muskets, or whatever we call them, are called tabacos by the Indians."/SLT].[5]

They did not find a village that had more than five houses, along the way, and everywhere they were given the same reception. The trees, plants, flowers, and birds, without animals, except the dogs that did not bark, remind us of what was described for the islands previously visited. They observed corn, and possibly greater stores of cotton than had been seen elsewhere.

The good, peaceful people, naked, except for the women, who only wore a piece of cotton large enough to cover their private parts; and all of good appearance, remind us of the natives previously described.

These words of Columbus contain a forthright and courageous statement directed to the Sovereigns: "I declare (says the Admiral here) that if they learned the language from devoted religious persons, soon they would all become Christians. And so I trust in our Lord that Your Highnesses will make a very careful decision in this matter in order to bring so many people to the Church, and that you will convert them, just as you have destroyed those who did not wish to confess the Father, the Son, and the Holy Ghost.[6]

"After your days, for we are all mortal, you will leave your kingdoms in a very tranquil state, free from heresy and wickedness, and you will be well received before the Eternal Creator, to whom I pray to give you long life and great increase of greater kingdoms and dominions, and the will and disposition to increase the holy Christian religion, as you have done thus far, Amen.

"Today I got the ship off the beach, and I am making haste in order to leave on Thursday, in the name of God, and to go southeast to look for gold and spices, and to discover land." All these are the words of the Admiral, who had been compelled by a contrary wind to remain on the beach, and was not able to get underway again until November 12th.

Cuba as Actually Observed

Monday, 12 November. They sailed from the port and the Río de Mares at daybreak. They directed their course in search of an island which the Indians on board affirmed repeatedly was called Babeque,[7] where as they related by signs, the inhabitants collected gold at night by torchlight upon the shore, and afterwards hammered it into bars.

The Admiral said that, on the previous Sunday, he had thought it would be well to take a few of the natives from the place where the ships lay, for the purpose of carrying them back to Spain, that they might acquire our language and inform us what their country contained, also becoming Christians and serving us as interpreters.

"I have seen and I know (says the Admiral) that these people have no religion, nor are they idolators, but they are very gentle, and they are without knowledge of what is evil. They neither kill or seize others. They are without arms and they are so timid that a hundred of them run away from one of our people, even though they may be joking with them.

"They are credulous, they feel that there is a God in the sky, and they firmly believe that we have come from the sky. They very quickly say any prayer that we tell them to say, and they make the sign of the cross. Therefore, Your Highnesses must decide to make them Christians, because I believe that, if you begin doing this, in a short time you will end up having converted a multitude of people to our Holy Faith, and you will acquire great dominions and riches, and all their people, for Spain.

"Without doubt, there is a very great amount of gold in these lands. These Indians that I am carrying on board say, not without reason, that there are places in these islands where they dig for gold, and they wear it on their necks, ears, arms and legs. There are very large bracelets, and also there are precious stones and pearls and unlimited spices. In this Río de Mares, from where I departed this night, there ⸺ a great quantity of mastic, and more yet if more ⸺ ⸺ted, because when these trees are planted, they take root easily. There are many of them, they are very large, and they have leaves like the lentisk [*lentisco*, a kind of mastic tree common in Spain/SLT] and fruit. They are larger, both trees and leaves, as Pliny says, than what I have seen on the island of Chios in the Archipelago.

"I ordered that many of these trees be tapped in order to see if they would yield resin that I could bring back. But, as it has rained constantly during the time I have been at this river, I have been unable to get any of it, except a very little which I am bringing to Your Highnesses. And also, it may be that it is not the time to tap them, for I believe that it is good to do this at the time when the trees begin to come out of the winter and are ready to flower. Here, the fruit is already nearly ripe now.

"Also, there must be a great quantity of cotton here. I believe that it would sell very well here, without transporting it to Spain, but rather to the great cities of the Great Khan, which will undoubtedly be discovered, and to many other cities of other lords who will be happy to serve Your Highnesses, and where other things will be taken from Spain and from the lands of the east, for these lands are west of us.

"Here there is also an endless quantity of aloes, even though it is not anything that will produce much profit. But, it is good to know about the mastic, because there is none other except in the island of Chios, and, if I do not remember incorrectly, I believe that they easily gain fifty thousand ducats from it.

"Here, in the mouth of this river, is the best harbor I have seen to date. It is clear, wide, and deep, and it is a good place and site to build a town and fort. Any ships whatsoever can stand in to shore here. The country is very temperate and high, and has very good water.

"Yesterday a canoe with six young men came alongside the ship, five came aboard the ship, I ordered that they be detained, and I am bringing them. After that, I sent some men to a house which is on the west side of the river, and they brought back seven women, small and large, and three children. I did this, because men behave themselves better in Spain when they have women from their own country than they do without them. Many other times it has already happened men have been brought from Guinea in order that they might learn the language in Portugal; and after they returned and it was hoped there would be some benefit from them in their own country, in return for the good association they had had and the gifts they had received, when they reached their country, they were never seen. Others did not act thus.

"But these men, having their women, will have a mind to do what they are asked to do, and also, these women will teach much of their language to our people. It is all one language in all these islands of India. All understand each other, and they all visit with their canoes. They do not have this situation in Guinea, where there are a thousand languages, so that one person does not understand the other.

"This night there came aboard in a canoe the husband of one of these women and father of the three children, a boy and two girls. He said that he wanted to come with them, and he pleaded with me. Now they are all consoled with him, because they are all related. He is a man of 45 years of age." All this is in the words of the Admiral.

Wednesday, 14 November. Stood off and on during the night, not judging it safe to sail among the islands in the dark. The Indians informed them yesterday that the distance from Río de Mares to the island of Babeque was three days voyage, this of course was to be understood as voyage in their canoes, which go about seven leagues or twenty-eight miles in a day.

The wind was light, and though their direction was east, it would not allow them to steer within a point of this course; these, and other hindrances which are related, kept them from making any progress before morning.

Problems with Indians and Spaniards

Saturday, 17 November. Today the two oldest Indians taken at the Río de Mares, and sent on board the *Niña*, made their escape.

Tuesday, 20 November. The Admiral was unwilling to proceed to the island he had named Isabela, which was about a dozen leagues off, and where he might have anchored that day, for two reasons: One, because he saw two islands to the south which he wished to examine; the other, because he feared that the Indians on board, whom he had taken from San Salvador or Guanahaní, as the natives called it, might effect their escape, as that island was only eight leagues distant from Isabela; this he wanted to prevent as he wished to carry them to Spain.

The Indians, as he informs us, were given to understand that in case the Spaniards met with gold they intended to set them at liberty.

Wednesday, 21 November. Today Martín Alonso Pinzón, in the caravel *Pinta*, left the other ships, without leave of the Admiral, incited by his cupidity, upon the occasion of an Indian on board his vessel offering to show him where he might find much gold. Thus he abandoned them without any excuse or necessity, or stress of weather, and the Admiral said: "He had, by language and actions, occasioned me many other troubles".

Monday, 26 November. They sailed this day thirty-two miles, which is eight leagues: In this course they saw and marked down nine very remarkable harbors, which the mariners affirmed to be excellent, also five large rivers were seen, the ships keeping close along the coast in order to have a good view.

The land seemed to consist of very lofty mountains of a delightful appearance, not rocky or barren, but smooth and abounding in beautiful valley, the whole most enchantingly covered with tall and flourishing trees, among which appeared to be many pines. Beyond Cabo del Pico, toward the southeast, were a couple of islets, each of about two leagues circumference, within these, three fine harbors, and two large rivers.

No towns were seen along the northeast Cuban coast, although there probably were some, to judge from the indications they encountered, for wherever they were on shore, they found fires burning, and other signs of inhabitants. The Admiral thought the land that was seen to the southeast of Cabo de Campana, was the islands called by the Indians Bohío [Española/SLT], as it appeared to be separated from that land [Cuba/SLT].

All the natives whom they hitherto met with seemed to entertain a great dread of the people of the place they called Caniba or Canima, and stated that they resided in this island of Bohío [Española/SLT], which the Admiral says must be a very large one, and thinks that the inhabitants plunder the lands and houses of the other Indians, who are very timid and are ignorant concerning weapons. It is on this account that he supposes the Indians are afraid to build their houses near the sea, in the vicinity raided by their enemies.

He relates that the Indians on board, when they perceived the Spaniards were directing their course thither, were speechless with fear, thinking they should be devoured. They were unable to shake off these apprehensions, and persisted in affirming that the men of this country had the faces of dogs, with only one eye; this the Admiral did not believe, and was of opinion that the people who made prisoners of these Indians, belong to the Great Khan.

Tuesday, 27 November. At the foot of the cape called Cabo de Campana they found an excellent harbor and a large river; a mile beyond, another river; half a league further, a third river; and another half a league onward, the fourth. Four additional rivers were seen within the distance of as many leagues, the last of them about twenty miles from Cabo de Campana, to the southeast. The most of these had safe entrances of great breadth and depth, and form excellent harbors for large ships, being free from rocks, shoals, and reefs.

Standing along the coast they discovered that southeast of the last river was a large town [Baracoa/SLT], which was larger than any they had seen; a multitude of people came down to the seashore shouting loudly; they were all naked and had spears in their hands. The Admiral desired to converse with them, and ordered the sails to be lowered. They came to anchor, and the boats were dispatched on shore with such preparation and order, that the Indians should neither receive injury, nor cause any to the Spaniards. Some trifles were sent in the boats for distribution among them.

Those on shore made a show of attempting to prohibit the landing of the Spaniards, but perceiving the boats fearlessly approaching the land they retired to a distance. The Spaniards thinking that a small number of the crew might approach them without causing any fear, three of their number advanced towards the Indians, calling out to them in the Indian language, which they had learned to some degree from those on board, not to be afraid. Notwithstanding this, they took flight, leaving not a soul behind.

The Spaniards proceeded to the houses, which were built of straw, after the manner of others they had seen, but found neither inhabitants nor furnishings. They returned to the ships and set sail at noon for a pleasant cape called Maisí [or Punta de Maicí/SLT], which they saw to the east, about eight leagues distant.

Having sailed half a league in the bay, they observed toward the south a very singular harbor [Puerto de Baracoa/SLT]. The country at the southeast presented a most delightful view, descending in an open plain from the mountains. Large towns and the smoke of many fires were seen, and the land appeared to be well cultivated. These determined the Admiral to put into the harbor above mentioned, and to attempt some intercourse with the people. This harbor he declared to be far superior to all he had yet seen, for the populousness and beauty of the country in the neighborhood, and the fineness of the air. . . .

Columbus adds these words: "I am not writing about how great the benefit may be from here. It is certain, Lord Princes, that, where there are such lands, there must be numerous things of benefit, but I am not lingering in any harbor, because I would like to see all the other lands that I can, so that I can report on them to Your Highnesses.

"Also, I do not understand the language, and the people of these lands do not understand me, nor do I or anyone else I have on board understand them. As for these Indians I am carrying on board, I often take one thing from them to mean the opposite. Nor do I trust them very much, because many times they have tried to escape.

"But now, the Lord be willing, I shall see the most that I can, and little by little, I shall come to understand and know this language, and I shall have it taught to persons of my household, because I see that up to here it is all one language.

"Then the benefits will be known, and there will be some effort to make all these people Christians, for it will be done easily, because they have no religion, nor are they idolaters. And Your Highnesses will order that a city and a fortress be built in these parts, and these countries will be converted."

A Healthy and Wealthy Land

"I assure Your Highnesses that I do not believe that there can be better lands under the sun than these lands in fertility, in moderation of cold and heat, and in abundance of good and healthful water, not like the rivers of Guinea [in Africa/SLT], which are all pestilential. Praise be to Our Lord, up to today, among all my people, there has been no one who has had a headache or who has been sick in bed, except one old man with kidney stones, from which he had suffered all his life, and he soon recovered at the end of two days. This that I say applies to all three vessels.

"Thus, may it please God that Your Highnesses send learned men here, or that they come, and that they will later verify the truth of everything. Earlier I spoke about the site of a town and fortress on the Río de Mares, because of the good harbor and the area, and it is certain that all I said is true, but there is no comparison between here and there or the Mar de Nuestra Señora. Inland from here there must be great settlements, countless people, and things of great value.

"This is why here, and everywhere else I have discovered and have hopes of discovering before I return to Castile, I say that all Christendom will trade with them, and Spain most of all, for all should be subject to Spain. And I say that Your Highnesses should not allow any foreigner, except Christian Catholics, to trade or set foot here, because this was the beginning and the end of the enter-prise, which was to be for the increase and glory of the Christian religion, nor should anyone come to these parts who is not a good Christian." These all are his own words.

Wednesday, 28 November. They remained in port all day because of the rain, although they might have sailed along the coast, for the wind was blowing from the southwest. But since the heavy weather would have hindered the view of the land, the Admiral thought best to remain at anchor, especially considering the danger from lack of familiarity with the coast.

The crews went on shore to wash their clothes, and some of them went a distance into the country. They found large villages with the houses empty, the natives having fled. They also dis-covered another river, larger than that at the harbor.

Thursday, 29 November. As it continued to rain and the sky was completely covered with clouds, they did not set sail.

Some of the Spaniards went to visit a town toward the north-west, and found in the houses neither people nor things. On the way they met an old man who was unable to escape, they took him, assuring him of their friendly disposition, and after present-ing him with some trifles, allowed him to depart. The Admiral was desirous of seeing him in order that he might give him some clothes and converse with him, for he was much delighted with the country and judged it to be very populous.

They found a cake of wax in one of the houses which they preserved for the King and Queen, and the Admiral was of the opinion that where wax was found there must be a great many other valuable commodities. In one of the houses a man's head was found hanging from a beam in a small covered basket, like they found in a house in one of the other villages. The Admiral thought these were heads of the principal men as the houses in which they were discovered were of a very large size, and that the persons to whom they belonged were relatives of the deceased.

Friday, 30 November. They could not put to sea, the wind being from the east and contrary. The Admiral sent eight armed men, with two of the Indians on board, to explore the country, and obtain some communication with the inhabitants. They came to many houses, without finding within them any person or thing, the inhabitants having fled. At length they discovered four young men digging in the fields, who perceiving the Spaniards, took to flight and could not be overtaken. They travelled a considerable distance and saw a great many villages; the land was very fertile and the whole under cultivation. Large streams of water were seen, and in the neighborhood of one, they saw a canoe very finely built of a single log, it was ninety-five palms in length, and capable of carrying 150 men.

Monday, 3 December. Passing a branch of a stream, they proceeded to the southeast and came to a creek or cove, in which they saw five large canoes, like *fustas* [a type of boat/SLT] very handsomely wrought. At the foot of the mountain they found the land all under cultivation. The woods were very thick, and in passing through them, they came to a shed very well built and tightly covered, so that neither sun nor rain could penetrate it. Under it they found a canoe made like the others, from a log, as large as a fusta of sixteen [sets of] oars; it was well shaped and very handsomely carved.

Having ascertained that they possessed no gold nor any precious commodity, the Spaniards returned to their boats. The country was found to be very populous, but most of the inhabitants fled through fear. The Admiral declared to the King and Queen that these people are so timorous that ten men might put ten thousand of them to flight. They carry no weapons save sticks with the ends a little hardened in the fire: these were very easily obtained from them.

Arrived at the boats, two men were sent off to a place where the Admiral thought he had seen a large beehive. Before their return, many Indians came to the boats where the Admiral was with his crew, and one of them jumped into the river and came to the stern of the Admiral's boat where he made a long speech, nothing of which was understood [by the crew] except that the other Indians held up their hands to heaven from time to time, and uttered loud cries. The Admiral was of the opinion that they were assuring him of the pleasure which his arrival gave them, but presently observed that the Indian on board changed color and trembled exceedingly, entreating the Admiral by signs to leave the river, for the natives were about to kill them all.

He [the Indian on board] then took a cross-bow from one of the Spaniards and held it out towards the Indian [from the group on shore], and uttered a speech which the Admiral understood to be a menace of hostility against them. He also seized a sword, and drawing it from the scabbard showed it to them, using the same language, which being heard by those on shore they all took to flight. The Indian [aboard] continued trembling and seemed overpowered with fear, although a stout, well-made fellow.

The Admiral was determined not to leave the river, but rowed for the shore toward a place where he saw many people, all of them naked, and stained red, some with tufts of feathers in their hair, and all having spears. "I approached them," says he, "and gave them some pieces of bread, demanding their spears, which they gave me for a hawk's bell to one, a little brass ring to another, and a few beads to another. In this manner they were all pacified, and came to the boats offering their articles for anything we chose to give them in return. A turtle had been killed by the sailors, and the shell lay in pieces in the boat. The ships' boys acquired the spears of the Indians with it, at the rate of a handful of spears for a piece the size of a fingernail.

"These people are like the others I have seen, and imagine we have come from the sky. They are ready to barter anything they possess for whatever we choose to give them, without objecting to the small value of it; and if they had spices or gold, I believe it would be the same.

"I saw there a handsome house of a moderate size, with two doors, as all the others have. I entered it and found a very singular contrivance in the manner of alcoves, which I cannot describe; from the ceiling hung cockle shells and other things. I took it to be a temple and called the Indians, inquiring of them by signs whether they offered up their devotions there, to which they replied in the negative, and one of them climbed up and gave me the ornaments which were hanging about; some of them I accepted."

Wednesday, 5 December. All last night they lay to off Cabo Lindo [Punta del Fraile/SLT], in order to examine the land which extended to the east, and at sunrise discovered another cape [cabo Maisí/SLT] in that direction, two and a half leagues distant, which having passed, they found the coast began to tend toward the south and southwest [the eastern extremity of Cuba called Punta de Maisí/SLT], and presently discovered a lofty and handsome cape in that direction, about seven leagues from the last.

The Admiral was inclined to steer that way, but his desire to visit the island of Babeque, which according to the Indians was to the northeast, restrained him. The wind, however, blowing from the northeast, hindered him from steering that direction; proceeding onward, therefore, he could see land to the southeast [Española/SLT] which appeared to be quite a large island, and according to the information of the Indians was very populous and called Bohío.

The inhabitants of Cuba, or Juana, and those of the other islands entertained a great dread of these people of Bohío [Española] imagining them to be man-eaters. The Indians communicated other remarkable things by signs to the Spaniards of which the Admiral does not avow his belief but thinks those Indians are more ingenious and artful than the others, as they were accustomed to make prisoners of them.

Cuba at the Time of Columbus

The aboriginal population of Cuba was somewhat different from that of the Bahamas. At the time of the Spanish incursion, the westernmost tip of the island of Cuba and small pockets elsewhere were still occupied by a remainder of the Ciboney. The eastern part of the island was inhabited by Taino, "who are said to have migrated from Hispaniola [Española/SLT] only fifty years before the conquest."[8] Elsewhere in Cuba lived people identified as Sub-Taino, who also apparently came from Española at a somewhat earlier date. The Cuban Arawaks, like those of the Bahamas, were a peaceful people. They lacked a number of the political and recreational features which had developed in Española and which are marks of the Circum-Caribbean tribes. The island was apparently more sparsely populated than Española or Puerto Rico. There may have been reasons for the Indians of Cuba and of the Bahamas to fear the more highly organized groups on Española, which seems to have been the center of power in the Caribbean.

Despite these differences, the people whom Columbus found in Cuba were similar to those on the islands of San Salvador, Santa María, Fernandina, and Isabela. There was little gold or other evidence of the kind of wealth that Columbus connected with the Indies of Marco Polo. The ships, merchants, and merchandise that were so eagerly anticipated did not materialize. Having followed the lengthy north coast of Cuba, with so little of the reward he desired, the Admiral must have been disappointed. Still, he kept following the trail which had been laid before him by his imagination and by the accumulated communications he had received from the Indians, both aboard ship and along the way.

4

Española and Guacanagarí

During the approach of the ship *Santa María* and the caravel *Niña* to the large island which Columbus called Española, the Spaniards observed several important geographical features. There seemed to be a wide channel separating Española from an island that Columbus named Tortuga. The land was not made up of rugged mountains but rose gradually to what appeared to be lofty elevations, most of the land seemed to be under cultivation, and the crops reminded Columbus of "the wheat fields in the plain of Córdova in the month of May."

The Admiral believed Española to be thickly populated, for there were many canoes and among them some as large as fustas, having fifteen banks of oars, which would be the length of a sizable barge. These were observed as the vessels entered the harbor called Puerto de San Nicolás because it was "the day of that Saint." Opposite the entrance to the harbor lay a beautiful plain, and a river flowed through the midst of that plain. As usually occurred, on the approach of the Spanish vessels, the Indians took flight.

The captive Arawaks aboard ship feared the people of Española and expressed distrust of Columbus because he had not followed the route that would carry them back to where they had been taken captive. The Admiral said he had no faith "in any of their representations," and so the lack of trust was mutual.

Columbus wanted to make contact with the people on shore, but uncertainty concerning the wind and the weather seemed to demand that he wait several days for suitable conditions. This he was not willing to endure, since he wanted "to make further discoveries" and to "find some good traffic in gold."

ABSTRACT OF THE JOURNAL OF COLUMBUS

Tuesday, 11 December. The wind blowing east and northeast, they did not set sail. Directly opposite the harbor, as stated above, lies the island of Tortuga; this appears to be a large island, and the coast runs in the same direction as the island of Española, the distance between them being at the most, ten leagues, that is to say, from Cape Cinquin to the extremity of Tortuga, after which the coast tends to the south.

The Admiral wanted to proceed along the channel between these two islands, in order to make a survey of Española, which affords the finest view in the world. The Indians also informed him that this was the course he must take to reach the island of Babeque, which they described as very large, with rivers, valleys, and lofty mountains.

The island of Bohío, they stated, was larger than that of Juana, which the inhabitants called Cuba, and was not surrounded by water, but as nearly as could be understood from them was mainland, and is situated behind Española, which they called Caritaba. [Lack of understanding is apparent here/SLT.]

The inhabitants of all these islands live in great fear of the people of Caniba [the cannibals/SLT], and the Admiral here repeats, as he has done in many places, that "Caniba means no other than the people of the Great Khan, who live somewhere in this neighborhood, and come in their vessels and make prisoners of the Indians, who not returning, their countrymen imagine their enemies [the Caniba] have devoured them."

"Each day," as the Admiral said, "they improved in their communications with the Indians on board, and conversed with them without such misunderstandings as formerly."

Indian Woman "Showed Reluctance to Leave the Ship"

Wednesday, 12 December. They were still unable to set sail, as the wind remained contrary. A large cross was set up at the entrance of the harbor, upon a beautiful spot on the west side "as an indication," in the words of the Admiral, "that your Highnesses possess the country and principally for a token of Jesus Christ our Lord, and the honor of Christendom."

This being done, three sailors went into the woods to view the neighborhood and presently heard sounds of the Indians, a crowd of whom they shortly after discovered, completely naked; they pursued and called out after them, but they all took to flight.

Having been directed by the Admiral to take some of the natives if possible, as he wished to show them some good offices and dissipate their fear, thinking from the fine appearance of the country that something valuable might be obtained here, the Spaniards kept on in pursuit and succeeded in capturing a female, handsome, and to appearance quite young; they brought her to the vessels where the Admiral conversed with her by the interpretation of his own Indians, as their language was the same. He likewise caused her to be clothed, and presenting her with glass beads, hawk's bells and rings of brass, dismissed her to go home with every civility. Some of the crew were sent with her, as also three of the Indians, for the purpose of communicating with the inhabitants.

The sailors who carried her ashore told the Admiral that she showed much reluctance to leave the ship, and seemed inclined to remain with the females on board, whom they had taken at Puerto de Mares on Juana [Cuba/SLT]. The Indians, with whom she was first in company, came in a canoe, and when they came to the entrance of the harbor and perceived the ships, abandoned their canoe and fled toward their houses, whither she now directed the Spaniards. This woman wore a bit of gold at her nose, which was an indication that it was to be found in the island.

Thursday, 13 December. The three men whom the Admiral had dispatched into the country with the woman returned, not having gone to the Indian town, by reason either of the distance or their fear. They affirmed that the next day many of the inhabitants would come to the ships, as they would be encouraged by the accounts which the woman would give them. The Admiral, as he wished to ascertain whether there was anything valuable here, which he was inclined to believe on account of the beauty and fertility of the country, and wishing to do everything for the service of the King and Queen, resolved to send again to the town, confiding in the relation which the female must have given them of the friendly disposition of the Spaniards. For this purpose, he selected nine persons from the crew, and dispatched them well armed and fitted for the enterprise, accompanied by one of his Indians.

They set out enroute to the town, which they found in an extensive valley four leagues and a half to the southeast. It was deserted, for the inhabitants, perceiving the approach of the Spaniards, had all fled, leaving everything behind them. The town consisted of a thousand houses and more than three thousand inhabitants.

The Indian who accompanied the Spaniards ran after the fleeing townsmen, calling out to them not to fear, for the strangers were not from Caniba but from the sky, and they gave many fine things to those whom they met. This had such an effect upon them that they took courage and came in a body of more than a thousand to the Spaniards, putting their hands upon their heads, which is a manifestation of great reverence and friendship. They stood trembling before them until the Spaniards, by many assurances, dissipated their apprehensions. . . .

While they were together with the Spaniards, they saw a great multitude of people, with the husband of the woman whom the Christians had taken and entertained. This female they were carrying upon their shoulders and they came to thank the Spaniards for the honor which the Admiral had shown her and for the gifts which he had given her. These people, according to the report of the men, were the handsomest and best disposed of any they had yet seen. The Admiral says he doesn't know how they could be better disposed than those of the other islands, assuring us that he had found them all of the very best disposition. As to beauty, the men stated that they exceeded the others beyond comparison, both men and women being of a much lighter color, and that two young females were seen as white as could be found in Spain.

Saturday, 15 December. They left the harbor again, to proceed on their course, but on putting to sea, found a strong easterly wind ahead, upon which they stood for Tortuga, and arriving at the island, stood about and steered towards the river which they had seen the day before and could not reach, but were again unable to make their way there. They came to anchor half a league to leeward, at a beach with a good anchorage. The Admiral went with the boats to view the river and entering an inlet nearby, found it was not the mouth. Returning, he discovered it at last, with only a fathom's depth of water and a strong current.

He entered here, with the intention of visiting the settlements which the men he had sent into the country had seen in this quarter. The end of a rope was carried on shore, and the boats were towed up against the current the distance of two lombard-shots [one thousand to two thousand yards/SLT], not being able to proceed any further because of the velocity of the stream. Some houses were seen, and the valley where the town was situated. A river, which was the one they had entered, ran through the valley, and the Admiral declared that he never witnessed a more beautiful prospect. At the mouth of the river they saw some of the inhabitants, who immediately fled.

The Admiral stated that these people must have been subject to frequent incursions from their enemies, since they displayed such a degree of fear. Wherever the Spaniards came, the inhabitants were observed to make signals by smoke, all over the country, more especially in Española and Tortuga. He named this valley, Valle del Paraiso [Paradise Valley], and the river, Guadalquivir, it being as wide as the river of that name at Córdova [in Spain]. The banks were rocky but pleasant and easy to travel.

Sunday, 16 December. At midnight, set sail with a light land breeze, and put to sea. At three o'clock, it shifted to the east, when they stood close upon the wind, and at a distance from the land, half-way between Española and Tortuga, met with a canoe containing an Indian, at which the Admiral was surprised, wondering how he could keep to the sea under so strong a wind. They took him on board with his canoe, and feasted him, presenting him with glass beads, hawk's bells and brass rings.

The vessels then steered to land towards a village [Port of Paix/SLT] near the shore about sixteen miles distant, where they anchored, finding a good place near the village. This appeared to be a new settlement; all the houses being of recent construction. The Indian went on shore, with his canoe, giving a favorable account of the Spaniards to his countrymen. They were already prepossesed in their favor, by the information they had received from the inhabitants of the town which they had visited previously.

The "King" Guacanagarí

Presently there came to the shore more than 500 people, and shortly after, their king. They assembled upon the beach near where the ships were anchored. Before long they came on board in crowds, but brought nothing with them, except a few, who wore bits of very fine gold at their ears and noses; these they readily gave to the Spaniards.

The Admiral ordered every civility to be shown them, "because" as he observes, "these are the best and most gentle people in the world, and especially, as I hope strongly in our Lord, that your Highnesses will undertake to convert them to Christianity, and that they may become your subjects, in which light, indeed I already regard them."

They saw the king on the beach, and the natives around him offering their respects. The Admiral sent him a present, which he received in great state. He appeared to be a youth of about twenty-one years, and was attended by an aged tutor and other counsellors, who gave him their advice and answered the questions put to them. The king himself spoke but little.

One of the Indians belonging to the vessels conversed with him, and informed him that the Spaniards had come from the sky and were going to the island of Babeque in search of gold. He answered that this was well and that in that island there was much of the same metal. To the alguacil [officer] of the Admiral who carried the present, he described the course to be taken, and informed him that in two days he might arrive there. He also added that if the Spaniards were in want of anything which his country furnished, he would give it to them with much good will.

The people here were all naked, king as well as subjects, the females without displaying any symptoms of bashfulness. Both sexes were handsomer than any they had hitherto seen, their color light, and if clothed and guarded from the sun and air, would be nearly as fair as the inhabitants of Spain, the temperature of the air being cool and pleasant to a high degree. The land is very lofty, covered with plains and valleys, and the highest mountains are arable. No part of Castile could produce a territory comparable to this in beauty and fertility.

The whole island, and that of Tortuga, are covered with cultivated fields like the plains of Córdova. In these they raise ajes [the yam or sweet potato/SLT], from slips set in the ground, at the foot of which grow roots like carrots; they grate these to powder, knead this, and make it into bread of a very pleasant taste like chestnuts; the stalk is set out anew, and produces another root, and this is repeated four or five times.[1]

In the evening the king [Guacanagarí] came on board; the Admiral showed him every honor and informed him that he was a subject of the King and Queen of Castile [and Aragón/SLT], who were the greatest princes in the world. Neither the Indians of the ship, who acted as interpreters, nor the king himself believed this, but continued in the opinion that the strangers came from the sky, where they imagined the Kingdom of Castile was situated, and not upon this earth. Food of the Spaniards was given to the king, of which he ate a mouthful and gave the rest to his tutor and counsellors and the others about him.

"Your Highnesses may be assured," says the Admiral, "that these lands are so extensive, so good and fertile, especially the island of Española, that no person is competent to describe them, and no one would believe what was said of them, without seeing them. And Your Highnesses may be assured that they are as much your own as the territory of Castile, for nothing is wanting to this purpose, but a settlement here and orders of what to perform.

"With the men I have with me, which are not in great number, I can traverse these islands without opposition, for I have seen three of my crew go on shore, and a whole multitude of the Indians take to flight without offering to resist them.

"They are all naked, and neither possess [European-type/SLT] weapons nor know of them. They are so timid that a thousand of them would not oppose three of us. Thus, they are very well fitted to be governed and set to work to till the land and do whatever is necessary. They also may be taught to build houses and wear clothes, and adopt our customs."

Monday, 17 December. At night the wind blew hard from the east-northeast, but the sea was not much agitated in consequence, by reason of the island of Tortuga which lay across and served as a shelter against the heavy sea. They remained at anchor all day, and the sailors were sent with nets to fish.

The Indians took great pleasure in their intercourse with the Spaniards, and brought them certain arrows which came from the people of Caniba, or the Canibales; these were long stalks of cane, pointed at the ends with sticks, which were sharp and hardened in the fire. They were exhibited by two Indians who had lost portions of flesh from their bodies; these, they informed the Admiral, the canibales had eaten, which he did not believe.

Some of the Spaniards were sent on shore to the town and for strings of beads bought some pieces of gold beaten out into thin plates. They saw a native whom the Admiral took to be the governor of the district and whom the Indians call *cacique* [an Arawak word for "leader" or "chief"/SLT]; he had a plate of gold as large as the hand, which he appeared desirous of bartering; this he carried to his house and arranged to have cut into pieces, which he traded away one by one; the whole disposed of he informed them by signs that he had sent for more, which would be brought the next day.

Tuesday, 18 December. They remained at the anchorage through the day, not having a wind; and because the cacique had told them he had gold to bring. The Admiral says he was not impressed with the amount of this metal that he was likely to obtain, but wished to know whence it came, as there were no mines in this place.

In the morning he ordered the ships to be dressed out with their flags and arms, for a festival in honor of the Annunciation of the Blessed Virgin, and fired many salutes. The king of the island left his home, which was about five leagues off, and came to the town nearby at the hour of terce. The Admiral had sent some of the Spaniards from the ship there to ascertain whether the Indians had brought their gold.

These brought information that more than two hundred men came with the king, four of them carrying him upon a sort of bier. The king with all his attendants came to the ship, and the

Admiral being at his meal in the cabin observed: "Your Highnesses would have been pleased to witness the honor and reverence they showed him, naked as they are.

"On coming on board and finding me at table in the cabin, he came in the most respectful manner and sat down by me, and would not allow me to rise, or to leave off eating. I thought he would be pleased with some of our food, and accordingly ordered a portion to be placed before him, which he ate.

"Upon entering the cabin he made a sign with the hand for his people to remain without, which they did with the greatest readiness and respect in the world, and all sat down upon deck, except two men of mature age, whom I took for his counsellors: these came and sat down at his feet, and the king would take a small mouthful of the food and give the rest to his attendants, who ate it; he did the same with the drink which was offered him, putting it to his mouth and then passing it to the others; all this was done with great state and very few words, which as near as I could understand his conversation, were uttered in a very sensible manner, his two attendants watching his countenance, conversing with him, and answering for him with the greatest degree of veneration.

"The meal finished, an attendant brought me a girdle shaped like those of Castile, but of different workmanship; this he presented to me and I accepted, along with two pieces of gold, beaten very thin, of which metal I am inclined to think they possess very little, although they are in the neighborhood of the place where it is produced in abundance.

"I saw that he was pleased with the hanging over my bed, and made him a present of it, with some fine amber beads which I wore upon my neck, and some red shoes and a flask of orange-flower water. He was wonderfully delighted with these gifts, and both he and his counsellors appeared to regret very much that we could not understand one another's language.

"By all I could understand from him, he informed me that if I desired anything of his, the whole island was at my service. I then produced a gold *excelente* [a Spanish coin], upon which the images of Your Highnesses were stamped, and showed it to him, letting him know, as I had done before, that Your Highnesses reigned over the first kingdom in the world and that there were nowhere so great princes.

"I also exhibited to him the royal standards and the banners with the cross, which he much admired, and he spoke with his counsellors respecting the great power of Your Highnesses, who had sent me such a distance from the sky to these parts, without fear. Many other things were said, of which I understood nothing, save that they manifested great wonder."

As it grew late, the king desired to return to land, whither the Admiral dispatched him in the boat, with great honor, firing a salute. Arrived on shore, he ascended his bier and went up into the island accompanied by the whole multitude. His son was carried behind him upon the shoulders of one of the most honorable men.

Wherever the Indians met with any of the sailors, they gave them food and showed them great respect. One of them encountered the troop accompanying the king home, and stated that he saw the presents the Admiral had given, each separate article carried before the king by one of the principal men, as judged from appearance.

The king's son followed his father with an equal train of attendants, as also a brother of the king, except that he went on foot, being led by the arms by two honorable men. This person came to the ship after the king had left her, and the Admiral made him a few presents, learning now, that the king was called in the language of the Indians "Cacique."

Friday, 21 December. Fields were seen under cultivation, indeed this was the case everywhere. Two men were dispatched from the boats and ordered to ascend a height and seek out the villages of the inhabitants, as none were seen from the sea, although it was judged that there were some in the neighborhood, by reason of a canoe with Indians which had come to the ship about ten o'clock the night before, to see the Admiral and the Christians. The Admiral presented these men with some trifles, which pleased them greatly.

The two Christians returned, informing us that they had discovered a large settlement at a little distance from the sea. The Admiral ordered the boats to be rowed in that direction, and presently saw several Indians coming down to the shore. They seemed to be fearful of the Spaniards, and the Admiral directed the boats to be stopped and the Indians on board to speak to those on shore and tell them they were friends, upon which the natives came closer to the water's edge, and the boats proceeded to land. The inhabitants now banished all their fears and came in such numbers as to cover the beach, extending a thousand pleasantries to the Spaniards, including men, women, and children.

Inhabitants Not Jealous of Their Women

The Admiral says concerning these people: "They are all as naked as they were born, both men and women: whereas in Juana [Cuba] and the other islands the females wear a small covering of cotton at the waist, like the flap of a man's drawers, to cover their private parts, especially those above a dozen years, neither old nor young practice it here.

"Elsewhere we have found the men anxious to conceal their women from the Christians, but here they display no such jealousy. The women of this place have very attractive bodies, and they were the first to give thanks to heaven upon our arrival, and bring what they had, especially food: bread of ajes, *gonza avellanada*, and five or six kinds of fruit."[2] These last the Admiral caused to be preserved for the King and Queen. They had received similar treatment from the women in other parts, before care was taken to conceal them.

The Admiral gave strict orders that the utmost care should be taken not to give offense to the natives in anything, and that no article should be taken from them without his permission; in this manner they were paid for everything they gave the Spaniards. The Admiral remarks that he believes no one ever met with a people of such a liberal and generous disposition, which was exercised to such a degree that they were ready to rob themselves of every article of property to oblige their guests, flocking to them with offerings wherever they arrived.

He sent six of his men to examine a town they had seen; to these the Indians showed every honor and presented such things as they had, not doubting in the least that the Admiral and all his crew had come from the sky, which the Indians on board also continued to think, notwithstanding what the Spaniards had told them. . . .

Columbus then left the place to return to the vessels, the Indians all calling out, men, women and children, and entreating him to remain among them. Several canoes full of men followed the boats to the ship; these the Admiral treated with much civility and gave them food and other presents. Great numbers came from the shore swimming about the ship, which was above half a league from the land.

While the Admiral was away, another prince came from the westerly part of the island, and not finding him, returned home. The Admiral sent some men to visit and obtain information from him; these he received very graciously, and conducted toward his town where he intended to give them some large pieces of gold. They went along with him until they came to a wide river, which the Indians passed by swimming, but the Spaniards, being unable to cross it, returned.

Saturday, 22 December. The sovereign of the country [Guacanagarí], who resided in the region, sent a large canoe full of men with one of his principal attendants. He invited the Admiral to come with the vessels to his territory, promising him anything he had. He sent a girdle by this messenger bearing a mask having the nose, tongue, and ears of beaten gold. The Indians in the canoe, meeting the boat, gave the girdle to a ship's boy, and proceeded on board the ship with their embassy.

Some time passed before these messengers were understood, the Indians on board not comprehending their message, since their language was somewhat different from that of the others; finally, they made their intentions known by signs, and thereby extended their invitation. The Admiral determined to accept it, and came to a resolution to sail the next day, which was Sunday, although he was not accustomed to put to sea on that day; this arose from devotion and not from any superstitious scruples. Besides, entertaining a hope that these people, by the willingness they manifested, would become Christians, and subjects of Castile, and already looking upon them in that light, he wanted to do everything he could to accommodate them.

Indians Liberal and Spaniards Greedy

Before their departure, he sent six of his men to a large village, three leagues to the west, the prince of that place having visited the Admiral the preceding day and saying that he had several pieces of gold. With these men, he sent his secretary, whom he charged to take care that the Spaniards did nothing wrong to the Indians, for these were so liberal and the Spaniards so immeasurably greedy, that they were not satisfied with receiving the most valuable of what the inhabitants possessed in exchange for a leather thong, a bit of glass or earthen ware, or other worthless trifle, and sometimes for nothing at all, which however, the Admiral had always prohibited.

Although the articles which the Indians offered were of little value, except the gold, yet the Admiral, considering the readiness with which they parted with them, such as giving a piece of gold for half a dozen strings of glass beads, ordered that nothing should be taken from them without paying for it.

The Spaniards having arrived at the town, the prince took the secretary by the hand and led him, accompanied by a great multitude of people, to his house, where food was set before them, and large quantities of cotton cloth and balls of yarn were brought to them. Late in the evening the Spaniards returned, the prince having presented them with three fat geese and some bits of gold. A great number of the Indians accompanied them back and insisted upon carrying their goods for them across the rivers and miry places.

The Admiral made the prince some presents, at which he and all his people showed the greatest pleasure and seemed to be happy in gazing upon the Spaniards, whom they believed to have come from the sky.

This day more than 120 canoes came to the vessels, all filled with people, and every one bringing something, particularly bread, fish, and water in earthen jars, as also some seeds which serve for spices; they put a grain in a cup of water and drank it, and the Indians on board the ships affirmed that it was very wholesome.

Sunday, 23 December. The want of wind compelled them to remain at anchor, and the Admiral dispatched the boats with his secretary to the prince from whom he had received the invitation the day before. While they were gone, he sent two of his Indians to visit the towns in the neighborhood. These returned, bringing a prince of the country with them, and information that gold was to be had in that island in as great quantity as could be desired, the people coming from other parts to obtain it. More people arrived who confirmed this account and showed the manner of collecting it. The Admiral understood this with difficulty, but still held it for certain that the metal must exist in abundance in these parts, and when the spot was found, it seemed that it might be had for little or nothing. He remarks that he is confirmed in this opinion because, in the three days he has been here, he has received many large pieces of gold and cannot believe it is brought here from other places. He then uttered these words: "Our Lord, in whose hands are all things, be my help, and order everything for thy service."

More than a thousand of the inhabitants visited the ships, every one bringing something. It was their custom, on arriving within half a bowshot, to stand up in their canoes holding their offerings out in their hands and exclaiming "Take! Take!" Besides these more than five hundred came swimming, for want of canoes, the ships being anchored about a league from the shore. Five princes with all their families came, along with the rest, to visit the Spaniards, to all of whom the Admiral gave presents, esteeming everything given well bestowed. "Our Lord in his mercy," says he, "direct me where I may find the gold mine, for I have many here who claim to have knowledge of it."

Monday, 24 December. Before sunrise they weighed anchor and put to sea with a land breeze. Among the Indians who came on board yesterday, and informed them that there was gold in the island, naming the places where it was found, there was one who seemed to display an uncommon degree of liking for the Spaniards; to him the Admiral was attentive, and he prevailed upon him to go along with them, and direct the way to the gold mines. This man was accompanied by another, his companion or relative, and both these, among other places they spoke of where the gold was obtained, named Cipango, which they called Civao [Cibao] and said it was very far to the east and possessed quantities of gold, and that the cacique of the country had his banners made of worked gold.

The Admiral says here: "Your Highnesses may be assured that there is not upon earth a better or gentler people, at which you may rejoice, for they will easily become Christians and learn our customs. A finer country or people cannot exist, and the territory is so extensive and the people so numerous, that I know not how to give a description of them. I have spoken highly of the people and country of Juana, which the inhabitants call Cuba. But there is a difference between these two countries as great as between day and night. I think no one who has seen these parts, can say less in their commendation than I have said.

"I repeat that it is a matter of wonder to see the things we have met with, and the multitudes of people in this island, which I call Española, and the Indians, Bohío; they are singularly pleasant in their intercourse and conversation with us, and not like the others, who when they speak appear to be uttering threats. They are well proportioned, both men and women, and their color not black, although they paint themselves, the most of them red, others of a dark hue, and others of still different colors, all which, I understand, is done to keep the sun from injuring them.

"The houses and villages are fair to see, and the inhabitants live in each settlement under the rule of a prince or judge [cacique], to whom they pay implicit obedience. These magistrates are persons of excellent manners and great reserve and give their orders by a sign with the hand, which is understood by all with a readiness that is wonderful." All these are words of the Admiral.

The Loss of the Santa María

Tuesday, 25 December. Christmas. Last night they kept along the coast with a light wind, from the sea of St. Thomas to the headland named Punta Santa, and at the end of the first watch, about eleven o'clock, being off this point about a league, the Admiral laid down to sleep, having gone without sleep for the past two days and night.

As the sea was calm, the man at the helm left his place to a boy and went off to sleep likewise, contrary to the express orders of the Admiral, who has throughout the voyage, in calm or storm, forbidden that the helm be entrusted to a boy.

The Admiral was free from any dread of rocks or shoals, because the Sunday before, when he sent the boats to the king, they had passed three leagues and a half to the east of Punta Santa, and the sailors had surveyed the whole coast for three leagues beyond that point and had ascertained where the ships might pass, a thing never done before in the whole voyage.

But as it pleased our Lord, at midnight, there being a dead calm and the sea being perfectly motionless, as in a cup, the whole crew, seeing that the Admiral had retired, went off to sleep, leaving the ship in the care of the abovementioned boy. The current carried the Santa María imperceptibly toward the shoals in the neighborhood, upon which she struck with a noise that might be heard a league away.

The boy at the helm, hearing the roar of the sea and feeling the current beating at the rudder, cried out, at which the Admiral awoke and sprang upon deck before any of the sailors perceived that they had run aground. Presently the master, whose watch it was, came up, and the Admiral ordered him and others who quickly made their appearance to hoist out the boat and carry an anchor astern.

The boat being hoisted out, the master and many others went into her, as the Admiral supposed to fulfill the order. Instead of doing this, they rowed off to the caravel, which was about half a league to windward. Those on board the Niña, however, with great propriety and justice refused to receive them, and sent them back, dispatching also their own boat which was first to arrive at the ship.

Meantime, the Admiral, finding his men deserting him and the ship down upon her side, with the water growing shallower, saw no other remedy but to cut away the mast and throw overboard everything they could spare, hoping that this would lighten and set her afloat, but in spite of all, the water continued to ebb and the ship to lie down towards the sea, which fortunately continued smooth, and presently she opened between the ribs.

The Admiral proceeded to the caravel to dispose of his crew, and as a slight breeze blew from the land, and much of the night remained, they lay to till day, not knowing how far the shoals extended. At daybreak he proceeded inside the reef to the ship, having first sent the boat to land with Diego de Arana of Córdova, alguacil of the fleet, and Pedro Gutiérrez, the King's butler or steward, to carry the news of his misfortune to the king [Guacanagarí], who had sent him the invitation the Saturday before, and whose residence was about a league and a half beyond the shoal where the ship lay.

Honesty and Benevolence of the Indians

This person, as they stated, shed tears upon hearing of the misfortune and dispatched the people of the town with large canoes to unload the ship. With their assistance the decks were cleared in a very short time, so great was the diligence of the king and his men. He, with his brothers and relatives, came to the shore and took every care that all the goods should be safely brought to land, and carefully preserved. From time to time, he sent his relatives to the weeping Admiral, consoling him and entreating him not to be afflicted at his loss, for he would give him of what he had.

The Admiral here observes to the King and Queen, that in no part of Castile would more strict care have been taken of his goods, not the smallest trifle was lost. The king ordered several houses to be cleared for the purpose of stowing the goods. A guard was set to watch over them throughout the night.

"The people as well as the king shed abundant tears," says the Admiral. "They are a very loving people and without covetousness. They are adaptable for every purpose, and I declare to Your Highnesses that there is not a better country nor a better people in the world than these. They love their neighbors as themselves, their speech is the most pleasing and sweetest in the world and is always spoken with a smile.

"Both men and women go naked, as their mothers gave birth to them, but Your Highnesses may be assured that they possess many commendable customs; their king is served with great reverence, and everything is practiced with such decency that it is highly pleasing to witness it. They have good memories and inquire eagerly about the nature and use of all they see." The Admiral says all this.

Wednesday, 26 December. At sunrise the king of the country visited the Admiral on board the Niña, and with tears in his eyes, entreated him not to indulge in any grief, for he would give him all he had; that he had already assigned the Spaniards on shore two large houses and if necessary, would grant others and as many canoes as could be used in bringing the goods and crew to land, which he had actually done the day before, without the smallest trifle being lost. "They are so honest and free from covetousness," says the Admiral, "and their king is pre-eminent in virtue."

While the Admiral was speaking with him, a canoe arrived from another place, with Indians bringing pieces of gold, which they wanted to exchange for hawk's bells, these being held in special value among them. Even before the canoe reached the vessel, the Indians called out, showing the gold and crying "take, take", for the hawk's bells, and seemed ready to go mad after them. Those in the other canoes standing off requested the Admiral to reserve a hawk's bell for them, and they would bring him in return four pieces of gold as big as his hand.

The Admiral rejoiced at all this, and presently a sailor came from ashore to inform the Admiral that the Spaniards were carrying on a great traffic with the Indians, purchasing bits of gold worth more than two castellanos [Spanish coins], for a strap of leather, and that this was nothing to what it would be within a month.

The king [Guacanagarí] was pleased to see the Admiral in good spirits, and understanding that he was anxious to obtain gold, informed him by signs that it was available in abundance nearby, and that the Admiral might be of good cheer, for he would give him as much as he wanted.

He gave him a further account of it, and told him it was available in Cipango which they called Cibao, in such abundance that it was held in no esteem. It was understood that it would be brought to him there, although in the island of Española, which they call Bohío, and in the province of Caritaba there were greater quantities.

The king took a meal on board the caravel and then went ashore accompanied by the Admiral, whom he treated with every honor, feasting him with several sorts of ajes, shrimps, game, and other foods which they had, and with their bread which they call cazabi [cassava]. Afterwards he conducted him into some groves of trees near the houses, where they were attended by a thousand people or more, all naked.

The king had on a shirt and a pair of gloves, which he had received from the Admiral, these last he particularly admired. In his manner of taking food, he showed a decency and cleanliness well worthy of his rank. After finishing his meal, which continued for some time, certain herbs were brought him with which he rubbed his hands for a considerable time, which was done, as the Admiral thought, to soften them; water was then brought to him for washing.

The meal completed, he went down to the shore with the Admiral, who sent for a Turkish bow and some arrows, these he gave to one of the crew who was expert in their use, and the exhibition of them much impressed the king, who knew nothing of weapons, his people neither using nor having them.

This all began, it is said, with a discussion concerning the people of Caniba whom they call Caribes; these, they stated, were accustomed to come and attack them with bows and arrows. It was ascertained that these arrows were not headed with iron, for neither iron nor steel are known in these parts, nor any other metal, except gold and copper, and the Admiral saw little of the copper.

The king was then given to understand by signs that the Sovereigns of Castile would send people to fight against the Caribes and bring them all prisoners with their hands tied. By order of the Admiral, a lombarda [cannon] and an espingarda [musket] were fired, and the effect of their shot struck the king with new wonder, frightening the Indians to such a degree that they fell upon the ground.

Afterwards a large mask was brought, with great pieces of gold, at the ears, eyes, and other places; this the king gave the Admiral, along with other ornaments of the same metal, which he placed upon his head and neck. Many other presents were also made to the Spaniards.

Fortress of Navidad

All these things had a great effect upon the Admiral in assuaging his grief for the loss of the ship, and he began to be convinced that our Lord had permitted the shipwreck in order that he might choose this place for a settlement. He says: "So many favorable things were offered to these purposes, that it cannot be called a disaster but a piece of great good fortune, for if we had not run aground, we should have kept off without anchoring here, since the place is in a large bay and within are two or three shoals. Neither should I otherwise have been induced to leave any men in these parts during the voyage, nor if I had, could I have spared them the proper provisions and materials for their fortification.

"Many of my crew have petitioned me for permission to remain, and I have today ordered the construction of a fort, with a tower and moat, all to be well built, not that I deem such a fortification necessary as a defense against these people (I have already stated that with my present crew, I could subjugate the whole island, which I believe to be larger than the kingdom of Portugal, with twice the population), but that I judge it proper. The territory is at such a distance from our country, and the natives who are naked, without arms, and timid, may thereby understand the genius of the people of Your Highnesses and what they are able to perform, so that they may accordingly be held in obedience by fear as well as love.

"For this purpose I have directed that there shall be provided a store of timber for the construction of the fort, with provision of bread and wine for more than a year, seed for planting, the longboat of the ship, a caulker, a carpenter, a gunner, a cooper, and many other persons, among the number of those who have earnestly desired to serve Your Highnesses and oblige me by remaining here and searching for the gold mine.

"To the undertaking which I have mentioned, things seem to have concurred very opportunely, in particular the ship's running aground in such a manner that it was not perceived until she was stuck, and this at a time when there was neither sea nor wind."

The Admiral relates other things to show that it was a piece of good fortune, and the determined will of God that the ship should be wrecked there, that the Spaniards might remain, for, as he states, had it not been for the treacherous conduct of the master and crew (who were mostly his countrymen), in not carrying the anchor astern to haul the ship off, as they were ordered, she would not have been wrecked, and thereby they should have failed to gain the knowledge of the country which they obtained during the stay, and by the men whom he intended to leave there.

His custom was to go on making discoveries and not to stay in any one place above a day, unless compelled by the wind, as his ship was a dull sailer and unfit for the purpose of discovery. He lays the blame for this upon the people of Palos, in not having complied with their agreement to furnish the King and Queen with suitable vessels for the expedition.

The Admiral concludes by observing that every piece of the ship was saved, there not being lost so much as a thong, board, or nail, she being as complete as when she first sailed, except what was caused by cutting her to get out the casks and merchandise. All these were carried on shore and well secured, as stated. He adds that he hopes to find at his return from Castile, a barrel of gold collected by them by trading with the natives, and that they will have succeeded in discovering the mine and the spices, and all these in such abundance that before three years the King and Queen may undertake the recovery of the Holy Sepulchre. "For I have before protested to Your Highnesses," says he, "that the profits of this enterprise shall be employed in the conquest of Jerusalem, at which Your Highnesses smiled and said you were pleased, and had the same inclination."

Thursday, 27 December. At sunrise the king came on board, and told the Admiral that he had sent for gold and wished he could cover him with it before his departure, or rather, that he would not depart at all. He took a meal with the Admiral in company with a brother and relative of the king; these two stated privately that they wished to go to Castile with him.

While they were on board, news arrived that the caravel *Pinta* was in a river at the end of the island. The cacique dispatched a canoe there, in which the Admiral sent a seaman. He [Guacanagarí] displayed such a degree of affection toward the Admiral that it was marvelous. The Admiral was already making diligent preparation for their return to Castile.

Friday, 28 December. In order to see to the construction of the fort and direct those that would remain, the Admiral went on shore. It seemed that the king espied him while he was embarked, for he entered his house in haste and sent one of his brothers to receive him. The Admiral was conducted to one of the dwellings given to the Spaniards, which was the largest and best in the place. Here there was prepared a seat made of the inner bark of the palm tree, upon which they caused the Admiral to sit. The king's brother then sent an attendant informing him that the Admiral was there, as if he were ignorant of it; the Admiral imagined that this was done to show him so much the more honor. The attendant having delivered his message, the cacique ran to the Admiral, carrying a great plate of gold in his hand, which he placed about his neck. He remained a night on shore, considering what was to be done.

"An Abundance of Gold" Available

Saturday, 29 December. At sunrise there came on board the caravel a nephew of the cacique, still a youth, but a person of good understanding and courage; and as the Admiral's constant object was to find the place where gold was produced, he made it a practice to question every one about it by signs, as they could converse in his manner. This young man informed him that at the distance of four day's journey to the east, was an isle [in reality a province/SLT] called Guarionex, and others called Macorix, Mayonic, Fuma, Cibao, and Corvay, and that they contained an abundance of gold. The names of these places the Admiral wrote down, and it afterwards came to the knowledge of the king's brother that the youth had given this information, whereupon some altercation ensued between them, as near as the Admiral could make out.

He had at other times understood that the king was exerting himself to prevent his learning where the gold was produced, lest he should go thither after it. "But there is such a quantity of it, and in so many places on the island of Española," says the Admiral, "that it is a matter of wonder."

At night the king sent him a great golden mask, begging for a washbasin and ewer; the Admiral supposed that he requested these, to have others made like them. The request was complied with.

Sunday, 30 December. The Admiral went to dine on shore, and found that five kings had arrived who were subject to Guacanagarí, the king above-mentioned. All these wore their crowns and went in great state, and the Admiral tells the King and Queen that Their Highnesses would have been highly pleased to observe their manners.

Guacanagarí came to receive him on landing and led him by the arm to the house where he was entertained the day before; here was an elevated space and seats, upon which he was told to sit; he then took his own crown from his head and placed it upon that of the Admiral, who in return took from his neck a splendid collar made of bloodstones and beautiful beads and put it upon the neck of the king. Also, divesting himself of a cloak of fine scarlet cloth, which he had put on that day, he clothed the king with it. He then sent for a pair of buskins which he placed on his feet, and a large silver ring which he placed upon his finger, having heard that the Indians had seen a sailor with a ring of that metal and had endeavored to obtain it. The king was greatly pleased with these gifts, and two of the other caciques came to the Admiral and each brought him a great plate of gold.

While he was there, an Indian arrived saying that two days ago he had left the caravel *Pinta* in a harbor to the east. The Admiral returned to his vessel, and Vicente Yáñez, the captain, told him that he had seen rhubarb, and that it was to be found on the island Amiga, at the entrance of the Sea of Saint Thomas, six leagues thence, and that he had recognized both the root and the branches. The description given of the rhubarb is that it sends forth branches and berries, which appear like green mulberries half dried; the stalk near the root is of fine yellow color, and the root itself like a large pear.

Tuesday, 1 January, 1493. The canoe which had been dispatched in quest of the Pinta returned without seeing her. The sailor who went in the canoe stated that at a distance of twenty leagues, they met a king who wore upon his head two great plates of gold, and as soon as the Indians who accompanied the sailor in the canoe spoke to him, he took them off.

The Admiral believed that Guacanagarí had prohibited all the others from selling gold to the Spaniards so that it might all pass through his hands. He had sent many canoes to collect it that day. The Admiral already knew the places as stated above, where it was so plentiful as not to be valued. The spicery, as the Admiral says, is also abundant, and more valuable than any available pepper. He left an order with those that remained to collect as much of it as possible.

Wednesday, 2 January. He went on shore in the morning, to take leave of Guacanagarí. He gave him one of his own shirts, and conversing with him about the Caribes, who made war upon the people of the island, he determined to give him a demonstration of the force of the fire-arms. For this purpose a lombarda [cannon] was ordered loaded, and fired against the side of the ship which was aground. The shot passed through her and struck the sea at a distance. He also presented for him a mock battle between armed members of the crew and then informed the cacique that he need not fear the Caribes, even if they should attack him.

All this was done, as he informs us, to strike a terror into the inhabitants and to make them friendly to the Spaniards left behind. He took the king and his attendants along with him to his house to dine. At parting, he gave a strict charge to Diego de Arana, Pedro Gutiérrez and Rodrigo Escovedo, whom he constituted his lieutenants over the force of the settlement, that everything should be well established and regulated for the service of God and their Highnesses.

The Cacique displayed great affection for the Admiral and showed a deep sorrow at separating from him, especially when he saw him about to embark. One of the Indians told the Admiral that Guacanagarí had ordered his statue to be made of gold, as large as life, and that it was to be finished in ten days. He went on board with the intention of setting sail, but the wind did not permit it.

He left in this land of Española, which the Indians called Bohío, a fort and thirty-nine men, whom he states were great friends of King Guacanagarí. Over these he placed Diego de Arana, a native of Córdova, Pedro Gutiérrez, the king's butler or steward, and Rodrigo de Escovedo, a native of Seville, and nephew of Fray Rodrigo Pérez, with all the powers the King and Queen had delegated to him. He left them all the goods which had been sent for bartering, which was a great amount, and everything belonging to the ship which had been wrecked. He directed that these goods should be traded away for gold. To these were added biscuit and wine for a year, and the long-boat of the ship, in order that they might, being mariners for the most part, at convenient opportunities undertake the discovery of the gold mine and a place proper for building a city, because this port did not suit him, and especially because the gold came from the east, and the further east they were, the nearer they would be to Spain. He also left them seed for sowing, his secretary and alguacil, a ships-carpenter and caulker, a good gunner and engineer, a cooper, a surgeon and a tailor, and all, he says, seamen.

Return Voyage

Thursday, 3 January. He did not set sail today, because last night, he says, three of the Indians from the islands, who had remained ashore, came aboard and reported that the remainder with their wives were coming. The sea was somewhat rough, not allowing the boat to go ashore.

The Admiral determined to sail, by the grace of God, the next morning. He says that if the caravel Pinta had been with him, he should have been certain of obtaining a barrel of gold, for in that case he should have ventured to coast along these islands. Being alone, however, he dared not do that, lest an accident should befall him and hinder his returning to Castile and informing the King and Queen of the discoveries he had made.

Even had he been certain that the Pinta would arrive safe thither, with Martín Alonso Pinzón, he should not have indulged his wish of surveying these parts further, for he feared that Pinzón might give a false report to the King and Queen, in order to escape the punishment which he merited for his misconduct in abandoning the Admiral without leave, and might thereby hinder the benefits consequent upon the discovery. He trusted that our Lord would grant him a favorable passage and a remedy for all evils.

Friday, 4 January. At sunrise they weighed anchor and stood out of the harbor with a light wind. They steered to the northwest passing the shoal by a channel much narrower than that by which they had entered.

There are very good entrances to sail into Villa de Navidad that contain from three to nine fathoms depth of water, extending from northwest to southeast. Here are shoals which reach from Cabo Santo to Cabo de Sierpe, more than six leagues, and which extend three leagues into the sea.

A league from Cabo Santo there are no more than eight fathoms of water, and within this cape, towards the east, are many shoals with navigable channels. All this coast runs northwest and southeast and has a beach extending its entire length. The land is very level for a space of four leagues from the shore, when it becomes diversified with lofty mountains, the whole very populous and abounding with large towns.

In the afternoon [Sunday, January 6th], the wind blowing strong from the east, a sailor was sent to the mast-head to look out for the shallows when he discovered the caravel Pinta bearing down upon them before the wind. There being no good anchorage in the neighborhood, the Admiral came about and stood back for Monte Christi, from which they had gone ten leagues. The Pinta kept him company, and Martín Alonso Pinzón came on board the Niña to make his excuses, saying he had parted company against his will. He offered several reasons for his conduct, which the Admiral says were all completely false, as he was motivated solely by his haughtiness and greed in abandoning him.

He confesses that he is unable to learn the cause of the unfavorable disposition which this man had manifested towards him throughout the voyage; but the immediate occasion of his deserting him, from information he acquired from an Indian the Admiral had placed on board his vessel, was that Pinzón had been told that in an island called Babeque he would find an abundance of gold. Knowing his vessel to be light and a swift sailer, Pinzón did not hesitate to abandon him as has been related. The Admiral concealed his resentment, so that he might not aid the machinations of Satan in impeding the voyage, as had hitherto been done.

It was ascertained that Martín Alonso, on arriving at Babeque, had not found any gold and had thence returned to the coast of Española, where from the information of the Indians, he expected to discover the mine. He coasted along the island for a distance of fifteen leagues, thereby approaching the Villa de la Navidad, spending over twenty days in all this. From this account, it appeared that the reports given by the Indians, of his being seen in the neighborhood, upon the strength of which king Guacanagarí sent the canoe after him, were correct.

The Admiral states that in this time Pinzón obtained much gold by trading, buying for a thong of leather, pieces as big as the two fingers, and at times as big as a hand. Of the metal thus acquired, he kept half himself and divided the rest among his crew. The Admiral states: "Thus I perceive, Sovereign Princes, that it was a providence of our Lord to ordain that the ship be cast away here, it being the best place in the whole island for a settlement, and nearest to the gold mines."

He adds that he had learned of another island behind that of Juana, toward the south, in which there was a still greater quantity of gold, and where it was found in grains of the size of a bean. In Española they are met with in the mines as large as kernels of wheat. This first mentioned isle was called by the Indians Yamaye [Jamaica/SLT].

From these places to the mainland, the distance was described as ten days' voyage in a canoe, which may be sixty or seventy leagues. It was said that the people of the continent wore clothing, and the Admiral says he was informed by many persons of an island toward the east inhabited solely by women [Matinino, identified with the island of Martinique/SLT].

Monday, 7 January. The Admiral's caravel was leaking; this day, he ordered her to be pumped out and caulked and sent the sailors ashore for wood. They found many mastic and aloe trees.

Tuesday, 8 January. The wind blowing hard from the east and southeast, he did not sail today, but continued providing wood, water, and other necessaries for the voyage. It was the Admiral's wish to coast along the whole island of Española, which he might have done upon his course homeward, but as he considered that the captains of the two caravels were brothers, namely Martín Alonso Pinzón, and Vicente Yáñez, and that they had a party attached to them, the whole of whom had displayed great haughtiness and avarice, disobeying his commands regardless of the honors he had conferred upon them—all such misdemeanors, as well as the treachery of Martín Alonso in deserting him, he having winked at without complaining, in order not to throw impediments in the way of the voyage—he though it best to return home as quickly as possible. He adds that he possessed many faithful men among his crews, but resolved to put up with the behavior of the refractory ones, and not undertake their punishment at such an unfavorable season.

THE FIRST "BATTLE" WITH THE INDIANS

As Columbus proceeded homeward along the north coast of Española, he came to the peninsula of Samaná. This area was occupied by the Ciguayo, who spoke an Arawakan dialect somewhat different from the language encountered elsewhere. These Indians were said to have some fifteen thousand warriors, which would suggest a total population of sixty thousand or more Ciguayans. We turn to Fray Bartolomé for a description of this encounter.[3]

HISTORIA DE LAS INDIAS, BOOK I, CHAPTER 67

Columbus sent the boat ashore for water and to gather gams from the farms that were there, and they landed on a beautiful beach. Also, the Admiral wanted to obtain some information about that land.

They found some men with their bows and arrows and stopped to talk with them. They bought two bows and many arrows from them, and asked one of them to come aboard the caravel and talk with the Admiral. He willingly agreed to do so.

The Admiral says that he was very unattractive, and that his face was all blackened with charcoal (this is not charcoal, but a certain coloring they get from certain fruit), because, he says, they are accustomed everywhere to painting themselves with various colors.

This man had all his hair very long. It was gathered and tied behind in a headdress of parrot feathers. He was completely naked like the others. The Admiral wondered if he was a Carib, like those who eat men but he was not, because there never were any Caribs on this island [of Española/SLT], as will be explained later when we tell about the island, God willing.

He asked the Indian about the Caribs, and the Indian indicated to him that they were to the east. He asked him about gold, and he also pointed to the east, in the direction of the island of San Juan [Puerto Rico/SLT]. The Admiral had seen the island of San Juan on the day before, before he entered this bay.

The Indian told him that there was much gold on that island, and he spoke the truth. A large amount of gold was taken from that island for some time. Not so much is found there anymore. Here they did not call gold "caona", as they did in the first part of this island, or "nozay" as they did in the small island of Guanahaní or San Salvador. They called it "tuob."

It should be noted here that a large section of this coast, more than twenty-five or thirty leagues, and fifteen or twenty leagues inland, as far as the mountains, making up the great valley of the north, was populated by some people who were called "Macoriges", and others who were called "Ciguayos", and they spoke a different language.

I do not remember if they differed from each other in language, as it was so many years ago, and there is no one today to ask about it. Although I talked on a number of occasions with both generations, more than fifty years have now passed. At least, I know this for sure, that the Ciguayos, in whose country the Admiral was now travelling, were called Ciguayos because they wore their hair very long, like the women do in our Castile.

The Indian told him about an island called Matinino which had much gold and which was inhabited only by women. At a certain time of the year, men would come. If the women gave birth to a girl, they would keep her, and if it was a boy, they would send him to the island of the men.

This was never confirmed later, that is, that there were only women in some country of the Indies. Therefore, I think that the Admiral took no notice, or that it was a rumor, just as he says here that he heard that there was another island that was called Guanín, where there was much gold, and there was not. However, there was much *guanín* in a part of that island, and this was a certain kind of gold of low quality that they called guanín. It has a somewhat violet color, and they prize it highly.

The Admiral ordered that the Indian be given food, and he gave him some pieces of green and red cloth and some glass beads. He ordered that he be put ashore by boat. When the

Spaniards came ashore, there were about fifty-five Indians by some trees. They were naked and were wearing their hair very long, in the same way, as has been said, as do women in our Castile. They were wearing their adornments of parrot feathers, and each one carried his bow. When the Indian who had gone to the ship landed, he persuaded them to lay down their bows and arrows and their weapons of palm wood, which are very hard and very heavy. They are made so that they are not sharp but flat, about two fingers thick all along. This weapon is hard and heavy as iron, so that, even if a man has his head protected by a helmet, his head will be crushed.

Those Indians came to the boat, and the Christians came ashore. They began to purchase the bows and arrows and the other weapons, because the Admiral had ordered them to do so. After having sold two bows, the Indians did not want to supply any more. Instead, they made ready to attack the Christians and to capture them. Perhaps they suspected that the Christians were buying the weapons from them so that they could attack them after that.

The Indians soon attacked, after getting their bows and arrows from where they had been keeping them. They got some cords or ropes, as if to tie up the Christians. When the Spaniards saw them approaching so boldly, few of them wishing to be martyrs, and not being off-guard, they forcefully attacked them. One of them stuck one Indian deeply in the buttocks with his sword, and another Indian was wounded in the chest with an arrow.

Having learned through this experience the difference between the weapons of the Christians and their own weapons, the effect that those weapons had in such a short time, and therefore, that they could gain little in the fray even though there were only seven Christians and more than fifty of them, the Indians all fled, leaving their bows and arrows here and there. The Spaniards might have unmercifully killed many of them, if the pilot who was in charge of the Spaniards had not interfered.

And this was the first battle to take place in all the Indies between Indians and Christians, where blood of Indians was shed. It is believed that the Indian with the arrow wound died, and that the Indian with the slashed buttocks was probably not too well off. Although little, it was the first blood to be spilled by the Christians.

5

Interlude

Columbus realized from the very beginning that his venture of discovery must show a return on the investments made by the Spanish Sovereigns, and he demonstrated that he was continually thinking of ways in which the indigenous Americans could be made useful. Throughout the first voyage, his journal repeatedly exhibits entries like the following: "They ought to be good servants and of good skill, for I see that they repeat very quickly whatever is said to them. I believe that they would easily be made Christians, because it seemed to me that they belong to no religion." Such statements were, of course, oversimplifications. One of the missionaries, Ramon Pané, would shortly learn of the native religious practices and write a report concerning them indicating that the religion of the islanders was more highly developed than the Admiral's first observations indicated.[1] Yet Columbus's frequent mention of the Indians' religion, or lack of it, shows the importance ascribed to future Christianizing of the inhabitants of these new lands.

In the same way, it was also indicated early that the Spaniards felt empowered to take possession not only of the lands of the Indians but of their persons as well. The taking of captives, ostensibly to serve as guides and interpreters, began almost immediately. On November 11, 1492, for instance, the Admiral's journal states: "It has seemed well to capture some of the people of that river [the Río de Mares in Cuba/SLT] to take to the Sovereigns to learn our language in order to find out what there is in the country, and on returning, to be interpreters of the Christians and adopt our customs and things of our faith." The captives taken included women and children as well as men, because, as Columbus explains, "the [Indian] men would behave better in Spain with women of their country than without them. . . .These [Indian captives], having their women, will find it good business to do what they are told, and these women will teach our people their language which is the same in all these islands." Many of these

Indians escaped from time to time and were replaced by others, yet the toll on the captives must have been great in ways that can only be imagined from matter-of-fact accounts such as the following: "This night there came aboard in a dugout the husband of one of these women and father of three children, a boy and two girls, and said that he wished to come with them, and begged me hard, and they all now remain consoled with him who should be related to all. He is a man of over forty-five years." This capture and forcible detention of the Indians seems, in a sense, incongruous in light of the great care taken by Columbus to ensure that the Indians property and homes were not disturbed.

Of course, the major theme running through the journal of the first voyage is the search for gold. As the journal tells us, Columbus "made it a practice to question everyone about it by signs," and the lure of gold and the desire to trade for it and to find its source figure prominently in his decisions on where and how to proceed in his exploration of the islands. Thus although Columbus himself is generous in his praise of these gentle, comely, and obliging peoples, it was clear from the very beginning that the tropical idyll of the Caribbean was intended for exploitation to the fullest possible extent.

The theory which allowed such exploitation of other lands by Europeans was founded in scholastic tradition. The Spaniards in the fifteenth and sixteenth centuries made use of the thesis set forth in the thirteenth century by Henry of Susa, cardinal bishop of Ostia, known to students of canon laws as Ostiensis or Hostiensis. According to this thesis, "heathen peoples had their own political jurisdiction and their own possessions before Christ came into the world. But when this occurred, all the powers and the rights of dominion held by heathen peoples passed to Christ, who, according to this doctrine, became lord over the earth, both in the spiritual and temporal sense."[2] This dominion held by Christ was subsequently delegated by Him to His successors the popes. Hostiensis believed that the Pope, as the heir of Saint Peter and the *Vicar of Christ* on earth, was supreme over all rulers, in temporal matters as well as in spiritual ones. This position was strengthened under Innocent IV, and Spanish as well as other European rulers would use this as a precedent which allowed "Christian princes" to take jurisdiction over territory held by non-Christians.[3]

Founded on such politico-ecclesiastical principles, the Bull of Donation and Demarcation of Pope Alexander VI, in 1493, asserts unequivocally the supremacy of the European:

> [It is] your duty to lead the peoples dwelling in those islands and countries to embrace the Christian religion; [then] out of the fulness of our apostolic power, by the authority of Almighty God conferred on us in blessed Peter and of the vicarship of Jesus Christ . . . [we do] give, grant, and assign to you and your heirs and successors, . . . all rights, jurisdictions, and appurtenances, all islands and mainlands found and to be found, discovered and to be discovered. . . . With this proviso, however, that none of the islands and mainlands, . . . be in the actual possession of any Christian king or prince.

We see from the Alexandrian Bull that the rights of "any Christian king or prince" are to be protected in "countries" and "islands or mainlands" which they may have possessed but that the rights of the native rulers and their peoples are apparently to be ignored. It is also evident that the papal bull not only recognizes the rights of Ferdinand and Isabela in what has already been discovered but extends this right to all lands to be found and discovered in the future. Accordingly, the grant is not only to them but to their "heirs and successors" likewise.[4] The right of Pope Alexander VI to act in this fashion was to be questioned by such persons as Francisco de Vitoria and Bartolomé de las Casas some forty years later, but to all appearances, no questions were raised in that fall and winter of 1492–1493. The first encounters between Europeans and the native peoples of the Caribbean were thus carried out in the context of a self-imposed European supremacy.

THE NAVIDAD EXPERIENCE

Columbus had not originally intended to establish a trading post in connection with his first voyage, but his plans were altered by the Christmas disaster, which resulted in the loss of the *Santa María* on a coral reef. The kindness and generosity of the Indians, their untiring efforts to succor the Europeans, and the sincere sympathy and affection of their king Guacanagarí led Columbus to view the wreck as providential rather than disastrous. As we have seen, he determined that God intended the wreckage, supplies, and trading goods to be used by a portion of the crew to establish a post, develop better trading relations, determine the source of the gold, and begin accumulating the wealth of the Indies, either by mining it themselves or through trade with the Indians. The account given by Las Casas in his *History of the Indies* reprises the description in Columbus's journal of the party left behind on Española and then continues to detail the very specific instructions and admonitions with which their Admiral left them.[5]

HISTORIA DE LAS CASAS, BOOK 1, CHAPTER 63

Columbus chose thirty-nine men to remain in this land and in that fort and town of Navidad. Among the men he had there with him, they were the most willing and happy that he could find, and they had the best strength and fitness for the work. As their captain, he left Diego de Arana, who was a native of Córdoba, a notary, and an alguacil, with full authority conferred upon him by the Catholic Sovereigns.

And in the event that he might die, he appointed to succeed him, Pedro Gutiérrez, the King's butler or steward. If he were to die, the responsibility would be assumed by Rodrigo de Escobedo, a native of Segovia and nephew of Fray Rodrigo Pérez.

He left a surgeon called Maestre Juan with the men to care for their injuries and to attend to their other needs as far as he was competent. He also left a ship's carpenter, a caulker, a cooper, and an artillery-man or good gunner who was well qualified. Also, a tailor remained with them. All the others were good seamen.

He provided them with enough hard-tack, wine, and supplies to last for one year. He left them seeds for planting, and the entire large amount of merchandise and barter-goods that the Sovereigns had ordered procured, in order that they could trade and barter for gold. He left considerable ordnance and arms, along with everything the ship had brought. He also left them the ship's boat so that they could fish and for whatever additional need they might have of it.

At this point, when he was ready to leave, he assembled everybody and he addressed those who were to remain. Being prudent and Christian as he was, his remarks included these principles:

First, that they consider the great favors that God had thus far bestowed upon him and everybody, and the benefits that He had given them, for which reason they should always be very thankful to Him, and that they commit themselves to His benevolence and mercy, being careful not to offend Him, placing all their hope in Him, and also praying for his [Columbus's] return. Columbus promised them that he would strive to return as soon as possible, and he trusted in God that they would all be very happy.

Second, he asked, charged, and ordered them, on behalf of their Highnesses, that they obey their captain as they would obey him [Columbus/SLT] himself.

Third, that they very much respect and revere the Lord and king, Guacanagarí, and his caciques and principals or nitainos and other subordinate lords, and that they avoid, as they would avoid death itself, rousing their anger or harassing them. They had seen how much they were obligated to him [Guacanagarí] and to the others and the need to keep them satisfied, staying as they were on their land and under their own rule. He asked that they strive and be careful, through their pleasant and reasonable association, to win his goodwill and keep his love and friendship, so that he would find him to be even more friendly and gracious when he returned than when he left him.

Fourth, he ordered them and beseeched them that they should not do any harm or violence to any Indian, man or woman, or take anything from them against their will. He especially ordered that they be careful and avoid doing any inury or violence to the women, because by doing so they might bring about a scandal and bad example for the Indians, and dishonor to the Christians, whom the Indians firmly believed were sent by the celestial powers and had all come from Heaven.

(If he believed these rules would be observed, the Admiral certainly trusted the Spaniards much more than he should have before his trust in them was violated. It must have been that he did not yet know them as well as he did after. And, I am not speaking of Spaniards alone, but of any other nation among those that we know of today (as the world now is). They may not have respected God, and they were in distant and strange lands and among people who did not believe in God.

He should not have trusted that they would observe the rules, as though their judgement and prudence would have been enough for them to live in such a way that they would not lose the esteem in which they were held. They were treated nearly like gods, and were given a very clear and gainful advantage, living as hypocrites). [This is Fray Bartolomé's comment/SLT.]

Fifth, he urged that they not scatter or separate into groups, or especially that one or two men not separate from the others, or that they go inland, but that they remain together until his return.

At least, they should not leave the land and dominion of that king and lord who loved them so much and who had been so fair and lenient to them.

Sixth, he strongly encouraged them to bear their solitude, which was little less than exile, although they had chosen it voluntarily. He inspired them to be virtuous, strong and brave in order to do the work that would face them. He spoke of the sufferings of their voyage, and how they were finally comforted with the happiness of the sight of land, and later, with the riches of gold that were being discovered more and more every day. He said that great things are never achieved except with great labors. . . . The greater the difficulty and the more laborious the way and means, the greater the satisfaction.

Seventh, he requested that, when they saw that it would be appropriate, they ask the king [Guacanagarí/SLT] to send some Indians out to sea with them in their canoes, and that some of them might go in the ship's boat, because they would like to see the land up the coast or shoreline. He requested that they try to discover the gold mines, because they thought that the gold which was brought to them came from the east, which would be that route up the coast. The Indians had told them that the gold came from there. At the same time, they could find some good location where it would be possible to establish a villa, because the Admiral was not satisfied with the harbor. Also, the Admiral requested that they barter for all the gold that they could easily and prudently barter for, so that when he returned, they would have obtained and accumulated an abundance.

Eighth and last, he assured them and promised to petition the Sovereigns that they grant benefits to those Spaniards who were deserving by having truly performed what he had requested of them, and he assured them that they would see how completely they would be rewarded by the Catholic Sovereigns, and God willing, relieved by him on his return.

(His pledge to the Spaniards to return, and his memory of them, which continued night and day, must have been a strong motivation for him to make the greatest effort in any way he could to expedite his return). [Fray Bartolomé's comment/SLT.]

They very willingly agreed to comply with what he had charged and ordered them to do. They placed in him, after God, all their hope for his help with the benefits which they were confident he would bring from the Sovereigns for their relief and comfort. They begged that he always keep them in mind, and as soon as he could, that he bring them that great joy which they expected to receive on his return.

The post at Navidad in Española during the months between Columbus's departure for Spain and his return on the second voyage proved to be a learning experience for both Indians and Spaniards alike. The Indians learned that their visitors had not, in fact, "come from the sky" but were instead possessed with very human greed and passions which even a willing and friendly indigenous population had trouble satisfying. When Columbus returned to find the burnt-out fort and to learn of the death of all thirty-nine men, he was shocked and grieved. The fact that those left behind in all confidence and optimism had been slain demonstrated, in the eyes of the Spaniards, that the Indians had lost their innocence. It also gave the lie to Columbus's numerous early statements that a handful of Spaniards would be able to control the thousands of Indians around them in any given region of Española.

THE MIXING OF RACES

The mixing of races, that inevitable accompaniment to conquest, began almost immediately in the Caribbean. Samuel Eliot Morison believes that a minimum of time was spent in establishing relations between the European men and the Indian women:

> Seamen being what they are, we may assume that Columbus's men "did not hold to the virtue of chastity," as Las Casas said. In the Bahamas, Cuba and Hispaniola they found young and beautiful women, who everywhere were naked, in most places accessible, and presumably complaisant. Yet we find nothing about such goings-on in Columbus's journal. He had special reasons for reticence, since everything that he wrote was destined for the Queen's eyes; but chastity in language was equally characteristic of other early Spanish voyagers and chroniclers. For lubricious details we must read the narratives of Italians like Michele de Cuneo, Amerigo Vespucci and Antonio Pigafetta. The first, in his Letter on the Second Voyage, describing the same Indians of the Pearl Coast and Brazil, repeats the charge with even less delicacy. Yet there is nothing in Columbus's Journal unsuitable *pueris virginibusque.* Under the date of November 6, 1492, he describes the women of Puerto Gibara, Cuba as *de muy buen acatamiento* (very handsome indeed) in their nakedness; and aboard the caravels there was certainly little privacy or protection for these Cuban girl captives. Elsewhere in Cuba there was not much contact with the

natives, but friendly relations were established in Hispaniola in December, where the wenches were whiter and more beautiful than those of Cuba. At Acul Bay they wore nothing at all, and "have very pretty bodies, and were the first come to give thanks to Heaven and to bring what they had," for the natives did not try to conceal their womenfolk out of jealousy as had happened elsewhere. Guacanagarí would certainly have considered the furnishing of choice young virgins as one of the duties of hospitality, although his subjects thought it a bit too much [later] when the Navidad garrison took five concubines apiece. Monte Cristi, where Niña lay from the fifth through the eighth of January, 1493, part of the time in company with Pinta, was probably the last place where there was any opportunity for wenching; for the natives at Samaná Bay (last port of call in the New World) were somewhat hostile. But the desire of Niña's men to sail thence directly to Spain instead of visiting the "Isle of Women" suggests that they had had their fill of that sort of thing.[6]

The Italian Michele de Cuneo, mentioned above, is introduced by Morison as "a jolly dog and good raconteur" who "belonged to a noble family of Savona" not far from Genoa, "and it is probable that he and Christopher were boyhood friends." He was with Columbus on the second voyage to the Caribbean islands, in 1493. His example of "race mixing" is of interest here because it was recorded by one of the male participants early in the discovery period and because the female participant was a Cariban woman. The Caribs were cannibals, and this fact later became an excuse for enslavement when it was illegal to enslave other inhabitants of the islands, but the taint of cannibalism did not restrain Michele Cuneo in this instance.

His letter concerning the second voyage, 1493–1495, bears the date 28 October 1495 and was written to a friend after he returned to Savona. While the Europeans were at anchor off an island inhabited by Caribs in the Lesser Antilles, there was an encounter between crew members in a ship's boat and a canoe carrying four Carib men, two Carib women, and two Indian slaves. Michele Cuneo explains that he "captured a very beautiful Carib woman, whom the said Lord Admiral [Columbus] gave to me, and with whom, having taken her into my cabin, she being naked according to their custom, I conceived desire to take pleasure . . . , but she did not want it and treated me with her fingernails in such a manner that I wished I had never begun. But seeing that (to tell you the end of it all), I took a rope and thrashed her well, for which she raised such unheard-of screams that you would not have believed your ears. Finally we came to an agreement in such manner that I can tell you that she seemed to have been brought up in a school of harlots."[7]

Along with encounters of this type, more long-standing relationships between European men and native women also grew up as soon as the Europeans stayed in one place for very long. As we shall see, the question of concubines figured prominently in the disastrous fate of the post at Navidad. Another early settlement experience was at Isabela, which was established as a trading station and town on the island of Española early in 1494. It was difficult for many Spaniards to survive there without foodstuffs from home. "Certain Spaniards were much more resilient than others. They managed to stomach cassava and yams, to mix with and live among the Indians rather than to cower, starving, within the forts; in short, to become wholly acculturated. . . . But such mixing actually began within a few weeks or months after the founding of Isabela in the north, and the result there and elsewhere was the rise of the mestizo population, born within and outside of marriage. At this time they were counted as whites and were specifically excluded from the subsequent forced labor system."[8]

The eagerness of the Spanish male to form temporary liaisons, as well as more permanent relationships, including marriage, with the Indian women, will be a continuing theme throughout the period 1492–1509. The eventual result of such race mixing is the extensive mestizo population which dominates Spanish and Portuguese America today.

6

Home from the Sea, Then Back to Española

On March 15, 1493, Columbus brought the *Niña* into the port of Palos, whence he had set forth less than eight months before. The crossing had been difficult and dangerous, and the two remaining vessels of the expedition had become separated. Both had made their first landfall elsewhere, but when Martín Alonso Pinzón arrived at Palos that same day in the *Pinta*, he found the *Niña* all snugged down as if she had been there for some time, and he became so upset that he went to bed in what proved to be his final illness.

Columbus dispatched letters to the Sovereigns, who were at their court in Barcelona, some eight hundred miles across the peninsula. While waiting for their official responses to reach him, Columbus took time to visit his friends and supporters, such as Fray Juan de Pérez, in La Rábida and neighboring communities. Then he made his way to Seville. The ships' crews had acquired samples of the birds and plants of the Caribbean to show the Sovereigns, and when they all reached Seville, the Indian captives were paraded through the streets in their native apparel, wearing such jewelry as bracelets on their arms and legs and collars around their necks. They carried the brilliantly plumed parrots and native foliage as they walked. Crowds thronged to see them, and wherever they went throughout their long overland journey to Barcelona, the reaction was the same. News had spread of the New World, and Spaniards were captivated and intrigued. Apart from seeing the Indians themselves, what seemed to attract the greatest attention was the discovery of gold, the fact that the people of the islands went about naked, and the idea that innumerable souls had been made available for conversion to Christianity.

Fray Bartolomé's *History of the Indies* gives a richly detailed account of the hero's homecoming with which Columbus was honored. This vast work has never been translated into English in its entirety. Part of the material used in the following excerpts is our own translation, and part comes from an earlier translation by

Andrée Collard. As we have explained in the notes to Chapter 1, when we show book and chapter number with no name following, it is our translation, and when the Collard translation is used, the name will be included in parentheses after the book and chapter number.[1]

HISTORIA DE LAS INDIAS, EXCERPTS FROM BOOK 1

Book I, Chapter 76 (Collard). My limited understanding and poor eloquence prompt me to think that the fruit of Columbus's labor speaks better for itself than I do. However, I want to say enough for the wise and clear-minded reader to draw his own conclusions, and what I particularize here in a few words stands for greater principles worthy of prime consideration above all others. Is there anything on earth comparable to opening the tightly shut doors of an ocean that no one dared enter before? And supposing someone in the most remote past did enter, the feat was so utterly forgotten as to make Columbus's discovery as arduous as if it had been the first time. But since it is obvious that at that time God gave this man the keys to the awesome seas, he and no other unlocked the darkness, to him and to no other is owned forever and ever all that exists beyond those doors.

Indians "Eminently Ready to be Brought to the Knowledge of their Creator"

He showed the way to the discovery of immense territories whose coastline today measures more than twelve thousand leagues from pole to pole and whose inhabitants form wealthy and illustrious nations of diverse peoples and languages. Their rites and customs differ but they all have in common the traits of simplicity, peacefulness, gentleness, humility, generosity, and, of all the sons of Adam, they are without exception the most patient. In addition they are eminently ready to be brought to the knowledge of their Creator and to the Faith.

It is then very clear that the boundaries of Christ's empire could be vastly extended by spreading the Christian religion to all its countless parts and by increasing the number of its worshippers to include such fine rational creatures in such great numbers. God chose the selected few even before He created the world—no

Catholic would dare deny this—picking souls then, now and forever, as He would grains of celestial wheat to enrich His divine granaries, or as more than precious living stones to build His divine house, and no amount of fiendish hordes and devices of the devil scattered over these parts would succeed in stealing away a single one of these souls.

What then, can be compared to this on the whole face of the earth? And what can one say of the abundance of temporal wealth in gold, silver, pearls and precious stones? To give an idea, Indian gold is what prevails on the market all over the world (this is not the place to speak of the disorder and accidental abuses of how it gets there). If some do not acknowledge this, at least it is clear that the nations of Christendom are infinitely enriched by the gold, silver, and pearls from our Indies, or would be, if God did not occasionally strike them down in punishment.

If the kings of Christendom were united in peace and conformity, they would be strengthened by this treasure, and the enemies of our holy Catholic Faith would not dare oppose it. Even if they should form armies as powerful as those of Xerxes, or any other of that magnitude, Spain alone could smash them with God's help and with the sinews of war, that is, monies derived from our Indies. According to historical authority, wealth helps rulers keep the enemy in check and in a state of submission.

It is fitting to stress that God most sublimely favored all of Spain over any other Christian nation, when he chose Christopher Columbus to give to Spain such a golden opportunity in every sense of the word. Not only scholars, great theologians, and eloquent and witty sermonizers but any plebeian idiot can, provided he possess a steady faith, some knowledge of doctrine and the ten commandments, mediate between Christ and a vast number of infidels, provided also that he live the life of a good Christian and show it by his actions. In this way anybody has the opportunity to be a holy Apostle, should he also receive such grace from above as to be content with helping to harvest the spiritual riches of these lands, since these universal Indian nations are so simple, so gentle, and so eminently ready to receive the Faith.

For this reason, every Spaniard ought to ponder gravely that this illustrious gift, denied to all other Christians, is a most powerful gift for which he will be asked to account on the Day of Judgment, together with the interest thereof; and on the day of his death he will have to give a precise and exact account of it, the scrupulousness of which will be made clear from the following chapters. And of all those distinguished and incomparable goods (as well as of those discovered daily which I shall make known later), that most worthy man Christopher Columbus was the cause, second to God but first in the eyes of men, being the discoverer and only worthy first Admiral of the vast territory already known as the New World.

Book I, Chapter 77. The Admiral departed for Seville [from Huelva and Palos/SLT] as soon as he could. From there, he sent a message to the King and Queen who were in the city of Barcelona at that time. He made know to their Highnesses the great fortune and happy conclusion that God had given him in his desired and promised discovery, and the tidings that were so new, the like and happiness of which had never been heard or believed by any prince in centuries past. When the Catholic Sovereigns received the letter, it really seems impossible to try to describe and to exaggerate the joy and happiness and satisfaction that they received. This can be gathered from the first letter and from many other letters which they sent to him in Seville. The first letter reads thus:

"The King and Queen—To Christopher Columbus, our Admiral of the Ocean Sea, and Viceroy and Governor of the islands which have been discovered in the Indies. We saw your letters and were greatly pleased to learn what you told us about the Ocean Sea, that God had given you such a good conclusion to your labor, and that He had guided you so well in what you began. He, as well as We ourselves and our kingdoms, will be well served by receiving so much benefit. May it please God that, besides your service to Him, you will receive many favors from Us, which you may be sure, will be given to you as your services and labors deserve. With the help of God, We want what you have begun to continue and to go forward. Therefore, We want you to come soon, in our service, and We want you to give the greatest possible urgency to your arrival here, so that there will be enough time to provide for everything that is necessary. As you see, summer has arrived, and before the time for your departure comes, you should see if any preparations can be made in Seville, or in other places, for your return to the land that you have found. Write to Us immediately by return mail, so that things can be provided during the time you are here, and so that when you leave from here, everything may be ready. From Barcelona, March 30, 1493—I the King—I the Queen—By order of the King and of the Queen, Fernan d'Alvarez." In the address it says: "By the King and Queen, to Christopher Columbus, their Admiral of the Ocean Sea and Viceroy and Governor of the islands which have been discovered in the Indies."

When he received the letter from the Sovereigns, he wrote again in compliance with their orders. He sent them a statement of what he thought was needed in readiness for his return and settlement of the island of Española, which was possibly said to be the most fortunate of all islands, and as large as Spain. The statement dealt with: so many caravels, so many provisions, so many people, and the other necessary things.

Indian Captives and Native Products on Display

Book I, Chapter 78 (Collard). Christopher Columbus, now Admiral, left Seville with as much finery as he could gather, taking with him the seven Indians who had survived the voyage. I saw them in Seville, where they stayed near the Arch of St. Nicholas, called the Arch of the Images. He had brought beautiful green parrots, *guaycas*, or masks, made of precious stones and fishbone, strips of the same composition admirably contrived, sizable samples of very fine gold, and many other things never before seen in Spain. The news spread over Castile like fire that a land called the Indies had been discovered, that it was full of people and things so diverse and so new, and that the discoverer himself was to take such and such a route accompanied by some of the Indians. They flocked from all directions to see him; the roads swelled with throngs come to welcome him in the towns through which he passed. . . .

Columbus hastened to Barcelona, where he arrived in mid-April. The Monarchs were very anxious to see him. They had organized a solemn and beautiful reception to which everybody came. The streets were crammed with people come to see this eminent person who had found another world, as well as to see the Indians, the parrots, the gold and other novelties. For greater solemnity, the King and Queen sat outside facing the public on Their royal thrones and next to them sat Prince don Juan and the highest nobility of Castile, Catalonia, Valencia, and Aragón, all of them beaming with happiness and anxious to greet the hero of the exploit that had caused so much rejoicing in all of Christendom. . . .

Columbus told them quietly about the favors God had granted the Catholic Sovereigns, and in particular recounted his tribulations, the discovery, the greatness and abundance of the new land, his certainty that much more of it still lay undiscovered—thinking as he did that Cuba was part of the continent—showing what he had brought of wrought but unpolished gold pieces and nuggets of all sizes. He gave the King the assurance that the land was infinitely rich, which meant the royal treasury was replenished as surely as if all were already under lock and key. But what is more important, he described some customs of the Indians and praised them as simple and gentle people ready to receive the Faith, as could be seen from those Indians who were present.

The King and Queen heard this with profound attention and, raising their hands in prayer, sank to their knees in deep gratitude to God. The singers of the royal chapel sang the *Te Deum laudamus* while the wind instruments gave the response and indeed, it seemed a moment of communion with all the celestial joys. Who could describe the tears shed by the King, Queen and noblemen? What jubilation, what joy, what happiness in all hearts! How everybody began to encourage each another with plans of settling in the new land and converting people.

They could tell how their Sovereigns, especially Queen Isabela, valued the propagation of the Faith by showing with words and actions that Their principal source of pleasure was having found such favor in the eyes of God as to have been allowed to support and finance (though with mighty few funds) the discovery of so many infidels ready for conversion.

Book I, Chapter 79. The following day, and for many days after that, the Admiral came to the place and spent many hours with the Sovereigns, reporting to Them in particular, things that had happened to him on his voyage, all the islands he discovered, which places and ports he saw in those islands, the disposition and peacefulness of the people of those islands [their docility as he observed it, how ready he believed they were to receive the Faith, and the fact that, from what he could observe, they had some knowledge of the existence of a God or Creator in the heavens. He told Them] about the very kind reception and the merciful and opportune assistance given to him by the most benign king, Guacanagarí, when he came to his kingdom and the ship in which he was sailing was wrecked. He told Them about the comfort that the king provided for him, and the other most truly hospitable things that he continued to do for him up to the time he returned to Castile.

He told Them of the hope that he had of discovering many more rich and extensive lands, especially the mainland. He contended that the island of Cuba was a continent, and that its beginning was a tip of Asia, although it appeared to be an island. He said many other important things in reply to the questions and inquiry of the Sovereigns. They discussed with him all the things that were needed for his return, for the settlement and for the discovery of what was still to be discovered. The Sovereigns ordered, commanded, provided and conceded everything that the Admiral advised and accordingly dictated, desired, and requested.

Then the Catholic Sovereigns declared that this subject for rejoicing should be spread throughout all Christendom, for the cause of happiness was common to all. This was to be achieved, and They gave a long and particular account of these divine treasures that God had granted Them, to the leader of Christianity, the Vicar of Jesus Christ, the Supreme Pontiff Alexander VI. Thus as true children of the church, these fortunate Sovereigns sent Their letters telling how They would send this distinguished man to discover that New World, a man who was chosen by God for such a rare, new, and most difficult venture, and who had discovered so many and such happy lands, filled with innumerable nations, and They told about all the success of the voyage and the admirable things that happened on it.

Who could doubt that the Roman Pontiff, with his entire holy and sublime College of the Cardinals, having heard such new tidings that were the cause of profound rejoicing, would experience inexpressible and spiritual happiness, seeing that such very large gateways of the Ocean had been opened to him, and that the concealed world had appeared, abounding with innumerable nations which had been hidden for so many centuries past, and in which it was expected that the empire of Christ would be gloriously enlarged and extended?

It is certainly believable that he gave praise and thanks to God, the giver of goods, because he had seen the way opened in his days for the beginning of the last preaching of the Gospel, and the calling or bringing of the laborers who were idle at the end of the world to the vineyard of the Holy Church. According to the parable of Christ, this is the eleventh hour. The entire Roman court is bathed in joy. From there, this heroic deed is swiftly proclaimed in all the Christian kingdoms. In all those kingdoms, it is not hard to believe that a most cheerful feeling was created by receiving news of the reason for such extraordinary rejoicing.

The Pope Designates Ferdinand and Isabela
for the Conversion of the Indians

Then the Vicar of Christ assisted with his apostolic generosity and support and with the fullness of his power. He trusted in God who holds all kingdoms in His hands, and whose authority he exercises on earth, with regard to what was incumbent upon him because of his Apostolic duty and the authority of the supreme papacy, in order to accomplish the necessary and worthy labor of converting such a great multitude of infidels that were so ready, and hopefully establishing the holy Church in these Indian territories that were so far wide-spread, as had already been initiated to some extent by our glorious Princes. This was to be accomplished by a most diligent effort, in an orderly manner and by appropriate means, and with apostolic authority and blessing, for the purposes of Christianity.

With this purpose, he ordered his bull with the lead seal to be issued. In it, he praises and extols the zeal and close attention which was shown by our Catholic Sovereigns toward the exaltation of the holy Catholic Faith, and which had been observed much earlier by the Apostolic See, even at the cost of spilling their own royal blood, as had been seen in the recovery of the kingdom of Granada from the tyranny of the Mohammedans.

The holy Pontiff also expresses congratulations for: the happy discovery of these lands and peoples in the days of his pontificate, with the support of the Catholic Sovereigns, and at their risk and their own expense; and for the diligence and labors of Christopher Columbus who was very deserving of all acclaim and praise. Especially, according to what the Sovereigns were saying, these infidel nations that were discovered might be very fit and ready to be persuaded and converted to the true God through the doctrine of His Faith, because they were so peaceful and gentle and had some knowledge of the Lord of the Heavens who provides all things.

He very strongly exhorts the Catholic Sovereigns before the Lord, and he entreats Them, by reason of the sacred baptism that They had received, obligating Them like any other Christians, and in the spirit of the Redeemer of the world Himself, to obey and to fulfill the apostolic precepts, as well as those of Jesus Christ.

In this entreaty and exhortation, a very rigid and obligatory precept is contained and included. Violation of this precept is no less than mortal sin. By this precept he orders and strictly requires that the Sovereigns very diligently pursue this pious venture and labor that is so acceptable to the divine will; and that, in pursuing it, They always and especially keep before their eyes the ultimate end that God is asking for, and that His Vicar and any Christian prince is obligated to ask for.

This ultimate end means that They are to influence and persuade the towns and kingdoms, and the people who live in or are natives of these islands and continents, to receive the Christian

Religion and Catholic Faith, attaching less importance to any dangers and hardships, and even less to individual temporal interests, that may arise in reaching or pursuing this end.

Their Highnesses are to have a strong faith in God, who showed and selected for Them, more than for any other prince in the world, so many infidel nations, so that They might bring them to know and worship Him, hoping that He will favor and will bring about the happy conclusion that is desired for all their thoughts and deeds and all that They propose to do in this happy venture.

By his own inspiration and apostolic privilege, the Pope ordained and appointed the Catholic Sovereigns and their successors in Castile and Leon as Supreme Sovereigns like sovereign emperors, over all the kings, princes, and kingdoms of all the Indies, islands, and continents, discovered and yet to be discovered, in the entire sphere west of an imaginary line or ray that runs north to south and is one hundred leagues west of the Azores and Cape Verde.

This was so that the Sovereigns could shoulder this trust and burden more freely and with more authority, and might better accomplish it, and so that They might work more or less in some way of their own with the hope of having some temporal advantage (which is what usually gives encouragement and enlivens the will, especially when there are hardships, difficulties and great expenses, and also so that no one will object to the cost and pay, as Saint Paul says).

He added a certain condition: that this is understood, provided that up to and including 1492 A.D., these lands that were discovered by the above-mentioned discoverer, Christopher Columbus, and by command and favor and at the expense of the Catholic Sovereigns of Castile and Leon, Don Fernando and Doña Isabel, had not been actually occupied by any other Christian king or prince. This was because, in such a case, it was not the intention of the Vicar of Christ, nor should it be, to deprive or make judgement against any Christian princes who might have previously held such a lawful right and authority.

Thus the Apostolic See granted, bestowed, and assigned to the Sovereigns and their heirs and successors supreme jurisdiction and authority over all the cities, towns, castles, places, rights, and jurisdictions, with all their appurtenances, as much as might be and may be necessary for the preaching, instruction, expansion, and preservation of the Christian Faith and Religion and the conversion of the residents and native inhabitants of all these lands, who are Indians.

Finally, the Supreme Pontiff granted, bestowed, and assigned all that he had and could give, grant, and assign. After having made this concession and assignment, he imposed a terrible and frightening precept upon Them. He ordered Them, in virtue of holy obedience, which is a necessity and carries with it the risk of their own condemnation, to provide and send to these islands and continents: persons, good and God-fearing men, learned men and specialists, who are well informed as to what is necessary for conversion, and who also are sufficiently experienced to instruct and indoctrinate residents and inhabitants, who are natives of these lands, in the Catholic Faith, and to teach and train them in good habits, applying all proper diligence to their conversion. (This was just as Their Highnesses promised to do, by their own spontaneous promise, when They rendered their previously mentioned account; and the Apostolic See did not doubt that They would do so, through their great devotion and royal magnanimity.)

Besides this, the Supreme Pontiff concludes his apostolic letters by prohibiting, under penalty of excommunication "latae sententiae ipso facto incurrenda" (which means that no other sentence or declaration, besides violation of the order, is necessary to be excommunicated), any Christian prince, whether he be king, emperor, or any other person of any rank or condition, from coming to these Indies, discovered or yet to be discovered, for trade or commerce, or for any other possible reason, without special permission from the Lord Sovereigns of Castile or from their heirs. The bull and apostolic letters of the concession and bestowal contain all these clauses and most of this chapter, according to the copy I have. This bull was issued in the holy palace near San Pedro, on May 4, 1493, in the first year of the pontificate of this Pope.

Preparation for
the Return to Española

Book I, Chapter 81. The bull and apostolic letters of bestowal and authority came from Rome at an opportune time, when the Admiral was being sent by Their Highnesses and provided with everything necessary that he had requested for his voyage. A few days before he left Barcelona, the Sovereigns ordered that the Indians he had brought be baptized. They were now well instructed in matters of the faith and in the Christian doctrine, for as soon as they had arrived, the Sovereigns had ordered that they

be instructed. Much attention was devoted to them, and they
requested baptism of their own free will.

The Catholic Sovereigns wished to offer Our Lord the first
fruits from this heathenism, with much festivity, ceremony, and
show, favoring them and honoring them with their royal presence.
To this end, the Catholic King and the most serene prince, Don
Juan, son of Their Highnesses and legitimate heir to the kingdoms
of Castile, decided to be their godfathers.

The prince wanted one of the Indians to remain in his house in
his service. Within a few days, God claimed him for Himself,
[Oviedo says he lived for two years/SLT], so that, according to
pious belief, he might be the first to enjoy the blessedness that
many from those nations were later to acquire and to have forever, by divine mercy.

The Sovereigns ordered that the people of these lands be
instructed in the matters of our holy Faith. For this reason, they
sent a friar from San Benito with the Admiral. He must have been
a noteworthy person, and according to what has been said, he
carried full authority from the pope in spiritual and ecclesiastical
matters.

The Sovereigns ordered the Admiral to bring clerics with him.
They also gave strict orders that the Indians be treated very well,
that they be induced toward our Christian religion by presents and
good deeds, and that if the Spaniards treated them badly, the
Spaniards were to be duly punished. This is apparent from the
instruction They gave him, an instruction from very Christian
Prices, directed principally toward the benefit and advantage of
the residents and native inhabitants of those lands.

The first chapter of the instruction is as follows: "First, it has
pleased God, Our Lord, by His holy mercy, to make known the
said islands and mainland to the King and Queen, our lords,
through the diligence of Christopher Columbus, Their Admiral,
Viceroy, and Governor, who has reported to Their Highnesses
that he knew that the people he found living there were very ready
to be converted to our holy Catholic Faith, for they have no religion or doctrine.

"This has very much pleased and is pleasing to Their
Highnesses, because, in all respects, it is a cause that is principally
in the service of God, Our Lord, and for the exaltation of our
holy Catholic Faith. Therefore, Their Highnesses, desiring that
our holy Catholic Faith be augmented and increased, order and
charge the Admiral, Viceroy, and Governor, to try to work, by all
ways and means possible, to attract the inhabitants of those
islands and mainland to be converted to our holy Catholic Faith.

"To assist in this work, Their Highnesses are sending the devout father, Fray Buil, along with other clerics that the Admiral is to bring with him. With the help and diligence of the Indians who come here, they shall see to it that they are well taught concerning matters of our Holy Faith, and they shall instruct them in our language as much as possible, for the Indians who came here probably already know and understand much of our language.

"Treat the Indians very well and lovingly"

"In order to better accomplish this mission, the Admiral shall take measures and require that, after the armada safely arrives, all who come in it, and those others who come from here later on, treat the Indians very well and lovingly, without offending them in any way. He shall see to it that they have much conversation and familiarity with them, and that they are as pleasant with them as they can be. Likewise, the Admiral shall gratuitously present them with some gifts from among the items of merchandise of Their Highnesses that he is carrying for barter, and he shall treat them very honorably.

"If it happens that any person or persons should mistreat the Indians in any way whatsoever, the Admiral, as Viceroy and Governor of Their Highnesses, shall punish them severely, by virtue of the authority that he has from Their Highnesses for that purpose." This, as we said, was the first chapter of the instruction that the Sovereigns gave to the Admiral.

This Fray Buil [Fray Bernal Boyl elsewhere/SLT] was a monk from San Benito, and a native of Catalonia. He must have been an abbot, and a principal religious person, about whom the Sovereigns must have had good reports, for They were in Barcelona at that time. I was unable to learn about him, because he was here for such a short time, as will be noted below. But I did get to know two clerics of the Franciscan Order who were with him. They were lay friars, but noteworthy persons [natives of Picardy or Burgundians, who came here only for their zeal of converting these souls, and although they were lay friars, they were very well-informed and learned, and it was known] that, through modesty, they did not wish to be priests, One of them was called Fray Juan de la Duela, or Fray Juan de Bermejo because he was reddish, and the other was called Fray Juan de Tisin. [They were good acquaintances of mine, and at least one of them was very close to me in friendship and conversation.] . . .

With the dispatches all taken care of, and having kissed the hands of the Sovereigns and the prince, Don Juan, the Admiral was attended by the great happiness of Their Highnesses and favors shown by Them, and he was fully escorted to his inn by nobles of the court. He finally left for the city of Seville in the month of June. Certain servants of the royal house went with him as workers in certain occupations, and many wanted to go for what they individually hoped to see and enjoy by simply seeing such new and acclaimed lands. Also, many did not expect to come to those lands in vain, but they expected that their travel and labors would pay them well, judging from the sight of the gold that the Admiral had brought, and believing that there was much more.

Book I, Chapter 82. When he arrived in Seville, the Admiral attended very diligently to his mission, for he did not know when he would reach these lands that he had discovered, especially this island of Española. For one thing, he wanted to see and give relief to the thirty-nine men whom he had left at the fortress in the land of the king, Guacanagarí. Also, he wanted to fulfill the desires of the Sovereigns, render more services to Them, and send Them all the riches that he could obtain, in order to show the considerable gratitude and obligation that he felt toward Them for the many honors and favors and gifts that he had received from Their Highnesses. For certain, I never felt or believed anything else about him, nor did I ever hear differently from any normal person. Rather, from all I have been able to conjecture, if he had any defect it was in wanting to please the Sovereigns more than necessary by shielding himself against the many and difficult obstacles that he later encountered.

Seventeen Vessels, Barter Goods, and Fifteen Hundred Spaniards

Seventeen large and small vessels and caravels were oufitted in the bay and port of Cádiz. They were armed with artillery and weapons, and they were very well stocked with provisions, hardtack, wine, wheat, flour, oil, vinegar, cheeses, all kinds of seeds, tools, mares and some other horses, hens and many other things that could multiply here and that would be useful. . . . They carried many chests of barter goods and merchandise to be given free to the Indians from the Sovereigns, and in order to exchange or barter with them for gold and other riches that they might have. They call this "rescatar."

Fifteen hundred men came, all of them or most of them paid by Their Highnesses, because few went without pay. I believe that there were no more than about twenty with horses, all of them of the working class. However, if the higher-ranking nobles and other persons were able to buy them, the number of horses for them would not be disproportionate. A great many were working people from the country who came to labor, plow, and dig, [and to extract gold from the mines (if they had known about this work, I really believe they might not have come), and finally to do everything] they were ordered to do.

There were workers for all occupations. The majority went with their arms in order to fight, if the need were to arise. Among all of these people, there were many noblemen, especially from Seville. There were other high-ranking persons, and there were some from the royal palace. [The Admiral brought his brother, Don Diego Columbus, with him. He was a virtuous person, very sensible and peaceful; and he was more open and more of good disposition than he was cautious or suspicious. He dressed very modestly, nearly like a clergyman. I really believe that he thought of being a bishop. The Admiral managed at least for the Sovereigns to give him an income through the Church.] By a new royal "cedula" [or order/SLT] the Sovereigns appointed the Admiral as Captain-General of the fleet [and of the Indies].

They appointed Antonio Torres, a brother of the nurse of the prince, Don Juan, [to go with the fleet and later to return with others]. He was a noteworthy person, sensible and qualified for such a responsibility. A royal constable, called Bernal de Pisa, came as comptroller of the island and of all the Indies. [He was a deputy of the chief comptrollers of Seville. They appointed their servant, Diego Márquez, as an inspector. He was a gentleman from Seville and a respected person of authority. Later, in 1513, he went with Pedrarias de Ávila as treasurer of the mainland. I am unable to remember the name of the treasurer at the time of this voyage. I believe his name was Pedro de Villacorta.]

Francisco de Peñalosa, a servant of the Queen, I believe, came as a military or field captain, and I think that also an Alonso de Vallejo came as a captain. They were considerate and courageous persons, especially Francisco de Peñalosa. After he had come to this island of Española and served as captain for three years, he returned to Castile, and the Queen, who liked him very much, ordered him to go with Alonso de Lugo, the first adelantado of the island of Tenerife, in order to take part in the conquest of the Moors on the Cape of Aguer and Azamor. . . . this Francisco de Peñalosa was my uncle. He was the brother of my father, whose name was Pedro de las Casas, and both of them came with the Admiral, on this voyage to this island of Española. My father remained with the Admiral when my uncle returned to Spain, and my uncle Francisco de Peñalosa probably died in 1499 or 1500. . . .

Also on that voyage came Gorbalán, a very spirited young man, and Luis de Arriaga, who was a man of courage and consideration, and who was well regarded and trusted by the Sovereigns. Many other noteworthy people came, seculars whose names I no longer remember, and who, according to the laws and regulations of the world, should be included in the enumeration, [all of whom swore on a crucifix and a missal, and they paid homage and agreed to be loyal and obedient to the Sovereigns, and to the Admiral in Their name, and to justice in Their name, and to the royal estate. All who came at that time, great and small, swore the same, each according to his condition.]

There were very few clerics and ecclesiastical persons who came [to preach to and convert these people]. The only friars were the ones I mentioned above, for I was not aware that any others came. There were three or four clergymen. This was all because there were no volunteers or persons who offered to come, considering the uncertainty and great distance of these lands and the little knowledge that existed about them; or it was because of the little diligence that was applied to looking for them and persuading them; or it was because of the little fervor and zeal that there was in the world at that time for the salvation of such an infinite number of these souls. Certainly, many came on that voyage at the sound of gold and through their curiosity to see these lands. (I believe that this curiosity was the lesser influence).

Book I, Chapter 83. When the Admiral departed from Barcelona, he left a book with the Sovereigns. I have been unable to learn what book this was, but I presume that it was probably: either a book in which he had assembled many secret notes from the ancient writers, notes by which he navigated, or the book of all his navigation and the courses or routes he had followed in his first voyage of discovery, a book to be copied for the royal archives. They arranged to return a copy of it to him after it was made. With this book, the Sovereigns and the persons who counselled them became more certain and gave more credit to the things the Admiral had told them, and more importantly, to the things that they expected to happen. . . .

As the Sovereigns were informed about the displeasure and grief of the king of Portugal for having lost out in such a way, They provided all the information that They thought was necessary for the Admiral to resist him if he interfered in any way. With this in mind, the Queen wrote the following letter to him:

"The Queen—To Christopher Columbus, My Admiral of the Ocean Sea, Viceroy and Governor of the newly discovered islands in the Indies. With this mail, I am sending you a copy of the book that you left here. It was very much delayed, because it was written secretly so that neither the people who are here from Portugal or anyone else might know about it; and for that reason, so that it could be done more quickly, it is "de dos letras", as you will see. Truly, according to what has been discussed and seen here with regard to this matter, each day it is realized that it is much greater, more important and substantial, that you have served Us well, and that We have a great obligation to you. Therefore, We trust in God that, besides what has been promised to you, which will be attended to and very completely fulfilled, you will receive much more honor, favor and advancement from Us. This is right, and your services and meritorious actions are deserving of it.

"If the navigation chart that you were to prepare is finished, send it to Me right away, and please make great haste in your departure, so that, with the grace of Our Lord, it may get underway without any delay, for you know how important this is. Write to Us and always keep Us informed about everything that happens there, and We shall keep you informed and let you know everything that happens here.

"On the subject of Portugal, no conclusion has been reached with them, although I believe that the king will come around to reason. I would prefer that you think the contrary, because in that way you will not be careless, nor will you fail to be on your guard, and thus you will not be deceived in any way. From Barcelona, September 5, 1493.—I the Queen.—By order of the Queen, Juan de la Parra."

This appears to have been the last letter that the Admiral received from the Sovereigns at that time before his departure. When he received it, he was already making final preparations, all the people were gathered, the captains were given orders, muster was completed, and he ordered all of them to embark. Each one of the pilots was given the course and route he was to follow, along with his instruction, and on Wednesday, September 25, 1493, before the sun came up, he set sail, and all seventeen vessels and caravels departed from the bay of Cádiz. He ordered that the vessels be steered to the southwest, which was the route to the Canary Islands, and on the following Wednesday, October 2, he anchored at the island of Gran Canaria, which is the principal one of the seven islands. But he did not wish to stop there, and therefore, at midnight he again set sail, and on the following Saturday, October 5, he made port at the island of Gomera, where he remained for two days.

During those two days, he very hastily took aboard [some livestock that he and others had bought, such as cows, goats, and sheep. Some who came had bought eight sows for seventy maravedís each. From these eight sows have been reproduced all the innumerable hogs that there have been and are today in all these Indies. They also took hens. This was the origin of all things from Castile that there are here today, the same as were the seeds of oranges, lemons, citrons, melons, and all garden stuff.] Water, firewood and beverages for the entire armada [were procured].

There he gave all pilots their instructions folded and sealed and containing the course and route they were to follow in order to finally reach the land of the king, Guacanagarí, where he had left the fortress and the thirty-nine Christians. He ordered the pilots that they were not to open their instructions, except in the event that the weather might force them to withdraw from their armada. In that event they might open them in order to know where they should go. Otherwise, they were not to open them, because he did not want anyone to know those routes, lest by chance the king of Portugal might be informed about them.

Book I, Chapter 84 (Collard). The fleet sailed on Monday, October 7, 1493, passed the last of the Canary Islands and from then followed a more southerly course than on the first voyage, sailing an estimated 450 leagues by the twenty-fourth of October. The men saw a swallow, then somewhat later, clouds and thunderstorms. They felt that the change in weather was caused by the proximity of land and the Admiral had some sails lowered, giving orders to keep a close night watch. At sunrise on Sunday, November 3, they could see land from all the ships and were as happy as if Heaven had suddenly opened up before them. [The Admiral named this first island Dominica, "because it was discovered on Sunday morning"/SLT.]

Book I, Chapter 85 (Collard). Sunday, November 10, they sailed northwest along the coast of Guadalupe toward Española, finding islands on the way. They named one Monserrat from its resemblance to the rocks of Monserrat in Spain; another Santa María de la Redonda for being round, with straight clifflike walls that looked inaccessible; and another Santa María del Antigua, that had some twenty miles of coastline. There were many more islands to the north, elevated and green; they stopped near one they named San Martín which had so much coral that it stuck to the anchors. Columbus does not mention the color.

On November 14, they anchored near an island they named Santa Cruz, and went ashore to see if they could find Indians and learn about the region from them. They came back with four women and two children, but on the way back to the ship, the boat met a canoe with four men and one woman who, seeing no other escape, fought to defend themselves and wounded two Christians; one of the woman's arrows even went through one of the shields. The boat ran into the canoe and turned it over. The Indians were captured, even though one of them kept shooting arrows from the water as easily as if he had been on dry land. They saw that one had been castrated and that it was the work of Carib Indians who meant to fatten him like a capon before eating him. . . .

When the fleet anchored at Monte-Christi [on Española/SLT] and the crew went ashore, they saw the corpses of two dead men, one old and one younger; the former was found with a Castilian rope around his neck and his arms tied to a pole as if on a cross. They could not be identified as either Indians or Christians, but Columbus suspected the worst. Tuesday, November 26, he ordered another search for the thirty-nine Christians left in the fortress. Indians met them in great numbers, showing no sign of fear. On the contrary, they came up to the Spaniards and touched their shirts and jerkins, naming them in Spanish, and this Columbus took as a good sign boding well for his men.

The Tragedy at Navidad

On November 27 at midnight, they reached the Navidad harbor. A canoeful of Indians came shouting "Admiral, Admiral!" but they would not board the ship until the Admiral appeared in person and they had recognized him. Two Indians climbed on the ship, each with a guayca or gold mask, of fine workmanship, as presents from their king, Guacanagarí. When asked about the fate of the Christians, they answered that some had died of illness and others had gone inland, taking many women along with them. Columbus knew then that all had perished, but he kept his feeling to himself and took leave of the Indians, giving them a present of brass pots and other trivia for their king as well as a few trifling things for themselves, with which they happily took their leave.

Book I, Chapter 86. Thursday afternoon, November 28, with his entire fleet, he entered the port of Navidad, near where he had left the fortress. He saw that it was all burned down, and this caused him very much grief and sorrow, for he saw sure signs of the death of all the thirty-nine Christians that he had left there. Not one person appeared on that day.

The Admiral went ashore in the morning of the following day, with great sadness and anguish at seeing the fortress burned down, and not seeing any of those whom he had left in such pleasure and contentment. There were some things left by the Christians, such as broken chests, rugs and some things that are called "arambeles" [cloths?/SLT] that laborers put on their tables.

Not seeing anyone whom he could question, the Admiral took some boats and went up a river that was nearby. He ordered that a well that had been dug in the fortress be cleaned out in order to find out if the Christians had hidden any gold there, but nothing was found. The Admiral found no one whom he could question, because all the Indians were fleeing from their dwellings. However, they found some of the Christians' clothing in those dwellings, and he turned back. They found seven or eight persons buried near the fortress, and three others in the fields nearby. They knew they were Christians because they were dressed, and it appeared they had been dead for a month or more.

While they were looking around there for writings, or other things, from which they might be able to get information about what had happened, a brother of the king Guacanagarí came with some Indians who already knew how to speak and understand our language to some extent. They referred by name to all the Christians who had stayed in the fortress. Also, through interpretation by the Indians that the Admiral brought from Castile, [especially one, whom he called Diego Colón, and whom I knew quite well], they gave him information and an account of the whole disaster.

They said that as soon as the Admiral had left, the Christians began to quarrel among themselves, to have disputes, and to fight with knives and swords, and each one of them took the women he wanted and the gold that he could get, and they separated; then Pedro Gutiérrez and Escobedo killed one Jácome, and with nine others, left with the women they had taken and their belongings; that they went to the land of a lord who was called Canabo, who was the lord of the mines (and I believe the spelling is wrong and that it should have been Caonabó, the very strong lord and king of Maguana, about whom more will be said later); and that he killed all eleven of them.

They also said that after many days the king, Caonabó, came with many people to the fortress where there was no one except the captain, Diego de Arana, and five others who had chosen to stay with him to guard the fortress, because all the others had scattered in the island; that at night he set fire to the fortress, and that, fleeing to the sea, the Christians drowned.

The king, Guacanagarí, fought against Caonabó to defend the Christians. Guacanagarí was seriously wounded and had not yet recovered. This was in complete agreement with the account given the other Christians whom the Admiral had sent elsewhere to obtain information about the thirty-nine Christians.

They arrived at the main village of Guacanagarí whom they saw to be suffering from the above-mentioned wounds. For that reason, he explained that he was unable to come to see the Admiral to give him an account of what had happened after he had left for Castile.

They realized that the Christians' deaths had come about because, as soon as the Admiral had gone, they began to quarrel and to have disagreements among themselves. They took women from their husbands and daughters from their parents, and they individually bartered for gold among themselves. Certain Biscayans joined in a group against the others, and thus they were separated in the country where they were killed for their offenses and evil doing.[2]

This is true, that if they had remained together in the land of Guacanagarí and under his protection, and if they had not angered the natives by taking their wives and daughters, which is most harmful and offensive anywhere, they might never have perished.

Columbus and Guacanagarí

Guacanagarí asked, through those Christians, if the Admiral might visit him, because he could not leave his house on account of his disablement. The Admiral went there and, with a very sorrowful face, Guacanagarí related to him all that has been said. He showed his wounds, and many of his people who had been wounded in that defense. The wounds looked very much as if they had been inflicted by the weapons that the Indians used, wooden spears which were like short lances with fish bones as tips.

After their conversation, he presented the Admiral with eight hundred small stone beads, which the Indians treasured highly and which they called "cibas", one hundred gold beads, a gold crown, and three small gourds, that they call "hibueras", filled with gold grains all of which were probably worth as much as four marks or two hundred castellanos or gold pesos.

The Admiral gave Guacanagarí many of our things from Castile, such as glass beads, knives, scissors, small bells, pins, needles, and small looking-glasses, all of which were probably worth as much as four or five reales, and with this, Guacanagarí thought that he was very rich. He wanted to accompany the Admiral to where he had his fleet. They honored Guacanagarí with a great celebration which he very much enjoyed. He was impressed with the horses and what the men did with them.

At this point, the Admiral says that he heard that one of the thirty-nine Christians he had left had told the Indians and Guacanagarí himself some things that were injurious and derogatory with regard to our holy Faith, and that he found it necessary to set him right in that matter. He had him wear a silver image of Our Lady about his neck, which is something he had not been willing to do before.

[The Admiral also says that the father, Fray Buil, and all the others, wanted him to imprison Guacanagarí, but although he says he could have done that, he did not want to do so, considering the fact that, now that the Christians were dead, the imprisonment of the king, Guacanagarí, could neither bring them back nor send them to Paradise, if they were not already there.

And he says that Guacanagarí ought to remain here, like the other Indian lords among the Christians; that some other Indian lords had kinsmen who might be harmed as a result of such imprisonment; that the Sovereigns had sent him to settle and had spent a great amount for that purpose; and that such an imprisonment would be an obstacle to settlement, because the Indians would make war against him and prevent him from settling. It would especially be a great obstacle in the way of preaching and conversion to our holy Faith, which was the main purpose for which the Sovereigns were sending him on this mission.

Therefore, if what Guacanagarí said was the truth, he would be doing him a great injustice, and the entire country might view him and all the Christians with hatred and enmity. They would consider the Admiral as not being grateful for the great good will shown him by that king on the first voyage, and also for defending the Christians at his own risk, as his wounds had testified.

Finally, he wanted first to settle, and after being settled and firmly established in the land, and after learning the truth, he would be able to punish him if he found him guilty, etc. These are the reasons that the Admiral gave for not following the judgment of those who advised him to imprison Guacanagarí, and his prudence was greater than that of those who held the contrary opinion.]

The Founding of Isabela

Book I, Chapter 88 (Collard). Although the Marien province had good waters and harbors, it seemed to lack building materials, therefore, the Admiral decided to backtrack in search of a good place to build a town. . . . He anchored in a large river port where there was an Indian village. Despite the exposure to northwest winds, he decided to leave the ships there and go ashore because the riverbanks looked green and fertile, and water could be brought to town by canals, thus making possible the construction of water mills and other commodities. Everyone was exhausted and worried, the horses were in bad shape; but everyone and everything found its way to a flat spot sheltered by a rock where they would build a fort, thus starting to found Isabela, the first Spanish settlement in the Indies named after Queen Isabela, for whom Columbus felt a deep devotion.

7

The Discovery of Cibao, South Cuba, and Jamaica

The tragedy at Navidad, which was quickly discovered after the arrival of the Spaniards on the second voyage, was naturally a tremendous blow to the expedition. Still, Columbus wasted no time in selecting the site for a new settlement, which was to be called Isabela after his royal patron. As soon as possible thereafter, he sent men to discover the location of the goldmines in the interior of Española, at a place called Cibao. At last the phantom that the Admiral had followed from island to island through the Bahamas, then to Cuba, and finally to Española had been found.

Close contact between the Europeans and the Indians led to a gradual change in attitude on both sides. The generosity of the indigenous Arawaks and their willingness to serve seemed to make the Spaniards first expect such service and then demand it. This attitude quite naturally provoked mistrust and resentment among the Indians. Native dissatisfaction was manifested in a number of small incidents, for which the Spanish punished the Indians. Eventually Columbus felt it necessary to go from village to village "in military formation," as Fray Bartolomé relates, "in order to instill fear in the land and to show the Indians that the Christians were strong enough to fight them and punish them if they tried anything." The loss of innocence which was rooted in the Navidad experience was already bearing its unfortunate fruit.

The initial contacts made during the second voyage were thus characterized by a significant change in tone. Nevertheless, relations at this point still continued to be overwhelmingly peaceful. As the Spaniards proceeded through the Indian communities, the Admiral observed that Fray Barolomé would call a "natural brotherhood among these people who were living without any knowledge of the true God" and how "God had prepared them" to accept Christianity "if we Christians would only pursue this main objective as we should."

When Columbus returned from Cibao, he found that the Spaniards who had remained at Isabela were "demoralized by the number of sick, dying, and hungry." The food which they had brought from Spain had deteriorated, and the Europeans had not learned to appreciate the native foods. It seemed that the very climate in this new world conspired against them, and the Spaniards died miserably, for they were a "people for whom having to work with their hands was equivalent to death, especially on empty stomachs."

As the Admiral proceeded with the exploration, he persisted in his belief that they were in the Indies. South Cuba extended so interminably that he felt certain it was the mainland. The Spaniards continued to marvel at the beauty and variety of the islands and to see and hear things which seemed to them miraculous.

HISTORIA DE LAS CASAS, EXCERPTS FROM BOOK I

Discovery of the Gold Mines of Cibao

Book I, Chapter 89. The Admiral had been informed by the Indians who lived in a nearby village that Cibao was close by, and while he was directing and occupied with the building of the town of Isabela, he decided to send explorers to find what everyone wanted so much, that is, the mines of gold, because he did not wish to lose any time or use up his supplies in vain, and because he wanted any news there was about the land, especially his Cipango. For this mission, he chose Alonso de Hojeda. . . .

Therefore, in the following month of January, the Admiral ordered him to go with fifteen men to search and to find out where the mines of Cibao were and to observe the nature of the land, its settlements, and its people. At the same time that Hojeda went, the Admiral also prepared to soon send the vessels that were to go to Castile. These were twelve vessels, leaving five—two large ships and three caravels—which he kept with him for requirements which might arise, and for exploration, as will be told later.

Alonso de Hojeda returned in a few days with good news that to some extent cheered all the Spaniards, amidst their hardships and illnesses, although many of them—and most of them or perhaps all of them—wished they were back where they were when they embarked in Castile, for now they could see that the possibility of their becoming rich with gold was slow in coming, [because they had thought they would find gold on the seacoast, to fill their sacks and carry away.]

Hojeda gave an account of his journey, saying that up to the second day of his travel from Isabela, all was uninhabited, and he had had some difficulty, but that, after proceeding through a pass, he had found many settlements, league after league, that the lords of those settlements and all the people there received them as though they were angels, that they came out to greet them, that they gave them lodging, and that they gave them their food to eat, as though they were all their brothers.

This pass is in the very productive mountain range which we spoke of earlier, and which forms the northern valley, all of which was populated. But the way by which they came was probably deserted, although everything was at a short distance, for it could not have been more than eight or ten leagues before they descended into the valley, which was surprisingly populated.[1]

Hojeda continued his journey, and he arrived at the province of Cibao in five or six days, which is only about fifteen or twenty leagues from Isabela. He had tarried in the villages because he was so well received. Having come to the province, he crossed the big river called Yaquí, which had been named Río del Oro by the Admiral on his first voyage when he saw its mouth in the port of Monte Cristi. Along its streams and brooks, the nearby natives and those who came with Hojeda as guides, in the presence of Hojeda and the Christians, gathered many specimens of gold which were sufficient to give credence and to give assurance that this was a land of much gold, as it truly became later on. From there, an untold amount of the purest gold in the world has been taken, and this will be related further on at greater length, if God be willing.

With this news, as I said, all the Christians were given a mixed but great unexpected joy, but the Admiral was the one who was the most delighted and he decided that after he had sent the vessels to Castile, he would go to see the province of Cibao with his own eyes and give everyone reason to believe what they might see and touch, like Saint Thomas.

He prepared a lengthy account for the Catholic Sovereigns of the land and its condition and where he had founded settlements. He sent Them the evidence of gold that Guacanagarí had given him and the evidence that Hojeda had brought, [and he informed them concerning everything that he considered to be appropriate].

Then he sent the twelve vessels, appointing as captain of all the vessels the previously mentioned Antonio de Torres, who was a brother of the governess of the prince, Don Juan, and to whom the Admiral gave the gold and all his dispatches. They set sail on February 2, 1494. Someone has said that he sent a captain named Gorbalán with those vessels, but that is not so, for I have seen how it is stated in a letter from the Admiral himself to the Sovereigns, a copy of which I had in my possession and which was written in his own handwriting.

Book I, Chapter 90. After the vessels had departed for Spain, and the Admiral had recovered from his indisposition and illness, he decided to visit the land, especially the province of Cibao. . . . He left his brother, Don Diego, in charge of the government, with men to advise and to help him. He brought with him all of the other men that he could who were in good health, some on foot and some on horses—laborers, masons, carpenters, and other workmen—along with the necessary tools and equipment, in order to prospect for gold, and to build a fort where the Christians could defend themselves if the Indians tried anything.

"To Instill Fear in the Land"
His Men Proceeded "in Military Formation"

On Wednesday, March 12, 1494, he departed from Isabela with all his men and with some Indians from the village that was close by Isabela. In order to instill fear in the land and to show the Indians that the Christians were strong enough to fight them and punish them if they tried anything, he ordered his men to proceed in military formation, with their banners displayed, with their trumpets sounding, and perhaps firing guns, [as a result of which the Indians would be sufficiently frightened]. He did this in every village he came to on the journey, both on entering and departing.

That day, he travelled three leagues on a smooth plain, camping at the foot of a somewhat rugged mountain pass. The trails that the Indians travelled were no wider than what we call paths, because they are only wide enough for travel by foot. The Indians are so little hindered by clothing or pack animals or carts that they do not have wide trails. The Admiral ordered certain *hidalgos* [a title given to lesser nobility/SLT] to go up the mountain with laborers for a distance of about two cross-bow shots, so that they could widen the trail with their spades and pick-axes, and could cut down and remove trees that were in the way. For this reason, he named that pass the Puerto de los Hidalgos.

On the next day, Thursday, March 13, having ascended the Puerto de los Hidalgos, they saw the great valley, which is something that I believe, without any question, to be one of the most admirable things in the world, and to be one of the worldly and temporal things which is most worthy of being extolled with all praise, and because of it, expressing boundless praise to its Creator who is the Creator of all things and who has added so many perfections, so many favors and so much beauty to it. It is eighty leagues long, and twenty or thirty of those leagues, from one side to the other, is seen from the top of that mountain range where the Admiral and his men were.

The view of that valley is such, being so refreshing, so green, so clear, so colorful, and so full of beauty, that when they saw it they thought they had come to some region of Paradise, all of them being surrounded by and regaled in profound and incomparable happiness. The Admiral, who regarded everything more profoundly, gave many thanks to God, and he named it the Vega Real [Royal Plain/SLT]. Later, when we speak about it in our description of this island, it will be seen how well it might deserve this name and any other more worthy name if it could bring its creatures to never stop praising their Creator.

Next, they descended from the mountain, which takes much longer than climbing it, with great rejoicing and happiness. They crossed the very happy valley, which was five leagues wide at that point, [passing through many settlements where they were received as though they had come from heaven], until they came to the great and beautiful river that the Indians called Yaquí. It had as much water and was as mighty as the Ebro by Tortosa or the Guadalquivir by Cantillana. The Admiral called it the Río de las Cañas, not remembering that on the first voyage he had named it Río del Oro when he saw its mouth at Monte-Christi.

Everyone slept that night on the bank of this river very happily and joyfully. They washed themselves and relaxed in it, enjoying the view and pleasantness of such a happy and beautiful land and such delightful climate, especially at that time, which was March. Although there is little difference from one season to another during the entire year in this island, as in many other places and in the greater part of these Indies, in those months, from September until May, the mode of life is like Paradise, and later, this will be spoken of at greater length, God be willing.

Natural Brotherhood among These People

When they came to and passed through the villages, the Indians whom the Admiral brought with him from Isabela entered the houses, and took everything they wanted, and the owners were very pleased with this, as though everything was for everyone. Then the Indians of the villages which they entered went to the Christians and took what they liked from them, thinking that this was also the custom with us in Castile.

From this it seems clear, although later known and experienced more clearly in ten thousand places in these Indies, how much peace, love, generosity, benign communication, and natural brotherhood there was among these people who were living without any knowledge of the true God, and how much God had prepared them and inclined them to be imbued with all the virtues, especially the Catholic and Christian doctrine, if we Christians would only pursue this main objective as we should.

By the next day, Friday, March 14, [mistakenly indicated in the text as Thursday/SLT], they had crossed the river Yaquí, the men and their supplies crossing in canoes and rafts, and horses crossing a deep ford, without having to swim, except where the water was high. One and a half leagues from there, they came to another large river, which the Admiral called Río del Oro, because it is said that they found some grains of gold in it while crossing it. This river seems to be the one that the Indians called Nicayagua, and it joins the river Yaquí, which was the big river behind them. It flows into it about one and a half leagues away. It is not large, except it must have been at the high water stage.

Three other streams join this river Nicayagua which by itself is a small stream. One ofthem is Buenicún, [which the Christians later called Río Seco], another is Coatenicuz, and a third is Cibú. The final syllables are stressed. These streams were very rich. They yielded the purest gold, and they were the main wealth of Cibao. [Or perhaps it was another very large stream, which was named Mao in the language of the Indians, and which also flows into the large Yaquí. This river is very beautiful and delightful, and it also had many rich gold mines. And I also believe it was Mao, not Nicayagua, by which the trail of the Puerto de los Hidalgos could descend to the Vega Real.]

According to the Admiral, they crossed this river with much difficulty, because it must have become much larger due to the incoming streams, as I have sometimes seen it. Besides being large itself, there was also a large settlement. A large number of the natives fled to the nearest forests when they became aware of the Christians. Others remained in the village, and went into their straw huts, and they very simply placed some reeds across the entrances, just as they might place guns by the openings in their ramparts, assuming that if the Christians saw that obstacle of the reeds placed across the entrances, they would know that it was not the will of the owners that they enter their huts, and that then they would refrain from entering.

What better proof of their innocence and plain simplicity? What greater custom could there have been in that golden age about which the ancient writers, especially the poets, sing so many praises and so much admiration? The Admiral ordered that no one should enter the huts, giving what assurance he could to the Indians. The Indians began to lose their fear, and they came out, little by little, to see the Christians.

The territory beyond the Yaquí is mountainous, and the Indians whom he brought with him had to guide them down the river to where it is all level, and it is about one league or sometimes half a league between the river and the mountains.[2] They had led the Christians to the main large settlements.

The Admiral left that settlement and came to another beautiful river which had such freshness that he named it the Río Verde. Its bed and banks had smooth stones and pebbles, all of them round or nearly round, which glittered, and nearly all of the rivers of Cibao are this way. The entire company rested here that night.

On the following day, Saturday, March 15, the Admiral came to some large settlements, and all the natives, except those who were absent, also placed sticks across the entrances, so that no one would enter, just as in the past villages.

That night they came to the foot of a large mountain pass that the Admiral named Puerto de Cibao because that part of the province of Cibao begins at its summit. The greater part of Cibao is beyond, to the left and toward the south. They were going down to the river Yaquí which would lead them toward the north or Arctic pole. They spent the night there because the men traveling by foot were tired. They were probably eleven leagues from the descent of the previous pass, which he had named after the hidalgos who ascended it when they left Isabela.

Book I, Chapter 91. Before climbing that mountain pass, the Admiral had the trail cleared as best he could, in order that the horses could pass, and from there he sent some pack animals to return to Isabela for provisions. Because the men were not yet able to eat from the produce of the land, much bread and wine was consumed. This was their main food, and it was necessary to supply these provisions. Then, on Sunday morning, March 16, they climbed the pass from where they again enjoyed the very beautiful view of the valley, because from that pass, for forty leagues on each side, it is even better than from the first pass.

They entered the land of Cibao, which is very rugged country with great and lofty mountains, all of which are covered with large and small stones. The Indians named it well, of "ciba", which is "stone," almost like a place or land of many stones. On the stones, a short grass has grown, but it does not quite cover the stones, although more of it has grown in some places than in others.

That entire province has innumerable rivers and streams, in all of which gold is found. There are few groves of trees. Rather, it is ordinarily very dry, except the low places by the rivers. But there is an abundance of innumerable pines. They are very slender, thinly scattered and very tall, and they bear no fruits. They are ordered by nature as if they were the olive trees of the Ajarafe of Seville. This entire province is very healthful and has a very mild climate. The water is beyond comparison, soft and very sweet. . . .

In every stream they passed, they found very small grains of gold, for all the gold of Cibao is ordinarily very fine-grained, although large particles have been found in some places and streams, and one nugget was found worth eight hundred gold pesos, weighing sixteen pounds. As stated in Chapter 89 above, the Admiral had sent Alonso de Hojeda a few days earlier to visit that province.

The natives of that province had already been informed of the arrival of the Christians, and they knew that the Guamiquina of the Christians was coming (they called the great lord "Guami-quina"). For this reason, they very joyfully greeted the Admiral and his Christians in all the villages through which they passed. They brought them presents of food and whatever they had, and especially gold dust which they had collected after they were informed that that was the reason for their coming.

By this time, the Admiral was eighteen leagues from Isabela. [According to what he says in a letter which he wrote to the Sovereigns, there he found and discovered many mines of gold, one of copper, another of pure lapis lazuli, another of amber, and some kinds of spices. We have no knowledge of any of these spices, other than pepper, which the Indians of this island called "axí". There was little lapis lazuli and amber. Certainly there has been much gold.]

Construction of Fort Saint Thomas

He could see that the further they penetrated Cibao, the rougher the country became and that it was most difficult to travel, especially for the horses. The mountains of Cibao and their height and roughness cannot be exaggerated. He decided to build a fort there where he was in order that the Christians might have refuge and might dominate that mining country.[3]

He chose a very beautiful location on a hill nearly surrounded by a wonderful, very refreshing river, [not a big river]. The water of that river seems purified, the sound of its flowing seems very soft to the ears, and the ground is dry and pleasant. This can bring complete happiness. This river is called Xanique, and not much gold had been taken from it, but it is in the center of many rich rivers.

There, he ordered that a fort be very well constructed of wood and brick, and on the side that was not encircled by the river, he dug a trench, so that the fort or tower was very strongly protected against Indians. At the foot of the location of this fort, there is a beautiful plain that the Indians called "sabana" [a plain/SLT].

Some years after it was vacated, I acquired a property or farm there, although I was living elsewhere. I found some gold in a small stream that faced the fort and flowed into the river Xanique. Where it flows into the river, this small stream forms a small island of very fertile and thick earth where, at that time, the first onions in the entire island of Española were produced from the seed which was brought from Castile and which those first Christians planted.

The Admiral named this fort Saint Thomas, thus denoting that the people who did not believe that there was gold in this island had come to believe it, after they saw it with their own eyes and felt it with their own hands. This idea has been mentioned above.

The Admiral and those who were with him were surprised by one thing, that is, that when they were digging the trenches for the foundations for a fort and had dug to a depth of at least one estado [the height of an average man/SLT], and had even broken through some large stone, they found some nests of straw which looked as though they might have been placed there only a few years ago, and amongst them, as if they were eggs, there were three or four round stones, almost like oranges, which appeared as though they might have been made to be cannon balls. . . .

To be captain and governor of the fort, he left an Aragonese nobleman and knight commander, whose name was Pedro Margarite and who was highly respected. He left fifty-two men with him [son Ferdinand says fifty-six/SLT]. [Later he sent more men, and there were as many as three hundred], including workmen, to finish the fort and others to defend it. Having left his instructions and having put things in order, he set out on his return to Isabela, with the intention of hurrying as much as he could in order to proceed with discovery. Therefore, on Friday, March 21, he left, and on the trail he met the pack animals returning with the provisions that he had sent them for. He sent them on to the fort.

Because the rivers were rising considerbly, and because it was raining a lot in the mountains, he had to go through the [Indian/SLT] villages more slowly than he wanted to. The men began to eat the cassava bread and yams and other foods that the Indians very willingly gave them. In return for the food, he ordered the men to give them beads and other things of little value that they had with them.

Problems with Spaniards and Indians Alike

Book I, Chapter 92 (Collard). Saturday, March 29, the Admiral returned to Isabela and found everyone demoralized by the number of sick, dying and hungry, which, to the healthy among them, was a sad and tearful spectacle. The situation was aggravated by lack of food because rations shrank every day, and they blamed the Admiral and the ship captains for having neglected precautions that would have kept the food from rotting on board when, in fact, the heat and humidity were as much a cause of food deterioration as anything else. Since they were running out of biscuits, the Admiral wanted to build a water-powered mill to grind the wheat they had brought from Castile. But the nearest place was a good league away and the manual workers were for the most part too sick and weak to work. Thus, everyone had to pitch in, hidalgos and courtiers alike, all of them miserable and hungry, people for whom having to work with their hands was equivalent to death, especially on empty stomachs.

The Admiral had to use violence, threats, and constraint to have the work done at all. As might be expected, the outcome was hatred for the Admiral, and this is the source of his reputation in Spain as a cruel man hateful to all Spaniards, a man unfit to rule.

Columbus's prestige declined steadily from then on, without one day of respite, until in the end nothing was left of it and he fell utterly into disgrace. This must be the reason for the Benedictine Fray Buil's indignation against Columbus when, as a prelate, he freely reproached Columbus for the punishments he was inflicting on his men, as well as for the strictness of his rationing principles. . . .

The Admiral received a message from Captain Pedro Margarite, of the fort of Santo Tomás, advising him that all the Indians were deserting their villages and that the Indian chief Caonabó was preparing to attack the fort. Columbus sent a reinforcement of seventy men—twenty-five as guards and the rest for the fort—chosen from among the healthiest sailors around him and given an additional supply of arms and food. Then he ordered Alonso de Hojeda to lead a squadron by land to the fort of Santo Tomás and spread terror among the Indians in order to show them how strong and powerful the Christians were. Hojeda was to take the direction of Vega Real because it was heavily populated; he was to see that Spaniards got used to the native foodstuffs, and he was to remain in charge of the fort in the post of governor.

Book I, Chapter 93 (Collard). On Wednesday, April 9, 1494, Alonso de Hojeda took some four hundred men inland and, after crossing the river that the Admiral had called Río del Oro (it must be the Mao river, for I know the land and the Indian names of rivers very well), Hojeda camp upon a town, chained its cacique [native chief], his brother and one of his nephews and sent them as prisoners to the Admiral. Moreover, he caught a relative of the cacique and had his ears cut off in the public square. The reason for this, it seems, is that the cacique had given five Indians to three Christians going from the fort to the ship to help them ford the river by carrying bundles of clothes. Supposedly the Indians left the man stranded in the river and returned to the village; the cacique did not punish them but instead kept the clothes for himself.

The cacique of the nearby town, trusting in the welcome he and his neighbor had given both the Admiral and Hojeda on their first visit, decided to accompany the prisoners to plead with the Admiral not to harm his friends. When the prisoners arrived and he with them, the Admiral ordered a crier to announce their public decapitation. What a pretty way to promote justice, friendship, and make the Faith appealing—to capture a king in his own territory and sentence him, his brother and his nephew to death, for no fault of their own! Even if they were guilty, the crime was so benign it begged for moderation and extenuating circumstances. Besides, how could their innocence or guilt be proven? Hojeda captured them on arrival and nobody knew their language. The same lack of justice may be observed in Hojeda's order to cut off the ears of one of the cacique's vassals in his presence. What good tidings all over the land, and such a show of Christian gentility and goodness!

To return to the story, when the other cacique, who was perhaps related to the prisoner, heard the sentence, he begged the Admiral to save them and with tears promised as best he could by sign language that nothing of the sort would ever happen again, and the Admiral granted his plea by revoking the sentence. Whereupon a horseman arrived from the fort with news of insurrection: the cacique's subjects had surrounded five Christians and meant to kill them, but he and his horse managed to free them and chase some four hundred Indians away, wounding some in pursuit and, I have no doubt, killing others as well.

What a reputation for Christians who had been held but a short while back to be men come from Heaven! This was the first injustice committed against the Indians under the guise of justice and the beginning of the shedding of blood which was to flow so copiously from then on all over this island, as I will show later.

No man in his right mind would doubt that the cacique and his people had a right to declare a just war against the Christians, and that their behavior toward the five Christians was indeed the beginning of their exercise of that right. With their lord taken away prisoner to the ship, perhaps they meant to ransom him with these Christian lives. What convincing reasons did the Admiral have when he came to this town, in the few hours he was there and especially not knowing the language, for the cacique not to believe he was acting well by allowing free passage on his land and welcoming him as he did? After all, the Admiral had come without permission, and Christians were such a fierce-looking novelty, trespassing with arms and horses that seemed so ferocious that the mere sight of them made the inhabitants tremble and fear they would be swallowed alive! In truth, this was an offense which everyone in the world today would take as such and seek revenge, on the strength of natural law as well as *iure gentium*. Also, would not the cacique think himself superior to the Admiral and his Christians? And to Hojeda also, who condemned the Indian thief for a dubious theft, acting as a supreme judge on foreign soil under foreign jurisdiction.

The worst and gravest crime was to capture a king living peacefully in his own domain, and to chain him was an ugly and atrocious crime. Reason itself says it was not right to trespass, not right to do it in a warlike manner, and not right that the Admiral leave the ship without first sending an embassy to notify the Indian kings of his intention to visit them, asking permission to do so and sending gifts, as he had been instructed to do by the King of Castile.

The Admiral should have taken pains to bring love and peace and to avoid scandalous incidents, for not to perturb the innocent is a precept of evangelical law whose messenger he was. Instead, he inspired fear and displayed power, declared war and violated a jurisdiction that was not his but the Indians'; and it seems to me this is not using the door but a window to enter a house, as if the land were not inhabited by men but by beasts.

Truly, I would not dare blame the Admiral's intentions, for I knew him well and I know his intentions were good. But, as I said above in Chapter 41, the road he paved and the things he did of his own free will, as well as sometimes under constraint, stemmed from his ignorance of the law.

There is much to ponder here and one can see the guiding principle of this whole Indian enterprise, namely as is clear from the previous chapters, that the Admiral and his Christians, as well as all those who followed after him in this land, worked on the assumption that the way to achieve their desires was first and foremost to instill fear in these people, to the extent of making the name Christian synonymous with terror. And to do this, they performed outstanding feats never before invented or dreamed of, as God willing, I will show later. And this is contrary and inimical to the way that those who profess Christian benignity, gentleness and peace ought to negotiate the conversion of infidels.

Exploration of South Cuba and the Discovery of Jamaica

Book I, Chapter 94. The king of Portugal saw that these Indies were discovered, and he realized that he had been mistaken in not having agreed to the undertaking that fortune had proposed to him and placed in his hands. He alleged that this sphere fell to Portugal in the demarcation and division that the Church had declared in the past between Castile and Portugal; and therefore he was making claim. (I do not know what demarcation that could have been, for I have had no knowledge of anything in the

Ocean Sea, other than Guinea.) [He even had an armada equipped
to come here, as was stated earlier.]

For this reason, when the King and Queen sent the seventeen
vessels on this second voyage for settlement, They very strongly
ordered and charged the Admiral: to try to proceed with discovery
as soon as he could, especially of the island of Cuba, which up to
then was thought to be mainland; and to discover as much more
mainland or islands as he could, so that the king of Portugal
might be prevented from taking any possession, especially considering that the Apostolic See had now specifically granted all this
sphere of the Indies, and had set limits and a demarcation or distribution of this part of the world between the Sovereigns of Portugal and Castile, as has been related previously in Chapter 79.

Thus, to follow the order of their Highnesses and to satisfy the
desire and inclination that God had given him, and to do what he
had been chosen to do, the Admiral decided to make haste in
order to proceed with discovery, to set up the government of the
Spaniards of Española, and to make arrangements with respect
to the Indians of that island, according to the knowledge and
judgement he had about them, in order to subjugate them.

He set up a council of those persons whom he thought to be
the most prudent and authoritative, and he appointed his brother,
Don Diego Columbus, as president. The other persons were: the
father Fray Buil, who it was said carried authority from the Pope
as his legate; Pedro Hernández Coronel a chief constable; Alonzo
Sánchez de Carvajal, councilman of Baeze; and Juan de Luxán, a
gentleman from Madrid and servant of the royal house. He
entrusted the entire government to these five persons.

He ordered Pedro Margarite who, as I said, had four hundred
men, to patrol, take over, and subjugate the entire island. All
were given orders that he considered appropriate at that time in
the service of God and Their Highnesses (as he says, speaking on
this subject).

He says that on Thursday, April 24, 1494, after eating a
midday meal, he departed in the name of the Holy Trinity, with
one large vessel or ship and two caravels, all three vessels being
well equipped. He left two vessels in the harbor for any requirements that might arise. He took the route to the west and
anchored in the harbor of Monte-Christi. On the following day,
he sailed to the harbor of Navidad, where he had left thirty-nine
Christians.

This was the land of the king Guacanagarí, who had shown
him such kindness, warm hospitality, and goodwill on the first

voyage, especially at the time of the shipwreck. Guacanagarí hid, fearing that Columbus had come to punish him because of the death of the Christians, of which he was not guilty, as stated above, although when the Admiral inquired about him of the Indians, who were his vassals and who soon came out to the vessels in their canoes, they pretended that he had gone in a certain direction and that he would soon return.

Finally, Columbus decided not to wait any longer, and he set sail on Saturday. He sailed six leagues from there to the island of Tortuga, where he was becalmed in the sea that prevails from the east, although the currents came from the west. He was stalled all night.

On Sunday, with a contrary wind, which I believe was a northwest wind, and with the currents which were coming from the west ahead, he was forced to go back and anchor by the river which he had called Guadalquivir on the first voyage, and which we spoke of earlier. Finally, on Tuesday, April 29, he arrived at the harbor of San Nicolás. From there he saw the point or cape of Cuba which he had named Alpha and Omega [Cape Maisí/SLT], when he discovered it on the first voyage, and which now, in the language of the Indians, is called the Punta de Bayatıquırı [Santiago/SLT].

He crossed that gulf, between Cuba and Española, which is eighteen leagues from point to point or cape to cape, and he began to skirt the southern part of the island of Cuba. Then he saw a large bay and large harbor, and he named it Puerto Grande [Guantánamo Bay/SLT]. Its entrance was very deep, and it was about one hundred fifty feet wide at the mouth. He anchored there, and the Indians came out to the vessels with canoes, bringing much fish and some rabbit-like animals of the island [hutias/SLT] which earlier, in Chapter 46, were called "guaminiquinajes."

He again set sail on Sunday, May 1, and proceeding along the coast, he continued to see marvelous harbors, such as that island certainly has. He saw very high mountains and some rivers that flowed to the sea. As he saw sailing very close to the shore, endless number of Indians of the island came out to the vessels in their canoes, believing that the Christians had descended from the sky.

They brought them their cassava bread, water, fish, and whatever they had, offering it to the Christians with such happiness and rejoicing, and without asking for anything in return, as if they might save their souls with all these things. But the Admiral ordered that they be paid for everything, by giving them glass beads, hawk's bells and other things of small value. They were very pleased with these things from the sky.

The Indians whom the Admiral brought with him tried to point in the direction where the island of Jamaica was, saying that there was much gold there. (I really believe that it is the island which they had called Banaque [Babeque/SLT] so many times on the first voyage, although I do not see that the Admiral makes any mention of Banaque here.) (I believe that Diego Colón was one of those Indians that Columbus had taken from the island of Guanahaní and had taken to Castile and brought back with him. Later, he lived many years on this island and talked with us.)

The Right of the Indians to Resist
Landings by the Spaniards

Thus, on Saturday, May 13, [son Ferdinand says May 3/SLT], the Admiral decided to turn to the southeast, and then follow a southern course. He sighted the island on the following Sunday, and on Monday, he arrived and dropped anchor, but not in a harbor. The Admiral says that when he saw it, it seemed to him to be the most beautiful and pleasant of all the islands that he had discovered until then. There were an endless number of large and small canoes that came out to the vessels.

On Monday, he looked for a harbor, continuing along the coast. When he was sending boats out to take soundings (that is, to cast a plumb in order to see how many fathoms deep the bottom is) of the entrances to the harbors, many canoes with armed men came out to defend their land against them and to prevent them from landing. They were like prudent people who, by natural law, have the right to defend their land against unknown people, until they see who the people are or what they are trying to do.

Every individual nation or private person has the right to suspect and to forestall any harm that might come from any new people or persons that they do not know. In the same way Joseph was right in saying to his brothers what he would say to strange people from another kingdom, and in pretending that he did not know them. In Chapter 42 of Genesis, he says "You must be spies in this kingdom of Egypt, who have come to see its nakedness, etc."

For the same reason, the emperors issued laws to the effect that, even though they had the right, the Romans were not to be so bold as to trade in or to go to the land of the Persians, with whom they were not at peace, or with whom they had no association. The reason for the law is stated in the law: "so that it may not appear to be said that the Romans are spies or observers from foreign kingdoms." This is in the mercantile law, "De mercatoribus et comercii".

So, when the men who were in the boats saw that the Indians were determined to prevent them from coming ashore and that they were armed, they returned to their vessels to avoid fighting. From there, the Admiral sailed to another harbor which he names Puerto Bueno.

It is said that when the Indians came out armed in that way to resist the entry of the men in the boats, the Christians, fearing that the Indians might become more audacious yet, decided to give them such a flurry of shots from their cross-bows that they wounded six or seven of them (and God knows how many more were wounded and killed), and that the Indians discontinued their resistance.[4] Then, a great number of canoes full of peaceful and humble Indians came from the neighboring areas to the vessels.

This was another great mistake. Instead of killing or wounding them, or breaking relations with them in any way, it would have been better by other ways or by signs or by sending to them the Indians that they had brought with them in the vessels, to give them to understand that they were not going to do them any evil or harm, just as the Indians were assured many times on the first voyage in many places in Cuba, in this island of Española, and in the Bahamas, as has been related in a number of earlier chapters. When they were unable to assure them in any of these ways, they were obliged to go elsewhere and to leave them, because the Indians had a just cause and the right to defend their land against all people.

No evil should be done, however small it might be, in order to achieve benefits that men want, however great the benefits might be, especially considering the long experience we have had by now with the good will and peacefulness of the Indians, and how easy they have been to pacify and satisfy, by persuading them or by giving them signs that the Christians were not coming to do them any harm, even though at first they resisted entry of the Christians out of simple fear. Here, they brought out their food and what things they had, and they gave it to the Christians for anything in return.

In this harbor, a leak was repaired in the keel of the Admiral's flagship. This harbor had the shape of a horseshoe. The Admiral gave the name Santiago [Saint James/SLT] to this island of Jamaica. On Friday, May 9, he sailed from this harbor. He sailed westward down the coast of Jamaica, keeping so close to shore that many canoes came out to the vessels, giving their things to us and receiving things from us, in all peace and happiness.

Young Indian Voluntarily Joins the Spaniards

Book I, Chapter 95. He could not sail along the coast of that island [Jamaica/SLT] any further, because he encountered very strong winds. For this reason, he decided to return to Cuba, and therefore, on Tuesday, May 18 [error in recording dates/SLT], he returned with the intention of sailing five or six hundred leagues along Cuba to determine if it was an island or mainland.

On the day the Admiral returned, a young Indian came to the vessels, indicating by signs that he wanted to go with them. Many of his relatives and brothers and sisters came after him to beg him not to go with the Christians. But they were unable to persuade him, although they very tearfully pleaded with him. Instead, he hid in secret places of the vessel, where he could not see them cry. Finally, he stayed aboard ship, and they went away disheartened and sad.

Surely one must believe that God chose to endow him with this inclination in order to save him in this way, because the Admiral probably would have him instructed in matters of the faith and would have him baptized, which could not happen if he had remained in his land.

The Admiral departed Jamaica with his vessels, and on Wednesday, May 18, [error in dates/SLT], he sailed to the cape of the island of Cuba which he named Cabo de Cruz. Proceeding along the coast, he encountered heavy and continuous rainstorms, with thunder and lightning, and he struck many shoals, and at every step he was afraid of running aground. . . .

The further he proceeded along the coast, innumerable small islands were more closely crowded together. Some were completely sandy, some were wooded, and many of them were completely under water. The closer they came to the island of Cuba, the higher, greener, and more lovely the islands were. They were one, two, three and four leagues in size. On this day, the Admiral saw many islands, and on the following day, he saw many more and larger islands. He called them all together the Garden of the Queen, because they were innumerable and he could not give a name to each one of them. On this day, more than one hundred sixty were counted on one side and the other—I mean, to the north and to the northwest and southwest. There were channels between them from two to three or more fathoms deep, through which the vessels were able to move. . . . In one of these small islands they saw a canoe with Indians who were fishing. When the Indians saw the Christians coming in the boat toward them, they seemed at ease as though they were looking at their brothers, and they gave signs to them to stop. The Christians stopped while they fished.

For fishing, they were using some fish that are called "revesos" [pilot fish/SLT], and the larger ones are about like a sardine. They have a rough place on their body, and wherever they attach themselves with it, they will be torn into pieces rather than become separated. The Indians would tie a thin cord, one or two hundred fathoms in length, to the tail of these fish.

These fish swim nearly at the surface of the water, or a little lower, and when they come to where the turtles are, they stick to the lower shell. The Indians pull on the cord and pull out the turtle that weighs four or five arrobas [100 to 125 lbs/SLT]. Finally, the fish remains stuck, if, as I said, they do not remove it. I do not know whether it would detach itself later if they were to leave it. . . .

When the fishing was over, the Indians came to the boat. The Christians made signs for them to come with them to the vessels, and they came very willingly. The Admiral ordered that barter items be given to them, and he learned from them that there were countless numbers of those small islands ahead. They gave whatever they had very freely and went away very happy. The Admiral still followed his course to the west, among the innumerable islands that there were, and with the heavy rainstorms and thunder and lightning storms. He sailed every day until the moon came up. . . .

Although he exercised very considerable diligence, care, and watchfulness, and put lookouts on the mast, the ship on which he sailed struck bottom many times and even got stuck, as a result of which he suffered new difficulties and dangers in order to free the ship, sometimes turning back and other times going forward. He came to an island that was larger than the others, and he called it Santa Marta. There was a settlement there, but none of the Indians of that settlement dared remain there, for fear of the Christians.

On that island they found much fish, and mute dogs that do not bark. In all the islands, they saw many flocks of very red cranes, parrots, and many other birds. Running out of water, the

Admiral discontinued sailing among those small islands, and on June 3, he came to the coast of Cuba where it was very dense with trees, and they were unable to see if there was any settlement.

A sailor went hunting birds with a cross-bow, and he encountered about thirty men armed with spears and darts. Some of their weapons were like swords that were not sharp weapons, but blunt at the ends. They are made of palm, for the palms there do not have fleshy leaves like they do here. They are smooth or flat, and they are so hard or heavy that they could not be more so if they were made of bone or nearly like steel. They are called "macanas" [usually thought of as a club rather than a sword/SLT].

The sailor said that among them he saw one Indian in a white tunic that came to his feet. Realizing that he was alone, near so many Indians, the sailor called to his comrades. The Indians fled as though they had seen a thousand men coming after them. Although on the following day the Admiral sent some Christians ashore to see if they could find anything, and they went inland about a league, they were only able to penetrate with difficulty, because the forests were dense, and especially, it seemed to them that there were marshes for nearly two leagues, as far as the hills and mountains.

From there, the Admiral continued westward, and after they had gone ten leagues with their vessels, they sighted some huts on the shore. The natives came in their canoes to the vessels with food and many gourds full of water. The Admiral ordered that they be paid for everything. He ordered that one Indian be detained, asking him and the other Indians through an interpreter if they could detain him until he showed the Christians the way, and until they could ask him some questions, and saying that after that, they would allow him to return to his hut.

They showed their willingness, although with some sadness, because they could see that if they were not willing, it would do them little good. This Indian verified to the Christians that Cuba was an island surrounded by the sea, and according to what the Admiral understood, he said that the lord of the western part of the island did not communicate with his people except by signs, but that anything that he ordered was immediately done [possible reference to the Ciboney who remained there and spoke a different language/SLT].

The idea that the lord who lived at that time was or was not mute, or was accustomed to communicate with signs, must be a fable, because for a period of fifteen or sixteen years, those of us who first came to discover the interior of the country and to settle it with Christians, never knew of any such situation or report. Thus continuing, the vessels came to a sandbar that was one fathom deep and that extended for a length of two vessels.

They were in such great distress and difficulty that, in order to reach a deep channel, they were very hard put to it to man all the capstans. They saw countless very large turtles, and the sea was crowded with them. A great number of cormorants came and darkened the sun. They were coming from the sea and flying to the land of Cuba. The same was true of countless pigeons and gulls and many birds of various species. On the following day, so many butterflies came about the vessels that the air was thick with them. They lasted until nightfall, and a heavy rainstorm drove them away.

The Old Cacique Lectures the Christians

Book I, Chapter 96 (Collard). On July 7, the Admiral went ashore to hear mass. An old cacique who seemed to rule the province arrived during the ceremony. When he saw the priest's rituals, the Christians' signs of adoration, reverence and humility, and the respectful way they treated the Admiral, he assumed that the Admiral was their chief and, presenting a pumpkin-like bowl of native fruit to him, squatted beside him—Indians "sit" in this fashion when not sitting on a dais—and held the following discourse:

"You have come a powerful man to these lands unknown to you, and you have inspired great fear wherever you have gone. I want to tell you that we believe in the life hereafter. Departing souls go in two directions: one is bad, full of darkness, where those who do evil to men go; the other is good and happy, and peace-loving people go there. Therefore, if you feel you must die and believe that every man answers for his deeds after death, you will not harm those who do not harm you. And this ceremony is very good, because it seems to me you are giving thanks to God by means of it."

They say he added that he had been to Española, Jamaica, and southern Cuba and had seen their native lords dressed like priests. The Admiral understood the speech through his Indian interpreters, especially one named Diego Colón, an Indian he had taken to Castile and brought back with him. The Admiral marveled at the Indian's wisdom which, to be sure, excelled that of any pagan philosopher. He answered he had learned this a good while back, that is, how the soul is eternal, and evil ones go to

Hell while good ones go to a place Christians call Heaven, adding how pleased he was to find out that the Indians believed it also. He said he had been sent by his King and Queen, the wealthy and powerful rulers of Castile, for no other purpose than to gather information about these parts, especially if it was true they were inhabited by man-eating cannibals or Caribs and if so, to prevent them from doing such evil, while defending and honoring the good people who lived in peace.

The wise old man heard these words with tears of pleasure and said that if it were not for his wife and children, he would go to Castile with the Admiral. He was given some trinkets and sank to his knees with signs of admiration for men of such quality that he was not quite sure whether they had been born on earth or in Heaven.

I took this from the writings of Hernando [Ferdinand/SLT] Columbus, the Admiral's son, and from the more lengthy account in Pedro Martyr's *Décadas*, for Don Hernando was only a small boy at the time of the event. It is likely that Pedro Martyr heard it directly from the Admiral himself, as he heard many of the things he describes, because he resided at court and was one of the King's protégés. The old man's speech is not surprising either since all Indians believe in life after death, especially the Cuban Indians, and we will have occasion to return to this topic later, if God wills.

Book I, Chapter 97. After leaving the place where the old Indian had spoken to him, it seemed that all the winds and water had conspired to fatigue him and to add anguish upon anguish, troubles upon troubles, and sudden assaults upon sudden assaults, because he had no time or opportunity to rest. Among the many rainstorms that he suffered, one sudden, horrible, and dangerous one that struck him was such that it forced the vessel below water.

With great difficulty, and it seemed only with the help of God, he was able to strike sail, and at the same time, to anchor with the heaviest anchors. Much water rushed in to the floor timbers, which is the lowest part of the ship, and this increased the dangers. The sailors were hardly able to pump it out, because, besides all of them being tired from continued toil, they needed food. They had been eating only one pound of rotten hardtack and a pint of wine or grog, except perhaps whenever they caught some fish.

They suffered great need, and it was much greater for the Admiral, who felt the need for himself and the others. He himself tells about it in these words in a letter he wrote to the Sovereigns concerning this voyage: "I am also on the same ration with the others. May it please God that this be for His service, because, as far as I am concerned, I would no longer subject myself to so many hardships and dangers. Not a day passes that I do not see that we are all facing our death."

With these dangers and continuous afflictions, the Admiral arrived on July 18, at the cape that he had earlier called Cabo de Cruz. The Indians received him very hospitably. With great happiness and pleasure, they brought him their cassava bread, fish, and fruits of the land, and everything they had. The Christians ceased labor and rested two or three days.

On Tuesday, July 22, the Admiral turned toward the island of Jamaica, because contrary wind did not allow him to return by the direct route to Española. He followed its coast down the west side, and everyone observed and praised God upon the sight of such agreeableness and such a beautiful and happy land. They saw all the coast and land full of settlements and excellent harbors league after league.

Countless Indians followed the vessels in their canoes, and they brought and served the Christians with many things to eat, as if they were all parents and children. The Admiral says that the men thought the food was much better than any they had seen up to that point. But every afternoon they were hit by the sudden assaults of the rainstorms and the distress they caused. . . .

The Admiral highly praised the beauty, fertility and fruits, and the rest of the things that the Indians brought to eat, and the many settlements of the island of Jamaica. He said that no other island that he had seen until then was equal to it. On the seacoast, he saw a very beautiful bay with seven small islands, and he saw that the island had a very high elevation, and he thought that it rose higher than the middle air zone where it freezes. The entire land was settled everywhere. . . .

"Almirante, Almirante"

The weather was favorable, and on Tuesday, August 19, he turned to the east, enroute to this island of Española. He gave the name Cabo del Farol to the last point of land of Jamaica that could be seen, which was a cape. On Wednesday, August 20, he sighted the cape or western tip of this island of Española, and he named it Cabo de San Miguel. Now it is called Cabo or Punta del Tiburón, and it is twenty-five or thirty leagues from the eastern tip of Jamaica.

On Saturday, August 23, a lord or cacique of that land came to the vessels saying "Almirante, Almirante", and other words. The Admiral deduced from this that the land he called Cabo de San Miguel must be part of this island, for he had not known until then that this was the island of Española.

At the end of this month of August, he anchored at a small island near this island. From the sea it looks like a sail because it is high, and the Admiral named it Alto Velo. It is twelve leagues from the small island called Beata. He had some of his men climb to the top of that small island, in order to locate the other two vessels that he had lost from sight. . . .

He waited there for the other two vessels, and they arrived in six days. Then, all together, the vessels sailed to the small island of Beata. From there, sailing along the coast they sailed until they came to a shore where there was a very beautiful valley full of settlements that were so close together that they all appeared to be one settlement. This land must have been the land which they now call Cathalina, after a cacica or señora whom the Christians came to know later as the ruler of that land. It is very beautiful country.

The Indians came from nearby in their canoes and reported that they had seen some Christians from Isabela and that they were all well. The Admiral was very happy and relieved by this. He sailed past the mouth of the Hayna River, which is three leagues from Santo Domingo, and near there, he had nine men sent ashore to cross over to Isabela, which is directly north from that coast, in order that they might report about his company and how they were safe.

From there, he sailed on ahead, still by the eastern route, and then a large settlement came into view, and he sent boats toward the settlement for water. The Indians came out against the Christians with bows and arrows poisoned with poison from plants [they also had some cords, and they made signs that they were going to tie the Christians up with the cords].

For this reason, I am sure that this land was the province of Higuey, because its natives were more warlike and they had that poisonous plant, and also because of the distance he had travelled and the place where he was. But when the boats came ashore, the natives dropped all their weapons, and they very peacefully offered to bring water, bread, and all they had, asking if the Admiral was coming. It is believable that the Indians had come out with weapons thinking that they were another strange people and not Christians, but that, after seeing that they were the Admiral and his men, they turned to acts of peace and friendship.

Book I, Chapter 99. The Admiral, in a letter which he wrote to the Sovereigns, says that on this voyage he intended to go to the islands of the cannibals in order to destroy them, but that he had suffered great and continuous hardships and lack of sleep, night and day, without one hour of rest, on his discovery of Cuba and Jamaica, and in going round Española until arriving at this small island of Mona. Especially was this so when he was going through the many small islands and shoals near Cuba which he named the Garden of the Queen and where he was thirty-two days without being able to sleep.

He says that when he departed from Mona, as he was nearing the island of San Juan, he was suddenly overcome by a pestilential drowsiness which totally deprived him of his senses and all his strength. He looked as though he was dead, and they did not think he would last more than one day. Therefore, the sailors, as quickly as they could, turned from the course that the Admiral was following and wished to follow, and they brought him to Isabela with all three vessels. He arrived there on September 29, 1494.

What the Admiral says here about destroying the islands of the cannibals, of whom it was said that they ate human flesh, perhaps did not please God who had created them and who had redeemed them with His blood, because destroying them was not the remedy that God wanted in order to save them. With time, through preaching of the Faith, and with human perseverance, for there are many ways to achieve temporal things, they might be reduced to such a life that some of them might be saved.

Who questions that God might not have predestined some of them, and perhaps even many of them? Therefore, perhaps for this reason, God chose to hinder him with this illness. And perhaps the writing was in error, and one who wrote it wrote "destruir" instead of "descubrir". This appears to have some semblance of truth, because neither he nor his men would have been inclined to destroy anyone, as weak as they were. They only wanted to rest.

8

The Subjugation of Española:
A Bitter Harvest

Without the presence of Columbus as an authority figure, the situation in Española began to deteriorate rapidly. What had at the beginning been a matter of small incidents by the Indians and saber rattling or mild reprisals by the Spaniards was soon to develop into full-fledged assaults leading to subjugation and destruction. Columbus was absent from Isabela for five months as a result of the Cibao expedition and the voyage of discovery along South Cuba and Jamaica. During that time, a disastrous campaign under Mosén Pedro de Margarite left the country in an uproar over the excesses of greed, violence, and debauchery perpetrated by the Spaniards.

Relations between the Europeans and the Indians grew steadily worse during the months that Columbus lay ill in Isabela, after returning from the voyage of discovery. Upon his recovery, the Admiral and his brother, Bartolomé, recently arrived, faced a desperate situation. The goodwill and generosity of the inhabitants which had so impressed Columbus during his first voyage had turned to fear, hatred, and open hostility. The Indians, well organized politically, had finally begun to strike back under the leadership of several powerful caciques. Bolstered by new letters from the Sovereigns which reaffirmed his authority and their confidence in his judgment, Columbus mounted a full-scale military campaign against the forces of the combined caciques and against the people of the villages as well.

For all their numbers and their proud leadership, the Indians were powerless before the horrors of European warfare: crossbows, swords, and arquebuses and horsemen armed with destructive lances as well as the attack dogs and horses' hooves, whose effect was fiendish against those masses of naked bodies. The outcome was inevitable, and the toll was staggering; with the destruction in battle and death from European diseases, Las Casas estimates that, by 1496, not a third of the original population of the island was left alive.

HISTORIA DE LAS INDIAS,
EXCERPTS FROM BOOK I

The Gathering Storm

Book I, Chapter 100. After he had arrived in Isabela in that way, the Admiral was very ill for five months, and at the end of that time, Our Lord restored his health, because He still had much to accomplish through him, and also because the Admiral still had to be subjected to or afflicted by many more hardships and tribulations, at a time when he thought he could be happy and rest in peace.

He found two new developments [which had different effects on his spirit]. One was that his brother, Bartolomé Columbus, had come, and the Admiral was very happy to see him. The other was that all the country was agitated, terrified, full of horror and hatred, and in arms against the Christians, because of the offenses, harassments and robberies to which the Indians had been subjected by the Christians after the Admiral had departed for this discovery of Cuba and Jamaica. . . .

The cause of the agitation and fright of all the natives of the island could well have been the justice and injustice done by Hojeda in the previous year, as it was related in Chapter 93. The Admiral wanted to clear the caciques who were seized and taken to Isabela, and finally, he released them, over objection, upon the plea of the other cacique. However, all the other Indians might have known or guessed what could and would happen to them in time.

It follows that, being more prudent, and for the greater cause of justice, they could and would have been more active and concerned in not allowing people in their lands who were so cruel, strange, and oppressive, and from whom they were beginning to see such bad motives and to suffer such offenses. It was a clear sign to them of the damage that could occur to their kingdoms, freedom, and lives.

From what the Admiral himself says about them in a letter that he wrote to the Sovereigns, the Indian residents and inhabitants of this island were wise and prudent people. He says: "It was evident that these people would try to regain their freedom and that although they are naked, without clothing, no other people without learning equals them in understanding." These are words from the Admiral.

At the time the Admiral was leaving on the said discovery, he had appointed persons to the Council, as related above in Chapter

94, and he had appointed Mosén Pedro Margarite as captain general over four hundred men to patrol the country and to subjugate the people of the island. As soon as the Admiral had gone, Pedro Margarite went off to the Vega Real with his men. [The Vega Real is two short days of travel from Isabela, which is about ten leagues.]

The valley was very full of many natives, villages, and great lords, the country was very happy and delightful, as related in Chapter 90, and the people were without arms, and by their nature, they were very gentle and modest. The Christians yielded to the very reckless life of men who are idle, and who find things in abundance, and who have no resistance against sensual pleasures. They enjoyed such absolute license that they exercised no restraint of reason or of law, living or dead. There was no order or limit.

The Indians did not work regularly nor did they want to have more food than they needed for themselves and for their families, and one of the Spaniards would eat more in one day than the entire family of an Indian would eat in a month. [What did four hundred Spaniards probably do?] (The land was so very productive of their sustenance that with little cultivation anywhere, they [the Indians/SLT] had plenty of bread, and as for meat, there was plenty, for there were hutias [rodents similar to rabbits/SLT] in their yards, and the rivers were full of fish.)

Greed amd Gluttony of the Spaniards

The Spaniards were not content, nor are they now content, with having only what is necessary. They wanted much more, and they threw much away without reason or purpose. Although the Indians might willingly give them whatever they requested of them, the Spaniards also threatened them, struck them, and beat them with sticks. They did this not only to the ordinary Indians, but also to the high-ranking and principal persons whom they called "nitaynos," and they also went so far as to threaten and to pay great disrespect to the lords and caciques.

Besides considering the Spaniards to be intolerable, terrible, fierce, cruel, and devoid of all reason, it seemed to the Indians that those people were born only to eat, that they must not have had food in their land, and that they came to these islands in order to save their own lives.

This was the first reason that the Indians began to feel that the conduct of the Christians was abhorrent to them, that is to say, mistreating them and causing them anguish by eating and wasting their food, and because their vice and sin did not stop nor was it appeased with just food, for having the food, they lacked temperance and fear and love of God, and they fell to the other sensual and more injurious vices.

Therefore, the second way that the Christians showed the Indians who they were was to take their women and daughters from them by force, without having any respect or consideration for any person, rank, status, matrimonial tie, or anything by which honor may be violated, other than whom he desires most and who is the most beautiful. [They also took their children from them for servants, as well as all the individuals they needed and they kept them in their houses].

The Indians found these many evils, injuries, and harassments against them to be insufferable. They offered good hospitality and services to the Christians, and from them they received little gratefulness and reward. Above all else, the lords and caciques were offended and disrespected, and they had the additional pain and anguish of seeing their subjects and vassals suffer outrageous harms and injustices, not being able to help them. They went away and hid, so as not to see what was happening. They kept out of view because they did not dare or try to resist the Christians or to take arms to avenge themselves, considering how many Christian people there were and their horses, which were the main thing that made them fearful.

Those who do not follow in the path of God might, according to that same divine judgement, encounter a number of pitfalls, or sins [because one sin leads to another sin], or corporal or spiritual punishments, all of which are punishment for offenses against God. Thus, they might still pay in this life, either to atone for crimes in this life or to begin punishment for what is to be punished forever.

At this time, Mosén Pedro Margarite began to disgrace himself with members of the council whom the Admiral had left to govern. He did not patrol the island and subjugate it in the way the Admiral had ordered him to do in his instruction, either because he did not want to be ordered by the council members, or because he wanted to order them, or because they blamed him for what he was doing and allowing to be done against the Indians, or because he was obstinate.

This discord was the cause of other greater harms, and to a great extent, or to the greatest extent, it was the cause of the rebellion and depopulation of this island which followed later. He had sent insolent letters to those who were governing, and perhaps he had been insolent in other ways and had committed wrongs deserving of reprimand.

Therefore, when certain vessels came from Castile, which I believe were the three vessels that brought the Adelantado [Don Bartolomé Columbus/SLT], he did not wait for the Admiral but deserted the four hundred men that he had with him, and he came to Isabela to embark for Castile.

The father, Fray Buil, who was one of the members of the council, and many others [some clerics among them], also decided to go with him. [I do not know if they were the Burgundians of whom I spoke earlier, and I might have learned about this, but I made no inquiry at that time.]

When they came before the Court, they debased and reproached the affairs of these Indies. They announced that there was neither gold or anything that could be of benefit, and that all that the Admiral was saying was a hoax.

When the men found themselves without their Captain, Mosén Pedro, they all scattered among the Indians, and in two's and three's they went inland. Although they were fewer in numbers, they did not cease to commit the violence, insults, and harms to the Indians that they had committed when they were all together.

The Lords and Caciques Began to take Revenge

When the Indians saw these offenses, harms, and injustices continue to increase, and they had no way to stop them, the lords and caciques began to take revenge themselves and to obtain justice, each in his own land and district, and in the jurisdiction accorded to him by natural law and the right of the people, and surely by Divine right. And thus they ordered the killing of as many Christians as possible, with the idea that the Christians were wicked offenders of their vassals and that they were bringing about disorder in their communities.

The prudent reader might consider at this point whether these lords and caciques were doing what good and righteous judges and lords should be doing, being lords with true jurisdiction, which, as has been said, was theirs by natural law, by the right of the people, and by Divine right, when they ordered that justice be done with regard to people who were causing them so many harms and offenses and who were usurping their peace, tranquillity, and freedom.

What people in the world are there, however barbarian or gentle and patient, or more exactly, bestial they may be, who would not do the same? For this reason, a cacique called Guatiguaná ordered that ten Christians be killed, and he secretly ordered that fire be set to a hut of straw where there were some men that were ill.

His settlement was large, and it was situated on the bank of the mighty river Yaquí, and because it was a very fine location, the Admiral had built near or next to it a fort that he called Magdalena. Magdalena was ten or twelve leagues from where the town of Santiago was established and is now located.

In other parts of the island, other caciques ordered that as many as six or seven Christians who were scattered about the island be killed because of robberies and acts of violence which they had committed.

These excessive acts of the Christians against the natives of this island, wherever, they were or wherever they went, were so much against natural reason and the right of the people (which naturally dictates to all that they should live in peace, that they should keep their lands and dwellings without harm of disturbance, as well as their properties, few or many, and that no one should commit any violence, injury, or any other evil against them), and there were such horrible and frightening reports of the severity, roughness, iniquity, restlessness, and injustice of that people who had come recently and who were called Christians, such reports having spread throughout all the kingdoms, provinces, places, and corners of this island, that all the common people were fearful, hated the Christians without seeing them, and wanted never to see them or hear them. Especially, the four caciques, Guarionex, Caonabó, Behechio, and Higuanamá, along with all the many other lesser lords or caciques who followed and obeyed them, wanted to drive the Christians out of this land and remove them from the world by killing them.

Only Guacanagarí never did any harm to the Christians. He was the cacique of Marien where the Admiral had a shipwreck on the first voyage, and where he left the fortress and town that he called Navidad. Instead, during all this time, he supported one hundred Christians on his land as though each one was his son or his father, and he suffered their injustices or ugliness, either because his goodness and virtue were incomparable, as is apparent from the reception he gave and the things he did for the Admiral and the Christians on the first voyage, or perhaps because he was low-spirited and a coward who did not dare to resist the fierceness of the Christians. But it is certain that he lived with considerable bitterness and that he grieved and wept over his and his vassals' afflictions.

Book I, Chapter 101. When the Admiral had recovered from his very serious illness and was very much cheered by the arrival of his brother, Bartolomé Columbus, he acted to institute and confer upon him the rank or royal office of Adelantado of the Indies, just as he was Admiral of the Indies. He did this as Viceroy, thinking therefore that he had the authority. But the Sovereigns did not approve of this, and they informed the Admiral that the office of viceroy did not have the authority to institute such a rank and that only the Sovereigns had this authority. However, to favor both of them, their Highnesses, in their royal letters, did appoint him as Adelantado of the Indies, and he held that rank and title until he died. [The royal decree that instituted this rank of Adelantado, granted by the Sovereigns to Bartolomé Columbus, was issued at Medina del Campo on July 22, 1497. Perhaps we will deal with its significance later.]

He was a person of very good disposition, and he was tall, though not as tall as the Admiral. He was likeable, but somewhat strict. He was strong and very forceful, very wise and prudent, cautious, and he had considerable general experience in all matters. He was a great navigator, and I believe, from the books and navigation charts which probably belonged to him or to the Admiral and which are commented on and noted in his handwriting, that he was so learned in that science that the Admiral had little advantage over him. . . .

As for the disposition of the Adelantado, it seemed to me, at the times when I met him, that he had a more severe and cold disposition than the Admiral and was not as gentle and gracious. The Admiral often followed his advice and judgement [with regard to things that he wanted to do] and with regard to problems of the country, and he did not do anything without him. It may be that the Adelantado was the cause of those things for which the Admiral was accused of severity and cruelty.

However, the Admiral and his brothers were foreigners and alone, and they governed Spanish people who, although they were very much subject to their native masters, are less submissive and patient and more unruly when they have superiors over them who are foreign to them, and especially when they are outside their own country and show more hardness and fierceness. Therefore, anything that might not be to the liking of everyone, especially to many noblemen who had come with the Admiral, and more so to officers of the King who ordinarily express their ideas more than others, was probably judged and held against them as being severe and less tolerable than if other governors of our own nation had done it or ordered it.

Thus, perhaps the Adelantado practiced those severities at that time, I mean with regard to punishment of the Spaniards. With regard to harms that were done to the Indians, little concern was ever felt that they [the Indians/SLT] might be harmed, and few accusations were made with regard to them.

Another View of the Loyal Cacique, Guacanagari

Book I, Chapter 102. At this time of the illness of the Admiral a few days after he had returned from his discovery of Cuba and Jamaica, the cacique of Marien, Guacanagarí, came to visit him, and he showed great sorrow over his illness and hardships and expressed his regrets. He said that he had had no part in the death of the Christians who had been killed by order of the other caciques and lords or in the warfare of the natives who were in the valley and other places. He said that he could give no greater proof of the good will and love that he had for him and his Christians than the hospitality that he had shown them in his land, the good services that they had always received from his vassals, and the fact that he had continued to have one hundred Christians in his land, who were provided for and served with all the necessary things that they had, as if they were his own children. He said that for this reason, he was hated by all the caciques and lords of the island, that they treated and persecuted his person and name and vassals like enemies, and that he had sustained many harms from them on that account.

As for the thirty-eight [thirty-nine/SLT] Christians who remained in the fortress on his land when the Admiral returned to Castile with the news of the discovery of these lands, he wept as though they were all his children, excusing himself from guilt and blaming himself for his misfortune in not having been able to protect them until the Admiral returned so that they might be alive.

The Admiral accepted his explanation, showed him courtesy, and had no doubt that all or the greater and principal part of what he was saying was true. The Admiral decided to march through the island with as many Christians as he could, in order to scatter the natives who were banded together and to subjugate the entire land. The cacique Guacanagarí offered to go with him and to bring all his people that he could to favor and help the Christians, and this is what he did.

For people who love truth and justice and who are devoid of all passion, especially temporal interest, it should be noted here that Guacanagarí might have favored and protected the Christians for their good and so that they might remain on the island, and to those who do not understand the basis of the matter, it may appear on the surface that Guacanagarí was doing properly and virtuously. In truth, however, he greatly transgressed and violated natural law; he was a traitor and destroyer of his country and of the countries of the other caciques of the island and of their entire nation: he sinned mortally by helping, supporting, favoring, and protecting the Christians, considering the obligation that all men have to the common good, freedom, and preservation of their country and its community, [as appears in the paragraph "De iustitia et iure" of the Veluti law [book 1, title 1, law 2/SLT], where it says that religion is owed to God and obedience is owed to the fathers and to the country. This is one of the natural precepts that we are obligated to follow, under threat of very serious mortal sin].

Consequently, all the caciques and lords and all the other natives of those kingdoms persecuted him justly and lawfully, and they waged a just war against him and against his kingdom as their mortal enemy and public enemy of all and as a traitor and dissipator of his country and nation, because he helped, favored, and protected the public enemies of his country and of all the other countries of the other kingdoms and states, these enemies being rough, hard-hearted, forceful, and alien people [the Spaniards/SLT] who molested, disturbed, mistreated, and oppressed them and put them in unbearable servitude and finally exhausted, destroyed, and killed them.

It was highly probable and most certain that those alien people, who did such things and who gave such evidence of themselves everywhere they went, would overthrow, destroy, and devastate the communities of all the kingdoms of this island, as soon as they settled and established themselves in the land, as they finally did and as is now very evident. Furthermore, his own kingdom and his own vassals and subjects could lawfully kill and justly oppose Guacanagarí as a traitor and destroyer of his country and the general welfare of his kingdom. He would be unjust if he were to oppose them and the other caciques who might persecute him for that reason. . . .

At this time, the Admiral waged war against the cacique or king, Guatiguaná, some of whose people the Christians had cruelly slaughtered because he had ordered that the ten Christians be killed, and he fled. Many natives were taken alive [they were nominally from a province considered to be in rebellion/SLT].

The Story of Hojeda and the Cacique Caonabó

It happens that, a little before this, Alonso de Hojeda came. . . . He had been sent alone on horseback by the Admiral accompanied by nine Christians on the pretense of visiting the king Caonabó, on behalf of the Admiral. He is the one of whom we spoke earlier as a great lord, much stronger than any other lord of this island. Hojeda was to ask Caonabó to visit the Admiral at Isabela and, if possible, he was to capture him by a ruse.

The Admiral and the Christians feared this king or cacique more than any other on the island because they had reports that he was trying to exhibit his bravery and position in wars and in other ways and that he took pride in having his royal majesty and authority seen and respected as a result of his deeds, words, and importance. And he was aided by having two or three brothers who were very brave men and many other people who strengthened him, so that in warfare, it was not considered so easy to conquer him.

The ruse was as follows: The Indians gave the name "turey" to our brass and to the other metals which we had brought from Castile, out of the respect that they had for it as something from heaven. They called heaven "turey," and so they made jewels from those metals, especially from brass. Therefore, Alonso de Hojeda brought as a present from the Admiral, some shackles and handcuffs that were very well crafted, slender and thin, and very polished and shiny. He said that it was turey from Biscay, as though it was a precious thing from heaven.

Hojeda came to the country and village of Caonabó, which was called Maguana and is probably about sixty or seventy leagues from Isabela. He dismounted from his horse, and all the Indians were frightened by seeing him, because at first they thought that man and horse were all one animal. They told Caonabó that Christians had come, having been sent by the Admiral Guamiquina of the Christians, and that they had brought him a present from the Admiral that was called turey from Biscay. By Guamiquina, they mean the lord or the one who was over the Christians.

When he [Caonabó/SLT] heard that they were bringing turey to him, he was very happy, especially because he had heard reports of a bell that was in the church of Isabela and because the Indians told him that they had seen it and that the Christians had "a turey that spoke." The Indians thought that it spoke, because all the Christians gathered at the church for mass in response to its sound. Therefore, he wanted very much to see it, and according to what has been said, he had sent requests several times to the Admiral for it to be brought to his place. So, he was pleased for Hojeda to enter where he was. And it is said that Hojeda knelt and kissed his hands, and that he said to his companions: "All of you do as I do".

He gave him to understand that he was bringing him turey from Biscay, and he showed him some very bright and silver-colored shackles and handcuffs. By signs and some words that he knew by this time, Hojeda gave him to understand that that turey had come from heaven, that it had a great secret power, and that the Guamiquinas or kings of Castile wore it as a great jewel when they did "areytos" which were dances, and when they celebrated.

Hojeda asked the king to go to the river to relax and to bathe, which was a very customary thing. (The river was perhaps more than a half league from the village, and it was very large and beautiful. It was called Yaquí, and it comes from a mountain with the other river that we spoke of earlier. It flows to Monte-Christi, and the Admiral had called it the Río del Oro.) He said that there he would put them on where they should be worn, and that then Caonabó would return as a knight on the horse, and he would appear before his vassals like the kings or Guamiquinas of Castile.

One day, Caonobó decided to do this, and with some of his servants and a few other natives, he went to the river. He was quite careless, and he had no fear that nine or ten Christians could do him any harm, because he was on his land where he had so much power and so many vassals.

After Caonobó had bathed and refreshed himself, he was very desirous of seeing his present of turey from Biscay and of testing its power. Hojeda had those who had come with Caonobó withdraw a short distance, and he mounted his horse. The Christians put the king on the horse's haunches and they were greatly pleased and happy to shackle him and apply the handcuffs. Hojeda made one or two turns where they were, to hide his intentions, and, together with the nine Christians who were with him, he took the trail to Isabela, giving the appearance that they were getting ready to return to the village.

Little by little, he withdrew until the Indians, who were looking at him from a distance, lost him from sight, for the Indians were still keeping away in fear of the horse. Thus, Hojeda laughed at them, and the trick was played. The Christians drew their swords and were ready to kill him [Caonabó/SLT] if he were not quiet and still so they could securely tie him up with good ropes that they had.

With all imaginable speed, they followed the trail and went through the mountains, and after many hardships and dangers and much hunger, they arrived and brought him to Isabela and turned him over to the Admiral.

It was publicly and widely known that Alonso de Hojeda had captured the great king Caonabó, one of the first principal kings and lords of this island in this way, with this ingenuity, and by this ruse of the black turey of Biscay. This was the talk, and after I came to this island [in 1502/SLT], which was six or seven years after the occurrence, we often spoke about it with much certainty.

There may have been other details besides those that I am relating here, or a different account about how they may have seized him at the river and shackled and handcuffed him, but at least I am writing this as I understand it, and as we considered it to be certain at that time, that is that Hojeda had captured him and had brought him to Isabela by the ruse of the shackles of turey of Biscay.

Ferdinand says that when the Admiral [his father] went to wage war against the Indians who were assembled in the Vega (which will soon be discussed), he captured him along with many other lord caciques, but I am not sure of this, in view of what has been said and for other reasons. One of the reasons is that Caonabó would not have gone so far from his land in order to wage war against the Spaniards. The Vega Real was seventy or eighty leagues away in the distant land of Guarionex, and this would present great difficulties because he had no animals to carry supplies. This was very much contrary to the custom and ability of the Indians, at least the Indians of those islands.

Pietro Martire [Peter Martyr/SLT] tells the story in another way in the first of his Decades: that the Admiral sent Hojeda only to ask Caonabó to come to see him, that Caonabó decided to come with many armed men so that he could kill him and all the Christians, and that Hojeda, in order to induce him to come to see the Admiral, warned him by telling him that if he were not friendly with the Admiral, he and his people would be killed and destroyed.

These are not words that Caonabó would tolerate, as he was a great lord and strong, and he had not experienced the might, spears, and swords of the Spaniards. Finally, Pietro Martire says that, when he came armed with his men, Hojeda captured him en route and took him to the Admiral. But this is all a fancy for many reasons that can be seen from what has been said. What we used to say at the time was that Caonabó replied to Hojeda: "Let the Admiral come here and bring me the bell of turey that speaks, for I do not have to go there".

This is more in accord with the seriousness and authority of Caonabó. What I say is further confirmed by something noteworthy that is as certain as the first thing that was said about him. It is as follows. When the king, Caonabó, was in irons and chains in the house of the Admiral, where all were looking at him from the entrance because the house did not have many rooms, and upon entry of the Admiral, whom all respected and revered, and who had an authoritative appearance (as was stated at the beginning of this History), Caonabó did not move or pay any attention to him. But when Hojeda, who was a small person, entered, Caonabó arose and wept, showing great respect to him.

When some Spaniards asked him why he did that, considering that the Admiral was Guamiquina and the lord and that Hojeda was his subject like the others, he replied that the Admiral had not dared to go to his place to capture him, but that Hojeda had dared to, and that for this reason, he owed this respect only to Hojeda, and not to the Admiral.

The Admiral decided to send him to Castile, and many others with him as slaves to fill the vessels [which subsequently went down at sea/SLT]. For this reason, he sent eighty Christians to Cibao and other provinces in order to forcibly capture any Indians they could. In my records I find that they captured six hundred Indians. . . .

When the brothers of Caonabó learned of his capture, and when they considered the things that the Christians were doing everywhere they went and that they would suffer if they did not protect themselves, they assembled as many people as they could, and they decided to wage as cruel a war as they could against the Christians, in order to liberate their brother and lord, who was now drowned, and to drive the Christians from the land and from the earth if they could do so.

[Losing the vessels caused great anguish and pain to the Admiral. Soon afterward, he had two vessels rebuilt, one of which I saw and which was called the India. . . .]

The Admiral Receives Praise
from the Sovereigns

Book I, Chapter 103. Antonio de Torres came to Castile with his twelve vessels after a very satisfactory and short voyage, for he left the port of Isabela on February 2, and arrived at Cádiz close to the beginning or the 8th or 10th of April. The Sovereigns were inestimably happy with the arrival of Antonio de Torres, knowing that the Admiral had arrived with his entire fleet in safety at this island, and also upon receiving the letters and report from the Admiral and the gold that he sent to them, gold which had been taken from the mines of Cibao by the men that the Admiral had sent with Hojeda to see and to discover the mines, and also upon seeing with their own eyes that there was gold in that land and that it had been extracted by the men's own hands. . . .

When Antonio de Torres arrived, They ordered that three vessels be sent with many of the things that the Admiral asked for in his letters. . . . With these vessels, the Sovereigns wrote this letter or epistle to the Admiral:

"The King and Queen.—To Christopher Columbus, Our Admiral of the Ocean Sean and Our viceroy and governor of the newly-discovered islands in the Indies: We saw the letters that you sent to Us with Antonio de Torres. We were highly pleased with them, and We give many thanks to God, Our Lord, who has acted so favorably and who has guided you so well in everything. We consider that what you have done there was a great responsibility and service. Also, We gave audience to Antonio de Torres, and We received everything that you sent to Us with him and that We were hoping to see, as a consequence of the great goodwill and affection from you that has been recognized and is recognized in matters of Our service.

"Be assured that We consider Ourselves very much served and supported by you in Our service, so as to grant you favors, honor, and advancement as your great services require and deserve. Antonio de Torres did not arrive here until now, and We had not seen your letters. He had not sent them to Us, but brought them to Us personally in the interest of better safeguard. Considering the haste of departure of these vessels that are now going, We ordered that they be sure to carry as many of the things that you asked for in your memorial as possible, without being delayed. This will be done and fulfilled.

"With regard to all else, We cannot reply to you as We would like to at this time, but when he leaves, God be willing, We shall reply to you and We shall provide for everything as appropriate. We have been angry about the things that were done there against your will, and We shall order that the things are remedied and that punishment is given. Send Bernal de Pisa on the first sailing that comes here. We are ordering him to get ready for his return.

Until his replacement is ordered from here, turn over the responsibilities he had to whichever person you and Fray Buil decide on. Because of the hasty departure of these vessels that are now going, it was not possible to attend to his replacement, but on the first sailing from here, God be willing, a suitable person will be appointed to that responsibility. From Medina del Campo, On April 18, 1494. I the King.—I the Queen—By order of the King and the Queen, Juan de la Parra."

. . . The Sovereigns ordered that four [additional] vessels be readied with all possible haste and diligence, so that Antonio de Torres could return with all the provisions and supplies that the Admiral had asked the Sovereigns for in his memorial. The archdeacon of Seville, Don Juan de Fonseca, attended to all this very completely. Everything was done precisely, so that by the end of August or the beginning of September, as I understand it, Antonio de Torres set sail with the four vessels. The Sovereigns sent with him this letter to the Admiral:

"The King and the Queen.—To Christopher Columbus, High Admiral of the islands of the Indies: We have seen your letters and memorials that you sent to Us with Torres, and We have had much pleasure in learning all that you wrote to Us in them. We gave many thanks to Our Lord for everything, because with His help, this your action will be the cause whereby our Holy Catholic Faith may be much further increased.

"One of the main reasons why this has pleased Us so much is that it was initiated and accomplished by your hand, labor, and diligence, and it appears to Us that the greater part of everything that you told Us at the outset could be accomplished has come true, as if you had seen it before you told Us. We trust in God that what remains to be learned will continue to be successfully discovered, and We shall be very much indebted to grant favors to you, so that you will be very well rewarded.

"We have seen everything that you wrote to Us, and We have been very happy and pleased to see everything, however much at length you have talked about it. But We would like you to tell Us more, so that We may know: how many islands have been discovered by now; the name of each of the islands that you have named, for although you have named some of them in your letters, those are not all the islands; the names given by the Indians to the other islands, everything that is in each island; everything that you have found in each of the islands; what has been reported to be in each of the islands; and what things that have been produced have been sent from there since you were there, for the time is now past when everything that was planted should be harvested.

"Mainly, We want to know all the seasons of the year, month by month, because it appears to Us, from what you say it is like there, that the seasons are very different from the seasons here. Some wish to know if there are two winters and two summers in one year. Write to Us all about this, and send Us all the other falcons that can be sent from there, and all the birds that are there and that can be obtained, because We would like to see all of them.

"As for the things that in your memorial you asked to be provided and sent from here, We have ordered all of them to be provided, as you will learn from Torres and will see in what he is bringing.

"If you agree, We would like for a caravel to sail from there every month, and for another to sail from here every month, in order for Us to hear from you and all the people who are there, and also so that you can be supplied all the time with what is needed, because the affairs with Portugal are settled and the vessels will be able to come and go safely. If it seems to you that this should be done, proceed, and tell Us the way you think that vessels should be sent from here.

"As for the policy that you should follow with the people you have there, what you have been doing thus far seems very good to Us, and you should continue that way. You should give them as much satisfaction as possible, but you should not allow them to violate in anything that they must do or that you order them to do by Our command. As for the settlement that you established, there is no one who can give a definite rule or change anything from here, because, being present, We would probably have taken your advice and opinion in the matter, even more so being absent. Therefore, We have turned the matter over to you. As for all the other things in the memorial that Torres brought, notations have been made on the margins of the memorial for your information.

"As for the situation with Portugal, an agreement was reached here with its ambassadors, and it has seemed to Us that there were no more difficulties. So that you may be informed at length in this matter, We are sending you a copy of the articles on the subject. Therefore, it is unnecessary to comment further on the subject, but We order you and We hold you responsible for watching that entire situation and for seeing to it that it is watched by everyone, as it is stated in the articles.

"As for the matter of the line or boundary that is to be established, it seems to Us to be a very difficult thing which requires much learning and trust. Therefore, if possible, We would like you to participate in it and to resolve the matter along with the others who are to be involved in it on behalf of the king of Portugal.

"If there is much objection to your departure for this, or if it would lead to any difficulty there where you are, see if your brother or anyone else you have there may have knowledge of the matter and fully inform them by writing, by words, and by drawings, and by all the methods by which they can be best informed. Send them here immediately on the first caravels that come, and We shall send others from here with them at the time agreed upon.

"Whether you leave for this or not, write to Us very fully with regard to all you know in this matter and what you think should be done, for Our information and in order that everything may be made available to Our service. See to it that your letters and those that you send later come promptly so that they may be sent on to where the line is to be established before the time is up to which We have agreed with the king of Portugal, as you will see in the capitulation. From Segovia, on August 16, 1494.—I the king.—I the Queen.—By order of the King and the Queen, Fernand Alvarez."

I have been unable to learn what was done subsequently in this matter. Only this is certain: that neither the Admiral nor his brother were able to leave, either because of the discovery of Cuba and Jamaica, the illness of the Admiral, and other adversities that befell them, or because the time of the agreement was past, and I still believe that it was mainly because of what will be discussed in the following chapters.

Subjugation of the Indians Continues

Book I, Chapter 104. Every day the Admiral knew that the entire land was taking up arms, although actually it was a mockery [because of the inadequacy of Indian weapons against the Spaniards/SLT], and he knew that their hatred of the Christians was increasing. He was unaware of the great reason and justice of the Indians [because he did not understand their rights under natural law/SLT], and he hurried as quickly as he could to march forth to scatter them, and to subjugate the Indians of this entire island by force of arms, as we have already said. To do this, he selected two hundred Spaniards who were the most healthy (for many were sick and feeble) to go on foot, and twenty on horseback.

They carried many cross-bows, firearms, spears, and swords, and one other weapon which, next to the horses, was more terrifying and frightening to the Indians. This weapon consisted of twenty hunting dogs. Within one hour after they were released or told "get him", each dog would tear a hundred Indians to pieces. Because all the natives of this island had the custom of being totally naked, from their heads to their feet, one can easily see what things the very ferocious dogs could do, when they were urged and forced by those who incited them against naked or completely nude and very delicate bodies, certainly more than they could do to tough-skinned hogs or to deer.[1]

This idea began here. It was thought out, invented, and arranged by the devil. It spread throughout the Indies, and it will come to an end when no more land is found on this earth and no more people to subjugate and destroy, just like other exquisite inventions which are very serious and very harmful to the greater part of the human race, and which, it would seem, began here and advanced and have moved toward total destruction of these nations.

Here it should also be noted that the Indians, as has been stated, went about naked in these islands and in many places on the mainland, that in all the other places their clothing might not have amounted to more than one mantilla of thin cotton, measuring one and a half yards or two yards at the most and that these things might have been their defensive arms in all the Indies (I mean their skins and the mantillas). Therefore, the cross-bows of the Christians, the old firearms, and the incomparable arquebuses of today are incredibly destructive to the Indians.

It is unnecessary to mention the swords that have cut and today are cutting through the bodies of naked Indians. The sight of the horses, to people who had never seen them and who thought man and horse were all one animal, was like being buried alive in hell. That suffering and fear has left its mark even today in persons, dwellings, villages, and kingdoms. It is true that only ten horsemen, at least on this island (and all the other places of the Indies, except the high Sierras), are enough to defeat with their spears 100,000 natives who might join in war against the Christians, as few as one hundred being able to escape. This could be done easily in the Vega Real of this island, because the land is as flat as a table, as was stated earlier in Chapter 90. All of the arms that we use against the Indians are highly destructive to them.

There is no point in talking about how offensive their arms are against us, because, as we said earlier, they are more like children's games.

When his men were assembled and he had all else that was necessary for warfare, the Admiral took with him his brother, Bartolomé Columbus, and the king Guacanagarí (I was unable to learn which of his vassals he brought with him), and on March 24, 1495, he left Isabela. After two short days travel—ten leagues, as has been said—he entered the Vega, where many natives were gathered. They said they thought there were more than 100,000 assembled. He divided his men between himself and his brother, the Adelantado, and they separated into two groups. They turned loose the cross-bows, guns, very fierce dogs, the violent force of the horsemen with their spears, and the men on foot with their swords. And thereby, they routed the Indians asunder as though they were flocks of birds.

They did no less to them than they could have done to a flock of sheep shut up in their pens. The horsemen speared a great number of them, and the dogs and swords tore others to pieces. All who were taken alive, and there were a great number, were taken as slaves. It is to be noted that the Indians are always deluded, especially those who have not yet experienced the strength, forcefulness, and arms of the Christians, because the first thing their spies do when they are sent out is to bring them a report of how many Christians there are. They bring back kernels of corn, which are like garbanzos, to show how many Christians there are. However many Christians there may be, there are no more, or never have been more, than 200 or 300 or 400 at the most, just a handful. When the Indians see how few the Christians are in number, and that their own number is so great, it seems impossible to them that so few might prevail against so many. But afterward, when they meet to fight, they find out through danger and destruction how mistaken they were.

Here one should note what Ferdinand Columbus [son of the Admiral/SLT] says about this, when first he condemns the departure of Pedro Margarite, and then he condemns the force and attacks that the Christians launched against the Indians. These are his words: "After the departure of Mosén Pedro Margarite, it came about that every man went out among the Indians wherever he wanted, plundering their property, taking their women, and committing such offenses against them, that the Indians sought to take revenge against those whom they caught alone or scattered. The cacique of Magdalena, called Guatiguaná, killed 10 Christians, etc."

Later, when the Admiral returned, many were punished, and although they were unable to capture Guatiguaná, more than five hundred slaves who were his vassals were captured and sent to Castile aboard the four vessels brought by Antonio de Torres.

Punishment was also given on account of six or seven other Christians who were killed by other caciques in other parts of the island. Further on, Ferdinand says: "Most of the Christians committed thousands of transgressions, and therefore, the Indians had a deep hatred of them and refused to submit to them, etc." These are his words, and he also says that after the Admiral returned, he ordered extensive punishment because of the death of the Christians and because of the rebellion of the Indians.

"Certainly, God was not Served by Such Detestable Injustice"

If Ferdinand concedes that the Christians plundered their property, took their women, and committed many offenses and thousands of other transgressions against the Indians, and if they had no judge, of natural law and right of the people, other than themselves, how could the Admiral punish them? (All the more since this was natural defense, which is known to apply even to beasts and inanimate stones, as Boethius proves in the fourth prose of Book I of his "De consolatione". And they did this, although they may have recognized the Admiral or someone else as their superior, for the Admiral did nothing to stop it.)

Also, if the Admiral had only been seen by the ten, twelve, or fifteen villages that were on the eighteen-league route that he took when he went to see the mines, and if the Admiral had not convinced or been able to convince anyone, by natural reason or by authentic scripture, that they were obligated to obey him as their superior, how, by any divine or human reason, would he, did he, or could he punish them for the rebellion, as Ferdinand says? The Admiral had not convinced them, nor was he able to do so. He did not understand them, nor did they understand him.

How can those who are not subjects be rebels? Could the king of France reasonably say to the natives of Castile that they are rebels against him, if the French committed violence, plunder, attacks, and transgressions against them, usurped their properties, and took their women and children from them in their own lands and homes, and if they defend themselves or try to escape from those who are doing them so many wrongs? I do not believe that Castile would acknowledge this to be a rebellion.

It is clear at that time, and even much later, as will be evident, the Admiral did not know what he should do and how far his power extended. And, Ferdinand Columbus missed the issue entirely. [He completely ignored the human and divine right which was to be achieved by] the discovery that his father made in these lands; the importance and ministry (although earned with difficulty and well deserved) that his father attained; the responsibility and powers that the Sovereigns gave his father; and everything else. These things should have been regarded as necessary steps, as we said previously in Chapter 93.

If Ferdinand had understood this purpose, and if he had comprehended the justice and right that the Indians had in defending themselves and their country, especially when they experienced so many wrongs and injustices every day from new and strange people whom they never offended but who were indebted to them for many good things, and if he had comprehended the little or no justice that the Christians had in entering their lands and kingdoms in that way, he would certainly have better reflected and considered what he said in this passage, and therefore, he would not have said what he said incautiously in praise of the Admiral. He said, "They sent the horses in one direction and the dogs in another. All of them, pursuing and killing, wreaked such havoc that God was served in a short time. Our men won such a victory that many were killed and others were captured and defeated, etc." Certainly, God was not served by such detestable injustice.

Book I, Chapter 105. As the Admiral himself says in various letters that he wrote to the Sovereigns and to other persons, he marched through a large part of the entire island for nine or ten months, waging fierce war against all the caciques and villages that did not render obedience to him. During those days or months there was a very considerable destruction or slaughtering of Indians and depopulation of villages. [This was especially true in the kingdom of Caonabó, because Caonabó's brothers were so courageous, and] because all the Indians tried with all their might to see if they could drive from their lands people who were so hurtful and cruel, and who, without any cause or reason and without having been harmed themselves, were depriving them of their kingdoms, lands, and freedom, their women and children, and their lives and natural existence. But they saw that they were dying cruelly and inhumanly every day.

Many were easily overtaken by the horses and quickly speared. They were cut to pieces and cut through with swords, and chewed and torn apart by the dogs. Many of them were burned alive. They saw that they were suffering all extreme kinds of mercilessness and impiety. Therefore, many provinces, especially those that were in the Vega Real where Guarionex ruled, and the province of Maguana where Caonabó ruled, which, as has been mentioned, were the main kingdoms and kings of this island, decided to yield to their unhappy fate. They put themselves in the hands of their enemies, to do with them as they wished, so that there would be no further extermination.

The Indians Burdened with Tribute

In many places and provinces of the island, there were many natives left who fled to the forests, and there were others that the Christians had not yet had time to find and subjugate. (As the Admiral himself wrote to the Sovereigns,) when the people of this island, who he says were countless, were subdued with force and skill, the Admiral brought all the villages to his obedience in the name of Their Highnesses, and they were all required to pay tribute with what they had in their own lands. This tribute was collected until 1496. These are all words of the Admiral.

I really believe that the prudent and learned readers will probably realize at this point how unjustly these tributes were imposed, whether they were legitimate, and how the Indians were compelled to pay! There had been many deaths and much havoc, along with losses of their properties, persons, women, children, and freedom of their entire existence, and the annihilation of their nation; and, with much violence, coercion, and fear, they were made to pay tributes, and they yielded to paying them.

The Admiral ordered all those who were fourteen years of age or older and who were in the province of Cibao, in the Vega Real, and near the mines, to pay a Flanders-type hawk's bell, I mean the hollow part of it, full of gold every three months, [and each month the cacique Manicaotex gave a guard half full of gold that weighed three marcos which are worth 150 pesos de oro or castellanos]. In the case of all the others who were not near the mines, each person contributed twenty-five pounds of cotton.

Surely, this was an unreasonable, very difficult, impossible, and intolerable burden and extortion, not only for people who were so delicate and not accustomed to hard labor and such vexatious responsibilities, who were so free and owed nothing, and who were to be brought and won over to the Christian Faith and

Religion through love, gentleness, tenderness, and kindly communication, but it would be most onerous and impossible even for cruel Turks and Moors, and for the Huns and Vandals who might have ravaged our kingdoms and destroyed our lives, and it would be unreasonable and abhorent.

Then a certain token of copper or brass was used, and it had a mark that was to be changed each time tribute was to be paid. Each Indian paying tribute was to carry the token around his neck so that it would be known who paid the tribute and who had not. He who did not carry the token was to be punished for not having paid the tribute, although it is said that the punishment was moderate.

But this idea, which appears to be what Augustus Octavius did at the time of our Redeemer, did not continue, because of the changes and disturbances which soon occurred, whereby God, in order to show that He had been disserved by such untimely impositions, reshuffled everything and cancelled those impositions.

At this point, it should be understood that the Indians of this island had no expedient or device by which to gather the gold that was in the rivers and in the ground, because they did not gather or get more than was found in the channels or banks of the streams or rivers, by pouring water, with their hands held together, on the dirt and gravel. This was very little—flakes or small grains and larger particles which they sometimes came upon by chance.

Therefore, to require them every three months to give a hawk's bell full of gold, which would contain at least three or four pesos de oro, each peso having been worth and today being worth 450 maravedís, was impossible for them in every way, because in six or eight months, or sometimes even in a year, they did not gather that amount, nor could they come near to that amount, for they did not have the means.

For this reason, Guarionex, the lord of the great Vega, told the Admiral many times that if the Admiral wanted, he and his people would develop a farm which would produce food for the king of Castile and which would be so large that it would extend from Isabela to Santo Domingo, a distance of a good fifty-five leagues from sea to sea (and this would be so much that all Castile would be supplied with bread for ten years). This would be on condition that the Admiral would not ask him for gold, because the vassals of Guarionex did not know how to gather it.

But the Admiral had a great desire to give a profit to the Sovereigns of Castile, and he chose to continue with the tribute: in order to compensate for the great expenditures which they had made up to then, which they were making, and which had to be made every day in this business of the Indies; and in order to hold back the slanderers and persons who were next to the Sovereigns, who always disfavored this mission, who dissuaded Their Highnesses from spending saying that all the money was poorly spent and lost and that they would get no benefit from it, and who, finally, showed as much disregard and indifference as they could with respect to the mission.

I believe the Admiral had good intentions, although I feel that he had little religious zeal and did not consider what the Sovereigns as Catholics owed to the conversion and welfare of those souls, even if they, the Sovereigns, made no profit. He was a foreigner and alone (as he said, he was disfavored), and it seemed that all of his support depended solely upon the riches that might come from these lands to the Sovereigns.

[Along with his great blindness and ignorance of justice, he believed that just because he had discovered these lands and the Sovereigns of Castile had sent him to bring the Indians to the Christian Faith and religion: they would all be deprived of their freedom; the caciques and lords would be deprived of their honors and dominions; and he might deal with them as badly as he wished, as if they were deer or young bulls in public pastures.]

He acted hurriedly, and perhaps he created more confusion than he might have. According to those who respect the truth and who had no great fondness or feeling for their own opinions, he was certainly Christian, virtuous, and of very good inclination.

Thus, he paid no attention to the remedy which Guarionex urged him to accept and the farms that he offered, but only to the hawk's bell of gold which he had levied. Later, when the Admiral realized that most of the Indians could really not comply, he agreed that the hawk's bell would be reduced by one-half and that the Indians were to pay tribute with that half full of gold.

Some complied, but it was not possible for others. Life became more depressing, and some fled to the forests. Others killed some Christians, because of certain injuries and tortures they received when the offenses, harms, and wrongs committed against them by the Christians did not cease. Revenge, which the Christians call punishment, was taken against them, not only against the killers, but against as many Indians as there might be in that village or province. They punished them by death and by torture, with no consideration of any natural, human, and divine justice and reason by which authority they did it.

A Desperate Attempt at Passive Resistance

Book I, Chapter 106. Every day the Indians saw their incredible misfortune increase, [and they saw that the Christians were building forts or walled structures and buildings, but no vessels, in the port of Isabela; and now they were worn out and bewildered, a very heavy sadness descended on them, and they did nothing but wonder if the Christians were thinking of returning to their land some time. They considered that] they had no hope of freedom or of softening, remission, or remedy of their afflictions, and they had found through experience that the Christians were very great eaters, that they had only come to these lands in order to eat, that none of them had come to dig and to do manual labor in the soil, that many were sick, and that they lacked supplies from Castile. Therefore, many of their villages decided to help the Christians along by means of a strategem or sign, so that they would all die or go away, for they knew that many had died and many had gone away. They did not know the nature of the Spaniards, who, when they are more hungry, have that much more tenacity and are more resistant to suffering.

The sign (although the results were contrary to what they thought they would be) was that: they would not plant or work their farms, and therefore, no crop would be harvested, they would withdraw into the forests where there were many good roots that are called "guayaros," that are good to eat and grow without being planted, and by hunting the hutias or rabbits that fill the forests and fields, they would nevertheless carry on with their unhappy lives.

Their stratagem had little success because although the Christians suffered very great hardships and dangers, from very great hunger, and from scouring the forests and pursuing the sorrowful Indians, they neither went away nor died. However, some died for the above reasons. Instead, all misery and misfortune fell on the Indians themselves because with their wives, and carrying their children on their backs, they were very much harried and pursued, they were tired, worn out, and hungry, and they had no opportunity to hunt or fish or look for their own food. Much illness, death, and misery fell upon them, because of the dampness of the forests and rivers where they always fled and hid, and an infinite number of fathers, mothers, and children died.

Thus, of the multitudes of people who were in this island from 1494 to 1496, it was believed that less than one-third of all of them survived, due to the killings in the wars, the hardships and oppressions that occurred later, the misery, and above all, the great internal affliction, anguish, and grief. Good vintage and very swiftly accomplished!

This depopulation and perdition [levied by Spaniards against the Indians/SLT] was greatly aided by the desire to pay the salaries of those [Spaniards/SLT] who worked here and to pay for supplies and other merchandise brought from Castile, by sending Indians as slaves, so as not to ask the Sovereigns to pay such great expenses and costs. The Admiral tried hard to do this for the reason stated above, that is, because he was disfavored and so that those who scorned this business of the Indies might not have so much influence with the Sovereigns, by telling them that they were spending money and would gain nothing.

But the fulfillment of the law of Jesus Christ might have been more worthy of consideration than the disfavor of the Sovereigns, justice more worthy than so much injury and injustice, and kindness and love of neighbors more worthy than sending money to the Sovereigns. The discovery of these Indies by the Admiral, his return to them, and everything else, were all ways of attaining the prosperity, temporal growth, conversion, and spiritual salvation of these people; and this purpose might have been more worthy than that of using force and violence, with so many killings and so much loss of souls and bodies and with such disgrace to the name Christian, in order to bring those who were caciques and natural lords and all their subjects, to obedience, subjection and payment of tribute to the King.

They never offended, saw, or heard the King, nor were they obligated to do these things for any lawful reason. [The Spaniards attacked them without cause when they were safe in their own lands, and they gave them no reason for it. They were very cruel and indifferent, and they were violent and wielded ruthless power.] Without any desire on the part of the Sovereigns, as will be shown later, many Indians were taken and sent as slaves to Castile, as stated above.

If Our Lord had not immediately anticipated and punished the Admiral with the adversities that soon befell him (which will be related, if God be willing) in order to show how much injustice and wickedness was being done to these innocent people and against their circumstances, lives, and existence, then, by this means alone of enslaving the Indians to meet the above-mentioned needs and to relieve the Sovereigns of so many expenses, most of the people of this island, of those left after the said vintage, might have been further reduced and expended.

Any person who is sensible and especially if he is moderately learned will probably understand and conclude that these Indians suffered unjust captivity and that none of them, or any one of them, could be justly regarded as a slave, because all the wars waged against them were highly unjust and were condemned by all human, natural, and divine law.

Enslavement of the Indians

In retrospect, the vehemence of Fray Bartolomé's judgment regarding this episode is remarkable. In that era, opinions such as his, calling on natural law and the rights of sovereignty and legitimacy, were surely like voices crying in the wilderness. For the most part, the right of Christian Europe to invade the Indians' territory, lay claim to their lands, violate the sovereignty of their rulers, and plunder their property went unquestioned, as did the savagery unleashed upon them in campaigns of slaughter and suppression. Yet surprisingly enough, one aspect of this exploitation did give rise to doubts and questions: the selling of Indians as slaves.

As a result of an uprising in Macorix country late in 1494, native prisoners were taken, and five hundred of these were sent with Antonio de Torres, who sailed from Española with four ships on February 24, 1495. On these ships went Spaniards who were critical of the Columbus administration, as were Fray Buil and the disloyal Mosén Pedro de Margarite, who had both returned to Europe the year before. The opinions of these two men had been influential with the Sovereigns, particularly with Ferdinand, who saw Margarite as a fellow Aragonese of long acquaintance, and Fray Buil, as someone whom he had entrusted with important decisions.[2]

The first reaction of the Sovereigns to the role of the Indians as slaves is given in a letter to Bishop Fonseca, April 12, 1495 (Armas, Document 76):[3] "As for what you wrote to us about the Indians who are on board the caravels, we think that they can be sold better there in Andalusía than anywhere else. You should attend to their sale in the way you think best." This immediate response apparently began to trouble the Sovereigns as a matter of conscience: "Could the Indians be sold as slaves, if they were from a territory the sovereignty of which had been confirmed by the Roman Pontiffs in return for the evangelization of the Indians?"

The Sovereigns decided that it was necessary "to be informed by counsellors, theologians, and canonists as to whether or not these Indians can be sold with good conscience." Thus by a letter of April 16, 1495, they advised Bishop Fonseca: "In another letter, we wrote you that you were to sell the Indians that the Admiral, Christopher Columbus, sent aboard the caravels that have now arrived. We would like to find out from scholars, theologians, and canonists whether these Indians can, in good conscience, be sold by you. And this cannot be done until we see the letters that the Admiral may have written to us, in order that we may learn the reason why he is sending them here as captives. Torres has these letters and has not yet sent them to us." The bishop was told to speed Torres on his way, to hold any money he had received, and in the meantime, "those who are buying are not to pay but are not to know anything about this" (Armas, Document 77).

Actually, it would be five years before the Sovereigns would have a final and complete response from their committee of scholars, but they apparently learned enough to take action in specific instances. For example, in a letter to Bishop Fonseca dated June 2, 1495, the Sovereigns wrote concerning certain Indians, "Also this Juanoto [Berardi] says that the Admiral, Christopher Columbus, sent him nine Indians to be turned over to certain people so that they might learn the language. Because these nine Indians are not to be sold, but to learn the language, we order that you have them delivered right away, so that he may do with them as the Admiral said" (Armas, Document 78).

In another letter to the Bishop, January 13, 1496, the Sovereigns gave instructions concerning the conveyance of fifty Indians for use in the fleet: "We have decided to order that fifty Indians be given to Juan de Lezcano as captain in our fleet, in order to man certain galleys that he has in our service. Therefore, we order and charge that from the Indians that you have there, you shall give fifty Indians, ranging from twenty to forty years of age, to Juan de Lezcano or to the person whom he sends with his letter for them. You are to take the letter of payment, from him or from whomever he sends for the Indians, indicating on the letter how many Indians he receives, and the age of each, so that, if the

Indians are to be set free, Juan de Lezcano will return those that are alive, and if they are to be captives, they will apply to the salary of Juan de Lezcano in the fleet. They are to be discounted in the amount that they come to, adding up the prices they are individually worth, according to their individual ages" (Armas, Document 80).

The uncertainty of the Sovereigns here centered on the conflict perceived between the expediency of enslaving the natives and the promise of Christianizing them. Antonio Rumeu de Armas characterizes the politico-religious context of this conflict as follows. "The Inter Caetera bulls do not adopt any posture with regard to the freedom of the American Indians. But considering the missionary nature of the bulls, the state of savagery of the Indians, their ingenuous customs, and their idolatry and limited threat, it might be possible to foresee what the final decision of the Crown would be with respect to their future juridical status. How could they reduce them to slavery the same as the enemy Saracen infidels? How could they hide the offensive trade of their bodies under conversion?" The Canary Islands were also under the suzerainty of the Spanish sovereigns, and there "the Church had prescribed slavery for the infidel neophytes and for the aborigines who were being converted."[4]

Columbus had gained experience with indigenous peoples in the Canary Islands and during trading expeditions along the west coast of Africa while he was a Portuguese resident, before he came to Ferdinand and Isabela with his "Enterprise of the Indies." It seems natural that he turned to that experience for guidance when similar situations arose in the Indies. As to the opinion of Columbus concerning the position of the Indians, Armas concludes that "Christopher Columbus did not depart in the slightest way from the Lusitanian [Portuguese] line of conduct, which accepted slavery and conversion of the infidel at the same time, without discriminations or subtleties of any kind. In this respect, he is a true disciple of Henry the Navigator. The Admiral had hardly set foot in the New World, when, not being wealthy, he clearly perceived that the sale of the aborigines in the European slave markets would be a most lucrative business."[5]

9

The Indians during the Final Years under Christopher Columbus, 1495–1500

It was probably impossible to administer the trading venture on Española successfully and continue the exploration of additional territory simultaneously, but Columbus and his Sovereigns had agreed he should do so. Complaints had already reached the Sovereigns concerning Columbus's management of the enterprise, and dissatisfaction was growing among the Spaniards in Española. Of no little significance as a cause of this discontent was the fact that, in the words of Las Casas, "the Admiral and his brothers were foreigners and alone." The inevitable jealousies and rivalries were aggravated by the difference in nationality. Columbus, an Italian, was in the position of having to give orders to well-born Spaniards, to force them to do manual labor, and to maintain discipline and order in the midst of great hardship. The unfavorable reports to the Sovereigns eroded their confidence in Columbus's leadership, and his star began to fall.

In March 1496, Columbus felt it necessary to return to Spain to answer charges that his critics had brought against him and to respond to any question that the Sovereigns cared to raise. He also wished to report personally the successes which he had achieved in the Indies and to secure additional assistance in order to accomplish the goals agreed upon between himself and the Sovereigns. To accomplish these things would require a two-year absence from Española, during which time, his brother, Bartolomé, the Adelantado, would remain in charge. With the existing discontent among both Indian and Spanish leaders, this would prove to be a time of trouble which would persist when the Admiral returned.

We continue to rely on the *History* of Fray Bartolomé de las Casas as a major source of firsthand information and we also introduce here the *General History of . . . the West Indies* of Antonio de Herrera y Tordesillas, written in the early seventeenth century and first published a hundred years later.[1] As "First

182

Chronicler of His Majesty for the Indies," Herrera (1559–1625) had access to the major sources of the period, including the unpublished manuscript of Fray Bartolomé's *History*. Despite his official ties to the Spanish Crown, Herrera's treatment of the Indians has been judged to be fair. We follow his presentation, synthesized and adapted for our purposes, in order to give the reader another point of view.

HISTORIA DE LAS INDIAS, EXCERPTS FROM BOOK I

The Falling Star

Book I, Chapter 107 (Collard). Columbus had arrived in Isabela [from the discovery of south Cuba and Jamaica/SLT] on September 29, 1494, and before his return to Spain, Fray Buil, Pedro Margarite and other noblemen went to Castile on the ships that had brought the Admiral's brother Bartolomé. They informed the King that he should not entertain any hopes of acquiring wealth in the Indies, for the whole affair was a joke, there simply was no gold on the island. They spoke so well that the King began to conceive of Columbus's enterprise as a waste of money, which was reinforced by the fact that these gentlemen had not brought any gold with them.

He was not thinking of course, that gold does not grow on trees but in mines under the ground and that nowhere in the world has gold ever been extracted without toil unless it be stolen from someone else's chests. Columbus had brought ample proof of the existence of gold both when he returned from his first voyage and when he dispatched Antonio de Torres back to Castile with the gold his men had extracted and the gold given him by Guacanagarí. He was busy founding Isabela when Fray Buil and Pedro Margarite left for Castile, and he had been there four months and a few days; how, then, could he have mistreated the Spaniards and what was his bad government? Why did his star begin to decline? God only knows. . . .

He left Isabela on March 24, 1495, at the precise time when the King was sending one of his servants, the Sevillian Juan Aguado, to spy on him, giving Aguado strong letters of recommendation. Aguado began by throwing cold water on the Admiral's pleasure and prosperity so that, while Columbus was tyrannically offending the Indians instead of converting them, Aguado was arranging the beginning of his punishment. That is how God operates and that is why all of us must take care not to offend Him, praying that He enlighten us as to our sins so that we may mend our ways.

So then, the King equipped four ships with the things the Admiral had requested for the people who earned the King's money on the island, and he made Aguado their captain, giving him instructions and a letter that read: "The King and Queen.—Knights, squires, and all of you in the Indies. We are sending Our servant Juan Aguado, who will speak for Us to you. We command you to trust and believe him. From Madrid, April 9, 1495. I the King.—I the Queen.—By order of Their Highnesses, Hernandálvarez."

Aguado arrived in October 1495, when the Admiral was engaged in the war against King Caonabó, in the province of Maguana where later on a Spanish town was built which still exists today named San Juan de la Maguana. Aguado took on airs of authority and liberties he did not have when he meddled in juridical matters such as taking prisoners, reprimanding the Admiral's officers, and treating the Admiral's brother Bartolomé, then acting governor, with little respect.

Then Aguado went looking for the Admiral. They say that whenever they met Indians he would tell them a new Admiral was coming because he had come to kill the old one. And since Indians around Isabela and Vega Real had been much aggrieved by the Admiral's slaughters and the gold tribute he had imposed upon them—work which they found unbearable—it seems likely that the Indians rejoiced at hearing this.

Poverty, unjust servitude and oppression cause people to thirst for novelties, because they are so intent on leaving their misery and so hopeful that something new will better their lot that they fail to think how that something new might bring about worse disasters. For this reason, there were large gatherings of Indian chiefs, especially in the house of Manicaotex, a chief I knew very well and for a long time, who ruled the land near the great Yaquí River, about three leagues from the present city of Concepción. They discussed the benefits that might result from a new admiral since the old one so mistreated them; but they were mistaken for every Spaniard who ever went to the Indies added new injuries to the old ones and drove them infernally until they were extinguished.

Columbus's Visit to Spain

Book I, Chapter 112 (Collard). [Columbus's audiences with the King and Queen seemed to vindicate him and to settle, for the moment at least, the controversy over his leadership/SLT.] The Monarchs asked many questions; Columbus satisfied them—we shall not waste time mentioning Aguado's reports since little attention was paid them. Columbus said he hoped to sail again, this time to discover the continent although, to tell the truth, he thought he had discovered it already when he found Cuba.

The Monarchs said They would be pleased to see the list of his requirements for the third voyage. They were: eight ships, two for carrying merchandise to Española—he was anxious to please the Christians there so that the whole Indian enterprise would prosper and become famous—and six for his own use; a plan to leave 300 persons on Española on a permament, though voluntary, basis (all in the King's pay), who would be distributed as follows: 40 squires, 100 peons as soldiers and laborers, 30 sailors, 30 cabin boys, 20 goldsmiths, 50 farmers, 10 gardeners, 20 handymen, and 30 women—these were to receive wages of 600 maravedís and a fanega of wheat per month, plus twelve maravedís a day for food; a plan to establish trade so that merchants would receive a loan from the King if they guaranteed to engage in trade and nothing else, the King to bear the risks of transportation and the merchants to keep the proceeds after reimbursement of the loan; as for the merchandise itself, it was to be taxed according to the Admiral's judgment—the wine tax was fixed at 15 maravedís an azumbre [approx. 2 liters] and the meat tax at 8 maravedís per pound; a plan to maintain friars and clergymen to administer the sacraments to Christians and engage in the conversion of Indians, as well as maintain a physician, a pharmacist, an herbalist, and musicians to provide entertainment to the residents of the island. . . .

To replace those who were unhappy on the island and wanted to return to Castile, the Admiral thought of recruiting people in Spain. But he feared that the King would restrict the funds reserved for wages and he invented a plan designed to save the King money by not paying the recruits. Thus, he requested that the King pardon Spanish criminals in exchange for a few years' service on Española, and the King issued two letters on the subject. One said that since, hopefully, the presence of Christians would spread the Catholic Faith in the Indies, and since it pleased him to show clemency, he entreated all delinquent men and women to join the Admiral and these were the criminals committed for homicide, assault, and other offenses, except heresy, lèse majesté, treason, arson, murder with fire and arrows, counterfeit, sodomy, and contraband.

The death penalty would be lifted in exchange for two years of service; other penalties required only one year, after which time they would be allowed to return acquitted to Castile. I have met some of these people on Española; I even knew one whose ears had been cut off for a crime in Castile, and his conduct here was beyond reproach. The other letter notified the courts of the kingdom that prisoners condemned to exile or work in the mines should be exiled to Española instead of the ordinary places.

The two letters were signed from Medina del Campo on June 22, 1497; they also specified that the Admiral was entitled to distribute land, forests, and rivers to the residents who promised to remain on Española for a period of four years, and that these grants were to be used for residences as well as the cultivation of vineyards, olive groves, cane fields, etc., and the construction of mills and other private and public buildings. Except when a fence surrounded a property, the rest of that land was to be free from civil and criminal jurisdiction and used as public pasture or the raising of common crops.

Brazilwood, gold, silver, and other metals found on such land was the King's property. The costs of the war and royal weddings made the grant of six million maravedís — four million for expenses, two million for wages — very difficult indeed, but it was nothing compared to the difficulties the Admiral experienced in drawing that amount when the time came for him to use it [on his third voyage, 1498].

ANTONIO DE HERRERA Y TORDESILLAS, GENERAL HISTORY OF . . . THE WEST INDIES, VOLUME 1: EXCERPTS AND SUMMARIES

The Founding of Santa Domingo

The three ships the admiral had seen sail from Cadiz, at the orders of the Sovereigns, arrived at Isabela early in July, 1496. The Spaniards were overjoyed by the provisions they brought, and the news that Columbus had arrived safely in Spain. Since hunger for food from home brought the greatest displeasure, nothing caused greater rejoicing or placated them more than the arrival of ships with provisions from Spain.

Don Bartolomé Columbus, also called by his title, Adelantado, prepared the ships for their return to Spain, and sent aboard them three hundred Indian slaves, for the Sovereigns, having been informed that some Indian caciques had ordered Spaniards killed, ordered that all found guilty of such actions should be sent to Spain for punishment.

The Admiral wrote to his brother Bartolomé from Cádiz ordering that he proceed with the establishment of the new city, with a good harbor, located on the south shore of Española near the new mining district. If it was a good location, he was to bring all that was then found at Isabela, and abandon it.

The site for the new city was located on the river the Indians called Ozama. The harbor would accommodate ships of more than three hundred tons burden. The new settlement was given the name Santo Domingo, which has survived, although the Admiral preferred to call it the New Isabela.

While the work was proceeding at Santa Domingo, Don Bartolomé decided to visit the Province of Xaragua, ruled by the cacique Behechio and his sister Anacaona. Thirty leagues from Santa Domingo, Don Bartolomé came to the Neyba River where he found a large force of Indians awaiting him. Behechio had decided to oppose the Spaniards, but when Bartolomé explained that he had not come to make war but to visit him and his sister, the Adelantado and the Spaniards were received with great honor and rejoicing.

INDIAN PROVINCE OF
XARAGUA PLACED UNDER TRIBUTE

All the leading men of Xaragua received Don Bartolomé and those accompanying him with singing, dancing, and other ceremonies to demonstrate their pleasure. First thirty of the king's women appeared, naked except for the clouts covering them from their waists to their knees, with green boughs in their hands, singing, dancing, and leaping modestly. Approaching the Adelantado, they kneeled and handed him their boughs, then the remaining people came forward singing and dancing.

Don Bartolomé was then conducted to the cacique's residence where a meal awaited them consisting of bread made of cassava and rabbit-like hutias, roasted and boiled, and a great quantity of fish taken from fresh water and from the sea. After dinner the company of Spaniards was conducted to their respective quarters, where their beds were richly fashioned cotton hammocks.

The next day in the square, with the cacique, his sister, and Don Bartolomé present, two parties of men appeared armed with bows and arrows, naked as always, and made a skirmish in the manner of those in Spain but using lances of cane rather than spears; then gradually the men began to warm to the encounter as if they were fighting their enemies. Soon a number of them were wounded, and four dropped dead. All this seemed to be done with satisfaction and without regard for the dead and wounded. Many more would have suffered the pains of battle if Don Bartolomé and the Spaniards had not asked the cacique to stop the demonstration. Anacaona, the sister of Behechio and formerly the wife of the cacique, Caonabó, was very agreeable and courteous to the Spanish visitors and a great friend to all Christians.

After the entertainment, Don Bartolomé told Behechio and Anacaona that his brother the Admiral was visiting the King and Queen, their Sovereigns in Spain, that many caciques of the island were already their tributaries, and that he had come to determine whether Behechio would give recognition and pay tribute to them. The cacique responded that he was unable to pay tribute since there was no gold in his province.

The Adelantado explained that it was his plan that tribute should only be paid of the products found in a particular province. This pleased the cacique, who then said he would give him as much cotton and cassava as he would demand. He immediately ordered that his people should plant cotton, for they were to pay tribute of it to the King and Queen of Spain, through the Admiral, and to his brother Don Bartolomé who was present in his house.

When the Adelantado had concluded his conference with Behechio, he decided to return by way of the mines of Cibao, the Vega Real, and Isabela. There he found that nearly three hundred of their men had died of various diseases. This troubled him greatly, particularly because additional ships had failed to arrive with provisions, and he ordered that the sick and infirm should be distributed among the forts and nearby Indian towns between Isabela and Santa Domingo. With the native food available, they would have only their displeasure at the lack of provisions from home to contend with and would not suffer from actual hunger. Leaving orders to continue building the two ships at Isabela, as ordered by the Admiral, he continued on toward Santa Domingo, gathering the Indian tribute as he went on his way.

Contention with the Cacique Guarionex

The Indians of Vega Real and those of Cibao, considering it an unbearable imposition to pay tribute and to provide for the Spanish "guests" at the same time, particularly since they ate so much, along with other demands on the part of Spaniards that they looked upon as grievances, complained to the cacique Guarionex, contending that it was his duty to liberate them from these oppressions.

Guarionex being a peaceable and prudent man, knowing the power of the Spaniards, the effectiveness of their horses in battle, and considering that the very capable cacique Caonabó had not been able to contend against them successfully, refused to engage in war. However, being importuned by his people who persuaded him that they could prevail against the Spaniards, and, it is said, their threatening to choose another leader in his place, he consented to commence the war, against his better judgment.

At the fort of Concepción, the Spaniards became aware of these agitations and sent word to the fort at Bonao, by means of Indians who had continued to support them. The Spaniards at Bonao relayed this information to Don Bartolomé at Santa Domingo.

One of the Indian messengers made use of deception in carrying letters to the Adelantado, with the help of a staff that was hollow at one end. The Indians of Guarionex, knowing that Spanish letters "spoke", endeavored to intercept messengers at the passes, but when this Indian was halted by the guards he pretended to be dumb and lame and had to respond to their inquiries by signs. The guards, supposing the staff was required by his lameness, sent him on his way and did not search it. Thus, the letters were carried safely to Don Bartolomé.

When the Adelantado arrived at Concepción, he advanced with the other Spaniards, sick and well, who had gathered there. They chose to fall upon the fifteen thousand Indians that comprised the forces of Guarionex and the leaders who followed him, by surprise at midnight. The Spaniards knew that the Indians posted sentinels but did not, by choice, fight at night.

The Spaniards captured Guarionex and many of the lesser leaders who fought under him. They killed many in their surprise attack, then executed those identified as ringleaders in contending for the war. They then started for Concepción with Guarionex as their captive. Over five thousand of his people followed, demanding the return of their cacique. Don Bartolomé, who knew Guarionex desired peace, took pity on them and returned him, along with other caciques whom he had taken captive.

The Cacique Behechio, His Sister Anacaona, and the Adelantado

The cacique Behechio and his sister Anacaona sent messengers at that time advising the Adelantado that their tribute of cotton and cassava was ready. Don Bartolomé decided to go to their province, Xaragua, to collect the tribute and to leave the Spaniards who had been maintained by the Indians of Vega Real there. This would give some respite to those who had been providing food and would shift that burden to the Indians of the province ruled by Behechio. The Spaniards, however, continued to be ill at ease for the want of clothing and other necessities that had to be brought from Spain.

Behechio, his sister Anacaona, and thirty-two lesser caciques came out to meet Don Bartolomé upon his arrival. The Indian leaders had ordered many loads of cotton, spun and unspun, to be brought, and had filled a large house with this cotton. They had also prepared an abundance of the rabbit-like hutias and roasted fish. The Adelantado thanked them for all of this, and they offered to fill another house, or houses, with cassava, from which bread was made.

Don Bartolomé sent orders to Isabela that one of the two ships should come to the port of Xaragua to carry the tribute away. That harbor is a large bay, or inlet of the sea, dividing the land in that region into two parts. One part forms Cape St. Nicholás, stretching out thirty leagues. The other stretches out much further to form Cape Tiburón, the inland portion or bottom of the bay reached within two leagues of Behechio's palace.

Those at Isabela having sent the ship (caravel), when it arrived in the port Anacaona persuaded her brother to come and see the Spanish "canoe." They spent the night at a half-way point, a little village where Anacaona had many things made of cotton, also chairs, vessels, and other wooden things, wonderfully worked and very valuable; the chairs were of fine wood finished to a glossy black that looked like jet, and there were four bottoms (bales) of cotton, so large that a man could scarcely lift one of them. All of this she presented to Don Bartolomé.

Although Behechio had two very fine canoes, Anacaona would not board them, but chose to go aboard the Spanish caravel. The firing of the cannon put the Indians in such a fright that they were ready to jump into the sea, but seeing Don Bartolomé laugh, they composed themselves. While they were aboard, the seamen played the tabor and pipe (small drum and fife) and other instruments, which pleased the Indians very much. They had looked about fore and aft, then went aboard the caravel, looked into the hold, and were altogether amazed at what they saw.

Don Bartolomé had the sails spread and ordered the caravel to take a turn about the sea then return to the same place. The cacique Behechio was filled with wonder and admiration that such a great vessel could make way without the use of oars and could go forward and backward with the same wind.

When they had returned to Xaragua, the caravel was loaded with cassava, cotton, and other things and went away to Isabela, while Don Bartolomé returned overland.

Francisco Roldán Raises a Mutiny

While the Adelantado was at Xaragua, Francisco Roldán, the chief Alcalde at Isabela, who had "forgotton the bread he had eaten at the Admiral's table," decided he would try to gain authority by creating commotions. He used for his excuse the fact that Don Diego Columbus, younger brother of the Admiral and the Adelantado, had ordered the caravel that had brought provisions to Isabela to be laid dry (put ashore) to prevent its being taken by malcontents to carry them away back to Spain.

Roldán commenced a muttering among the laboring men where he had a following, since he had been their overseer, and also among the seamen, others who were contentious by nature, and still others who for various reasons were the most discontented. He said that the caravel would be better in the water and ought to be sent away to Spain with letters to their Catholic Majesties, for the Admiral had been away so long that they should have their wants relieved so they would not perish with hunger or be destroyed by the Indians.

The malcontents held that the Adelantado, Don Bartolomé, and his brother Don Diego would not send away for assistance because they planned to revolt, keep the island for themselves, and hold all of the Spaniards as their slaves. They would use them to build houses and forts, to assist them in gathering tribute from the Indians and in enriching themselves with gold. The men finding their already existing displeasures encouraged by the Chief

Alcalde, an authority figure, had the impudence to repeat things in public which previously had only been whispered in corners.

Francisco Roldán, now that these men had declared their feelings, required that they should all sign a paper expressing their opinion that what they were requesting was for the public good. Roldán, knowing that it would be a disadvantage to have their Sovereigns informed that he was a ringleader in the mutiny, sought other reasons that could be held as the basis for action against the Columbus brothers (who they said were not really Spaniards but were of Italian descent). He, therefore, convinced the malcontents that they should secure the friendship of the Indians to themselves by relieving them of tribute. They had received information that the Indians under Guarionex did not pay the tribute and that there were signs of discontent among them.

Don Diego, who had authority over Roldán at Isabela and thought he would thus keep him from advancing his plans, sent him and a number of the men away to Concepción, where it developed that he was better able to carry the mutiny forward, and abused and disarmed those at Concepción that would not follow him. Then returning to Isabela, he took the key to the royal magazine by force, broke the locks in pieces, and crying out, "Long live the King!" took what arms and provisions he thought necessary for his followers.

Don Diego came out with some honest men to try to appease the mutineers, but Francisco Roldán behaved so insolently that Diego thought it best for him and those with him to retire into the fort. The mutineers went away into the Indian towns saying they had quarreled with the Admiral's brothers because of the tribute they required, and saying that they would defend them if they stopped paying tribute.

A number of causes are said to have brought Francisco Roldán to that state of insolence, but the chief of them seems to have been the ambition to command and to be subject to no man nor to the rules established at Isabela; also he believed that the Admiral would not return because of the information that Juan Aguado carried to the Sovereigns against him. He had determined to place himself in authority. He had seventy well-armed men as followers, and they posted themselves in a town of the cacique Marque, two leagues from Fort Concepción. He planned to take that fort, to gain mastery over Don Bartolomé, who feared more than any other because he was a man of great valor, and then to kill him.

From Marque, Roldán approached the town where Guarionex lived, whose wife he was said to have debauched. Captain García de Barrante, who was there with thirty soldiers, shut himself up in a house so that he might not be required to talk to them, and bid him to go about his business, for those thirty men were in the King's service. Roldán threatened to burn him and his men and ranged about as he saw fit raiding his stores and provisions, then went on to Concepción, about a league away.

The Alcalde Michael Ballester shut the gates against him, and Don Bartolomé, who about this time came to Fort Magdalen, where he heard of Roldán's insurrection, went on to Isabela where he kept himself close, observing that the number of Roldán's men increased and fearing that all the Spaniards were of the same mind. He learned that Diego de Escobar, Alcalde of the Magdalena, Adrian de Mójica, and Pedro de Valdivieso, principal men, had already joined the rebels. Alcalde Ballister, however, advised the Adelantado to come to Concepción to avoid being killed, and he was able to traverse the fifteen leagues distance in safety.

Don Bartolomé then sent Malaver to ask Roldán to consider the confusion he had caused in the island, the disservice to their Sovereigns that resulted, the way he had obstructed the payment of tribute, and the danger he brought on the Christians by encouraging the Indians to take sides against them. The effect of the message was that Roldán had an interview with Don Bartolomé, after security was given. They spoke to each other at a window, the Adelantado asking why he led those people about in such a scandalous manner, resulting in the obstruction of their Majesties' service. Roldán answered that he only drew them together to defend himself against him, for it was reported that he designed to kill them all. The Adelantado answered that he had been misinformed. Roldán replied that he and his companions were in the King's service, and he might say where he would have them serve.

Don Bartolomé then ordered him to go to the town of cacique Diego Colón. He answered that he would not because there were no provisions there. Don Bartolomé commanded him to quit the office of Chief Alcalde, and required that he not act as such, or bear the name, since he did the King disservice. Whereupon Roldán went away haughtier than he had been before, to the lands of the cacique Manicaotex, from whom he drew three or more marks of gold, saying it would be paid to the King. Roldán called the cacique brother, and to keep him submissive, he led his son and nephew about with him. All who followed him were allowed to behave in a lewd, libertine, and arrogant manner, for the Indians lived in dread of them and made themselves available at their command.

As men daily resorted to Roldán, he grew more haughty and obstinate, resolving to get Don Bartolomé into his hands by besieging him at Concepción. With this state of affairs existing for the Adelantado, he took pleasure in being advised that Pedro Hernández Coronel, chief Alguacil of the island who went to Spain with the Admiral, had arrived in port with two caravels of provisions sent by the Admiral, February 3, 1498.

These were the first two of the eight ships that Columbus had requested from their Majesties, sent ahead to relieve the want he judged existed in the island. He, of course, had no knowledge of the insurrection, which apparently had its roots in the negative communications and actions of Juan Aguado, which had planted in Francisco Roldán's mind the belief that the Admiral and his brothers, Bartolomé and Diego, would be replaced by the Sovereigns as their representatives in the island.

Don Bartolomé decided to go to Santo Domingo to receive the caravels, and Francisco Roldán, when he learned the ships had arrived, proceeded to that city with his men. Fearing that the inhabitants and those arriving on the caravels would favor the Adelantado, Roldán and companions halted five leagues from Santo Domingo.

As soon as Don Bartolomé had read his dispatches, he informed the people that the Soveriegns had confirmed the title of Adelantado which his brother, the Admiral, had conferred upon him, and also reported the many favors their Majesties had granted to Columbus, who would soon leave Spain with six additional ships. This all gave great satisfaction to those who had remained loyal.

The Adelantado, since he wanted the Admiral to find the island at peace upon his arrival, sent Pedro Hernández Coronel to persuade Roldán to submit himself to the Sovereigns' representatives and to offer him a pardon for past crimes. At Coronel's arrival the guards presented cross-bows to stop him and said, "Stand off traitors, for if you had stayed away one week longer, we would have all been equals."

Coronel conferred with Roldán, stressed to him the disservice that was being done to the Crown, the mischief that this caused, the danger he would be in, and how much better it would be if they were all able to live in peace. He was sent away with haughty and scandalous responses, and Roldán with his followers went away to Xaragua. There, because of the richness and fertility of the country, they were able to continue living in their unrestrained and licentious manner.

The Adelantado, believing Roldán's actions to be unalterable, decided to use legal processes against him. Therefore, he made proclamation requiring him and his followers to submit themselves and declared them to be rebels and traitors. Ninety laboring men had come over in the caravels to work in the mines, cut brazilwood, and work the land, with the understanding that they would pay a certain portion of the gold they found to the King. Don Bartolomé was concerned that these men might be tempted to join in the free and irresponsible life followed by the mutineers.

Conflict with Guarionex
and the Loyalty of Mayobanex

The Indians of the Plain (Vega Real), although they were much molested by the rebels and suffered some vexations from those who remained loyal, withstood all patiently, without causing any commotion, even though they were encouraged to it by the mutineers, for their cacique Guarionex was of a peaceful disposition and chose to leave his country and go into the land of the cacique Mayobanex in Ciguayo rather than become involved in the conflict between the Spaniards who followed Roldán and those who were loyal to the Adelantado.

Mayobanex welcomed Guarionex, with his wife and children, and when the Spaniards at Concepción missed him they sent word to Don Bartolomé at Santo Domingo that he had revolted. The Adelantado took ninety of his ablest men, some with horses, and went into Ciguayo where he understood a large number of Indians was prepared to engage him.

Soon they came into view, shouting after their manner and shooting great flights of arrows. The Spanish horsemen had soon wounded such a large number with their spears that they withdrew into the mountains within the province of Ciguayo. The Spaniards remained there that night and the next day when they were informed by an Indian that the town where Mayobanex resided was four leagues away and that he was there with a large force ready for battle.

The Indians concealed themselves in the mountains and when they caught the Spaniards off guard, wounded some with their arrows. The Spaniards went in pursuit and killed a number, but their adversaries courageously continued the conflict. Don Bartolomé sent word to Mayobanex, by one of the Indians taken prisoner, that he had not come to make war on him and that if he would deliver up Guarionex the Spanish forces would leave his country as friends, otherwise they would bring ruin on him. Mayobanex sent as his answer: "Tell the Christians that Guarionex is a good and virtuous man, that he has never done harm to any man and therefore deserves compassion, and that they are wicked usurpers of the lands of others, and therefore I do not value their friendship, but will protect Guarionex."

With that answer the Adelantado continued to lay waste to the country around him in the province of Ciguayo, then again sent word to Mayobanex that he did not want to destroy him and that a representative should be sent to discuss terms of peace. Mayobanex sent one of his leading men, attended by two others. Don Bartolomé told him that he only required that they send Guarionex to him, for he was guilty of an offense in that he had refused to pay tribute to the King of Spain, and that, if they would turn him over, they would be assured of the Adelantado's friendship.

Mayobanex informed his people of this demand, and they answered that Guarionex should be delivered over to avoid war. Their cacique replied that it was not reasonable to give him up to his enemies since he was a good man, had wronged no one, had always been his friend, and had even taught him and his wife how to do the Areito of the Magua (that is, to do the "dance of the plain," where Guarionex's province was located, a ceremony that was highly valued), and most importantly because he had come to him and his province for protection, and he had promised to defend him.

Mayobanex then called Guarionex to him, they both wept, and he promised to continue to protect him even though he lost his province as a result. Mayobanex then ordered spies to lie in the routes of entry to their lands, posted guards with orders to kill any strangers who tried to pass them, and continued to try to comfort and reassure Guarionex.

The Adelantado again sent two messengers to Mayobanex, one of them a prisoner taken in his land and the other his acquaintance from the Vega Real, and a subject of Guarionex. Don Bartolomé then followed with ten foot soldiers and four horsemen, and they soon came upon the dead bodies of both messengers. The Adelantado then resolved to attack Mayobanex with no further clemency, but as he proceeded into his province with the Spanish forces the Indians of Ciguayo refused to support their cacique and to expose themselves to the cross-bows, spears, and swords of the Spaniards.

When Mayobanex observed that none would support him but some of his friends and relatives, he withdrew into the mountains. The Ciguayans were incensed against Guarionex for having placed them at odds with the Spaniards and resolved to deliver him up. Being aware of this, Guarionex also fled into the mountains, where the Spanish forces were at great disadvantage. They endured much hunger and thirst during the three months and pursuit continued, and for this reason, they asked the Adelantado to permit them to return to the Vega Real since the Indians had been routed.

Don Bartolomé approved, remained there himself with thirty men, and went about from town to town and hill to hill, seeking the two caciques. He accidentally met two Indians going to get provisions for Mayobanex, and although they kept the secret of his hiding place through great punishment, were finally forced to tell where he was, and twelve Spaniards offered to go after him.

The Spaniards stripped and anointed their bodies with a black and somewhat reddish dye from the fruit of a tree called "bisa" which the Indians use when they are at war or going about the country, to protect themselves from the sun. They took guides and proceeded to the place where Mayobanex thought he was secure, with his wife, children, and close family. The Spaniards then drew their swords, which they had concealed under leaves of the palm trees called "aguas," and took him and those with him away to Don Bartolomé, who went, with them in his company, to Concepción.

A verty beautiful kinswoman was taken with Mayobanex, who had been given in marriage to a lesser cacique who ruled over a certain portion of Ciguayo. When her husband, who was also hidden in the mountains, heard what had happened, he went in tears to entreat Don Bartolomé to return his wife, which he freely did. The Indian husband was so grateful that he brought four or five thousand Indians with "coas", which are staves hardened in the fire and used for digging sticks in the place of spades, and offered to plant corn wherever they wanted it; and the Indians prepared a plantation that would have then had a value of thirty thousand ducats.

The Ciguayans seeing that Don Bartolomé had set at liberty this lady who was famous in all the country, thought they might also gain freedom for their cacique Mayobanex. Many of them went to the Adelantado with presents of the rabbit-like hutias and fish, which was the best their country had to offer, to beg and promise that he should ever after continue in obedience. The Adelantado set the wife, children, and servants at liberty, but would not release the cacique.

Guarionex being distressed when his needs were no longer supplied, came out of hiding about that time to find something to eat, and being seen by the people of Ciguayo, they informed Don Bartolomé, in confidence, while they were there visiting Mayobanex, and the Adelantado had Guarionex taken and brought to Concepción. Thus the Adelantado had both caciques as his prisoners, as a result of the collusion of the people of Ciguayo.

Columbus Prepares His Return to Española: The Discovery of the Mainland

Ferdinand and Isabela were involved with a multitude of matrimonial and diplomatic affairs during the two years Columbus was present, 1496–1498, and thus it took the Admiral more than a year to conduct the conferences necessary to receive the privileges, orders, and patents essential to his conduct of affairs in the Indies, and much of another year to receive the funding, recruit the personnel, and acquire the ships and supplies that had been approved.

At length, he sailed from Sanlúcar de Barrameda, Wednesday, May 30, 1498, and headed for the Canary Islands. After ordering three of the ships to sail directly to Española, since the people there would be in need of provisions, he with the other three ships proceeded on the third voyage of discovery.

They took a course to the southwest and continued until they experienced such great heat that the hoops popped off of the casks of wine and water, and the food spoiled. He continued sailing, suffering much personal discomfort from the heat and lack of rest. On July 31, Columbus sent a sailor aloft who spied land to the southeast about fifteen leagues in the distance, which appeared to be three mountains. It was an island and was named Trinidad.

It was on this voyage that the Admiral discovered the mainland of South America, the Pearl Islands, other islands occupied by cannibals in the Lesser Antilles, and then sailed on to Santo Domingo where he learned that Francisco Roldán had raised a mutiny, and that the three ships separated from him at the Canary Islands had encountered the mutineers when they reached Española, having missed the port of Santo Domingo.

Columbus immediately examined the process being used by the Adelantado against the mutineers and altered it to include proof that the insurrection had arisen from the wicked inclination of Roldán and that neither the Adelantado nor any other person had given him just cause to complain or wronged him in the least.

The other three ships arrived some days after the Admiral as well as the caravel Don Bartolomé had sent out to find them. One ship had struck a shoal, lost the rudder, and was in very bad condition; they had taken so long that most of the provisions were spoiled; and when the Admiral learned that forty men from the ships had remained with Roldán, he was much troubled, for he believed that this show of success would make him even more haughty.

Columbus decided, however, to try him by fair means and to forgive him of his offenses, for he knew that his own enemies in Spain would make much of this new rift within his ranks. Also the Admiral had word that Roldán would submit himself to him when he returned. At this time Captain Alonso Sánchez de Carvajal arrived after discussions with Roldán at Xaragua and reported that all he had said to him proved to be without effect.

Francisco Roldán, knowing that the Admiral was in Santo Domingo, went from Xaragua to Bonao, where he was only about twenty leagues' distance from him. Columbus continued to try to bring about an accommodation. Michael Ballester and Alonso Sánchez de Carvajal, representing the Admiral, continued to try to negotiate with Roldán, and finally they learned that there was some dissension within the ranks of the mutineers. Francisco Roldán and those he called the "gentlemen" were willing to reach a settlement and would have liked to return to the service of the Sovereigns but there was another group who enjoyed the libertine and licentious life that they had become accustomed to among the Indians and did not want to give it up.

The negotiators and Roldán, having failed to get those they called the "meaner sort" to listen to reason, Roldán wrote a letter demanding a safe conduct at the hands of the Admiral and his brother, and reporting that he was convinced that all but the "gentlemen" would forsake him. The Admiral was concerned when he learned this, and soon found that it was true, for having issued an order to march to Bonao where most of the mutineers were located he learned that only seventy of those that were with him said they would obey his orders, and he had little confidence in some of these.

In this situation, Columbus issued a proclamation stating that all those who would return to their duty within thirty days would be kindly received and that no notice would be taken of what was past. In addition, all those who wanted to return to Spain would be given free passage. At the same time, he sent a safe conduct to Francisco Roldán and all who would come in with him to Santo Domingo.

The ships were detained eighteen days beyond the time agreed upon, awaiting decisions on the part of the men involved, some of the slaves on board had died, and Columbus finally had to release the ships for the return to Spain. He sent word to the Sovereigns of the rebellion of Francisco Roldán and the trouble this had caused. He also requested that more clerics be sent to instruct the people, and a lawyer for the execution of justice. Francisco Roldán and his followers also wrote to the Sovereigns hoping to vindicate themselves.

In the eventual settlement between Columbus and Roldán, the mutineers were to be restored to whatever rights they enjoyed before the rebellion. This meant that Roldán had the office of the Alcalde Mayor returned to him, and he began to exercise it with the greatest insolence. His remaining followers behaved themselves in a similar manner. Those who chose to return to Spain had been allowed to do so, as the Admiral had promised.

The First Repartimientos in the Indies

In October of 1499, Roldán petitioned the Admiral that the 102 men who remained as his followers should have land assigned to them in Xaragua. Since Columbus did not want all of them to remain together, some received land in Xaragua, some in Bonao, others in the Vega Real, and still others in the vicinity of Santiago. This was the first such distribution of lands in the Indies and became the example for the grants that followed. These repartimientos, or grants of land, included an assignment of Indians under the local cacique. They would till the assigned land and perform other labor for the Spaniard to whom they were entrusted.

Francisco Roldán had lands assigned to him near the town of Isabela, on the north side of the island, with two cows, two calves, twenty sows, and two mares, all of these belonging to the King and sent over so that they might begin to breed livestock for the island. Indians were assigned to Roldán as to the others.

Michael Ballester and García de Barrantes were sent with the ships to the Spanish Court to present the process against Francisco Roldán and his followers. They reported that Roldán and the other mutineers were wicked men, "corrupters of married women, ravishers of maids, robbers, murderers, false and perjured persons," and detailed the mischief they had caused.

Roldán's representatives, on the other hand, made grievous complaints against the Admiral and his brother, the Adelantado, saying "they were cruel, punishing men inhumanly for slight offenses, and that they designed to take upon themselves the sovereignty of the Indies and to secure all the gold," along with many more scandalous allegations, to excuse their own villainies.

As Columbus feared, this incident and the reports representing both sides of the issue, fairly or unfairly, were eventually detrimental to his cause. With a reminder that Columbus had asked that qualified persons be sent to assist him in carrying on the government, their Majesties chose Francisco de Bobadilla, Comendador of the Order of Calatrava, a native of Medina del Campo, and gave him the title of Commissioner and Examiner, under which he was to arrive in Española, and also the title of Governor, to be published and made use of at the appropriate time. The Sovereigns had decided that Columbus was not able to carry on and administer the routine affairs of government in an acceptable manner.

Although this decision was made late in 1499, and the necessary dispatches began to be prepared, they were not delivered until June 1500. Among the papers delivered to Francisco de Bobadilla were a number of blank warrants, signed by the Sovereigns, that he might fill in and make use of as he should see fit.

Another matter that was damaging to the cause of Columbus arose when Queen Isabela heard that the Admiral had sent three hundred Indian slaves to be shared by the Spaniards who chose to return on the two ships that brought word of mutiny. The Queen was highly offended, and asked by what right the Admiral, or any person, should assign her vassals to another as slaves.

The Queen had a proclamation issued that all those who had received these Indians should see that they were returned to Española, on pain of death, and that these particular Indians should be returned, for others sent earlier were said to be held legally, and she was informed that they had been taken as a result of war.

Concerning the Freedom of the Indians

Five years passed, from April, 1495, to June, 1500, before the Sovereigns secured from the commission of canonists, theologians, and other scholars the requested opinions concerning the enslavement of the Indians. This opinion was to make it possible for them to reach a decision and issue instructions concerning the Indians that had been held awaiting their decision. On June 20,

1500, the following order (one example of several) was given:

"Pedro de Torres, contino [an ancient office in the royal house of Castile/SLT] of our house: You are aware that, by Our order, you are holding in sequestration and on deposit, some Indians from among those that were brought from the Indies and sold in this city and within its archbishopric and in other places in Andalusia by order of Our Admiral of the Indies. We now order that they be set free.

"We have ordered the Comendador, Fray Francisco de Bobadilla, to take them to the Indies, and to do with them what We have ordered him to do. Therefore, as soon as you see this Our cedula, give and turn over to him all those Indians that you are holding, without any exception, for inventory before a public notary. Obtain the bill from him showing how he receives them from you.

"With this, and with this our cedula, We shall order that the Indians not be requested or claimed from you again. Do not do anything to the contrary." (Armas, Document 92)

The report of the commission had been turned over to the Sovereigns, then misplaced, so we do not have any of the details of their deliberations available to us. However, we do have other instructions concerning the treatment of the Indians which will be introduced at appropriate places as examples of royal responses to particular situations.

"The first shipments of Indians that were liberated arrived in Santo Domingo in August of 1500 aboard the fleet that brought the Magistrate Bobadilla to the New World."[2]

Francisco de Bobadilla Arrives at Española

The Roldán controversy was still not completely quelled when, on August 23, 1500, two caravels arrived from Spain with the new official, Francisco de Bobadilla, aboard. Bobadilla landed the next day, with all his men. They went to the church, and after mass, in the presence of Don Diego Columbus and the people of Santo Domingo, read a commission signed by their Majesties appointing him to enquire into all offenses committed in the island and to punish those whom he found guilty.

Having published his commission, he required Don Diego and others in authority to turn over to him the five prisoners held in the fort to be hanged for insurrection, alleging that he came to examine all such affairs. Those with Don Diego answered that the

Admiral's authority was above that of a judge and that they did not have power to comply with his demands.

Bobadilla, seeing that the title of judge carried inadequate authority there, resolved to make use of the title of Governor at once. The next day he came out of the church where the people were assembled, and caused the commission to be read in their presence, proclaiming him Governor in the name of their Majesties, and commanded all persons to obey him.

When the commission was read, he took his oath as Governor and again commanded Don Diego and those in authority with him to turn over the prisoners that were to be hanged. Don Diego and his men responded that they obeyed the orders of their Sovereigns, but that the Admiral had other orders of greater authority, and that they were not empowered to make any innovation.

Upon this refusal, thinking that he would draw the people to him and away from the Admiral, Bobadilla had an order read commanding the Admiral and all others to turn over arms, stores, provisions, horses, cattle, and other things belonging to the Crown, and another order enjoining him to pay all persons that had anything due them from the Crown out of the revenue of those islands.

This last order was very agreeable to all that were in the Sovereigns' pay, who were now ready to stand by Francisco de Bobadilla. He again ordered those who held the fort to deliver everything into his hands and threatened the use of force if they refused. With the support of the majority of the people and meeting no opposition, he broke open the gate of the fort, which was not strong, and took possession of the prisoners.

The Admiral, being informed of what had happened, could not imagine that the Sovereigns, whom he had served successfully and faithfully, had given such orders against him. He proceeded to Bonao, where Bobadilla sent a letter from the King and Queen merely ordering the two of them to confer. While the letter was on its way, and the answer returning, Bobadilla confiscated all of the Admiral's possessions, moved into his house, and seized his papers. He never restored any of these things, pretending that it had been done in order to pay the men, but it was suspected that he kept much of it for himself.

Having drawn the people to him, and after hearing witnesses against the Admiral and his brothers, Don Bartolomé and Don Diego, Bobadilla had the three of them seized, without having personally conferred with them about the charges brought against them, and ordered them placed in irons. The Admiral afterward kept his fetters and ordered that they should be buried with him, to show the ingratitude of the world.

Governor Bobadilla then ordered that the Admiral and his brothers should be sent to Spain as prisoners aboard the two ships that had brought him over. Those who commanded the ships treated the Admiral and his brothers very well and would have had the fetters removed, but he would not consent to it until it was done by order of the King and Queen.

When Columbus arrived, Ferdinand and Isabela were at Granada. Hearing how he had been treated they seemed concerned, ordered his release, and sent a thousand ducats to pay his expenses to come to their court. He arrived December 17, 1500, and the King and Queen welcomed and comforted him, saying that his confinement and harassment was done without their approval and promising to redress his grievances, but not offering to return him to the government of Española.

Governor Bobadilla soon concluded the proceedings against those that were to be hanged, clearing them of charges, along with Francisco Roldán and others that were guilty. This was disagreeable to those who had behaved themselves. These inferred that if they had been disorderly and brought ruin to the island, they would have been rewarded.

Since Bobadilla had freely granted that the Crown should have only the eleventh part of the gold that was produced, along with other liberties, the Spaniards had the courage to ask for Indians to help work the mines and till the ground. He advised them to join two and two in partnerships and assigned Indians to them under the authority of particular caciques, advising them to make the best use of them, for no one knew how long that arrangement would last.

The new Governor showed little regard for the oppression of the Indians, and the Spaniards were better pleased with the liberties he granted them than the discipline they had known under the Admiral.

In Spain, the Admiral brought so many complaints against Bobadilla, demanding justice for the wrongs done him that the Sovereigns decided to send another Governor to Española. Their choice was Fray Nicolás de Ovando, Comendador de Lares, whom they considered to be a discreet person. He had a look of authority, although he was small of stature; was a lover of justice, modest in his behavior, not covetous, and was humble. Some years later when he had the title Comendador Mayor of Alcántara conferred on him, he would not consent to be referred to as "his Lordship."

When the Comendador de Lares agreed to accept the assignment, the Sovereigns appointed him for two years. He was ordered to hear charges against Bobadilla, to examine the case against Roldán for insurrection, and what had been laid to the Admiral's charge, and to report all this to the Sovereigns.

The Queen charged Fray Nicolás particularly that the Indians of Española should not be enslaved and that none should molest them but that they should enjoy freedom and protection like their vassals in Spain and that they should be carefully instructed in the Christian Faith.

10

Governor Nicolás de Ovando
and the Indians, 1501–1509

*THE TRANSFER OF POWER ON ESPAÑOLA, ADAPTED
FROM HERRERA AND LAS CASAS*

The fleet that brought Nicolás de Ovando was under the command of Antonio de Torres. It carried twenty-five hundred men, most of them well born, and ten Franciscan friars. The fleet sailed from Sanlúcar de Barrameda on February 13, 1502. After eight days, a great storm came upon it, of such severity that it seemed all the ships might be lost. The remains of the wrecked vessels and stowage that had been cast overboard to relieve the ships' burdens were carried to the coast of Cádiz. The wreckage was of such magnitude that it was thought the entire fleet had been destroyed. The Sovereigns, receiving news of it, went into seclusion for eight days and would see no one.

When the storm had subsided, the ships gathered at the island of Gomera in the Canaries. Here Nicolás de Ovando divided the fleet into two parts, ordered the fastest ships to proceed with him, and told the rest to sail under the leadership of Antonio de Torres. The new governor arrived at the Port of Santo Domingo on April 15, 1502. When the townspeople saw the ships, they hastened to the shore, inquiring what news the passengers brought. They were told that the comendador de Lares had come to govern the island.

The townsmen gave news of happenings on Española. They were particularly pleased that an abundance of gold had been found, with one "grain" so large that one of such size had never been seen before. It was said to have been as big as one of the loaves of bread baked at Alcalá to be sold in Seville, and of a similar shape, including the stone mixed with the gold, "which would certainly in time have been converted into that metal," for "almost all the grain looked like solid gold."

Governor Bobadilla during his year-long tenure had given the Spaniards liberty to form partnerships and thereby to secure the labor of the Indians. Accordingly, many of them were taken to labor in the new mines near Santa Domingo. Francisco de Garay and Miguel Díaz had their Indian laborers at breakfast one morning, and an Indian woman, eating near the stream, was striking with a bar on the ground when the "grain" began to appear. She called the Spanish miner, and they were so happy with the discovery that they celebrated by roasting a pig and served it on the lump of gold, saying that no king had ever eaten from such a dish. Bobadilla took the gold to send to Their Majesties, compensating Francisco de Garay and Miguel Díaz for its value.

After examining Bobadilla, the new governor sent him aboard the fleet along with the mutineer Francisco Roldán and those who had participated with him in making the insurrection. The cacique Guarionex, lord of the Vega Real who had been taken by Don Bartolomé Columbus, was also sent aboard ship to be brought to court for trial. Gold with a value of about 2 million castellanos, including the gigantic "grain," was carried in this fleet of thirty-one ships.

Meanwhile Columbus had arrived anew in the Indies on his fourth voyage. Upon his departure from Spain, the Admiral was instructed not to put in at Santo Domingo until the return voyage, but since he was having trouble with one of his ships, he asked permission to enter the port to make a trade or buy another ship. Nicolás de Ovando denied his request. When Columbus learned that the returning fleet was ready to sail, he advised the new governor not to send it out for eight days, for a great storm was coming up. Governor Ovando would not believe it, and the pilots made a joke of it, calling Columbus a prophet.

The ships set sail in early July, and within forty hours there arose the most violent storm known in many years. Twenty ships were lost without a single man aboard them being saved, and the town of Santo Domingo, not yet built of stone, was blown down. Francisco de Bobadilla, Francisco Roldán, the cacique Guarionex, and the great store of gold, including the large grain that had been discovered, were lost with the ships that went down. The worst ship in the fleet, which had aboard four thousand pesos belonging to the Admiral, escaped the storm and was the first to arrive in Spain. The Admiral's ships, denied entry in the port of Santo Domingo, were dispersed by the storm and were in great danger, but they all came together in Puerto Hermoso, and "thus the Admiral and his ships escaped, and the fleet perished because they would not believe him."

GOVERNOR OVANDO'S INSTRUCTIONS CONCERNING
"THE GOOD TREATMENT OF THE INDIANS"

The new governor brought specific instructions from the
Sovereigns concerning the Indians of Española:

The King and Queen, Granada, September 16, 1501 "In the
islands and Tierra Firme (mainland) of the Ocean Sea, where you
are to be Our governor, you Fray Nicolás de Ovando, Comendador de Lares, of the Order of Alcántara, are to do as follows:

"First, you will strive with great diligence for the things that
are of service to God, and see to it that the divine services are
observed with great honor, order, and respect, as appropriate.

"Also, We desire that the Indians be converted to our Holy
Catholic Faith, and that their souls be saved, for this is the greatest good that We can wish for them, and for this reason it is necessary that they be informed in the matters of our Faith, in order
that they may come to know it. Therefore, you will take great
care to see to it, without using any force, that the clerics who are
there inform and advise them very lovingly, in such a way that
they may be converted as quickly as possible. And, to this end,
you will provide all the support and help that is needed.

"Also: In accordance with Our orders that you have, you will
see to it that the residents and inhabitants of the islands and
Tierra Firme personally and on the part of their people, will
submit to your authority, and will obey you as Our governor in
all the things that you order them on Our behalf. You will take
great care to see to it that all may continue to live in complete
peace, harmony, and justice, administered to all alike, without
any individual exception. You will assign good and capable ministers and officials to this end, and render punishment when it is
due.

"Moreover: You will see to it that the Indians are well treated,
that they may go safely throughout the land, and that no one may
use force against them, or rob them, or do any other evil or harm
to them. You will decide on punishments that you think are necessary, you will see to it that those punishments are given to those
persons who are guilty, and you will issue the necessary proclama-
tions and prohibitions.

"Also: On Our behalf, you will tell the caciques and other
principals that We desire that the Indians be well treated like Our
good subjects and vassals and that no one shall dare to do them
any evil or harm. You are to order this to be proclaimed on Our
behalf. From now on, if anyone does any evil or harm to them, or

takes anything from them by force, the Indians should notify you, so that you will render punishment in such a way that no one will dare to do them any further evil or harm.

"Also: We are informed that some Christians in those islands, mainly in Española, have taken from those Indians, their wives, daughters, and other things, against their will. As soon as you get there, you will issue an order that all that was taken from them against their will shall be returned to them and you will prohibit, under serious penalties, that anyone shall dare to do such a thing from now on. If they wish to marry Indian women, it shall be with the will of both parties and not by force.

"Also: It is Our will and mercy that the Indians pay the tributes and taxes that they must pay Us. But the way these things are paid and collected depends upon the conditions of the land. You will speak for Us with the caciques, the other principal persons, and other Indians as you think appropriate, and you will reach an agreement with them as to what tribute each one of them should pay to Us each year, in such a way that they know there is no injustice being worked against them.

"Also: It will be necessary to avail Ourselves of the service of the Indians, in order to get gold and to do the other labors that We order to have done. You will compel them to work at tasks in Our service, paying every one of them the wage that you think they should rightfully have, according to the conditions of the land." (Armas, Document 122)

Remember that Fray Bartolomé de las Casas, to whom we owe so much for our knowledge concerning the discovery and the early years following the arrival of the Spaniards in the New World, came with Governor Ovando in 1502, and that during the following decades, he was an eyewitness and close observer of what happened there. The chapters of his *History* relating to the things he saw firsthand constitute a particularly moving portrayal of the plight of the Indians and a powerful indictment of the Spaniards.

HISTORIA DE LAS INDIAS, *EXCERPTS FROM BOOK II*

Book II, Chapter 6 (Collard). Now let us return to the events that followed the arrival of Comendador de Lares on the island. Bobadilla had come to greet him with the people of this town and, after the usual ceremonies, they took him to a fort of adobe where they had prepared his lodgings. He presented his credentials to

Bobadilla in front of the mayors, aldermen, and the town council; they acknowledged them and according to custom, solemnly swore to honor them. He then began to govern with prudence and began his investigation of Bobadilla's case.

You should have seen Bobadilla! He remained alone and disgraced, going to and from the governor's house to appear for judgment, unaccompanied by any of the men he had favored by saying: "Take advantage of this, you don't know how long it will last," "advantage" meaning Indian sweat and labor. Truly, he must have been a plain and humble man by nature. I never heard anyone criticize him; on the contrary, all spoke well of him. Since he had given his three hundred Spaniards license to exploit the Indians, he gave them cause for esteeming him. If he had any defects, nobody spoke of them even after the investigation, his departure, and his death.

Comendador de Lares also investigated the case of Francisco Roldán and his supporters. I believe (I do not remember too well) he had him sent to Castile, a prisoner but not in chains, so that the Monarchs might determine the punishment he deserved. But divine Providence intervened by calling him first for a higher and subtler justice. [He went down on one of the ships lost in the storm/SLT]. I mentioned . . . how Bobadilla ordered that anyone exploiting the mines with Indians should pay the King 1 peso on 11. However, either the Monarchs resented this as an action taken without Their consent and gave orders to Lares to this effect, or Lares took it upon himself to tax all gold miners a third of their profit, regardless of their previous payments.

The Gold Seekers in Española

Since the mines were rich and new then, everyone wanted tools and cassava bread to be able to put more and more Indians to work. . . . Those most eager to mine gold would spend two or three thousand of their gold pesos for these things, and when asked to pay a third of their harvest, or rather, the harvest of the Indians whom they oppressed, they would find themselves penniless. Thus they would sell for ten pesos what they had bought for fifty, and the more gold they found, the greater their loss. Those who chose to farm fared much better since they paid nothing.

In general, then, miners lived in need and even in prison for debts, while farmers would have lived in peace and abundance had they not been given to excess in matters of dress, trappings, and other vanities which in the end prevented them from prospering. They spent money like air since they acquired it unjustly

through Indian sweat and labor, with little or no thought of punishment. At that time, farms raised only pigs, cassava, and other
edible roots like ajes and potatoes. From then on the monarchs
levied a fifty percent tax on the gold mined. And since nobody
came to the Indies except for gold—in order to leave the state of
poverty which plagues all classes in Spain—they had no sooner
disembarked than they set out for the mines, eight leagues from
the city, thinking there was no more to it.

You should have seen each of them fill his pack with Spanish
biscuits and carry it on his back with picks, pots, and pans. The
roads to the mines were like anthills. If they had no servants, they
carried their own pack but some caballeros had servants to carry
things. Once at the mines, since gold does not grow on trees but
underground, lacking knowledge and experience, they grew tired
of digging and washing dirt because, in the first place they had
never dug anything in their lives. They rested and ate too often.
Hard work made them digest quickly, so they would eat again; in
the end, nothing came of their labor. A week later, having
exhausted their food supply, they returned to town emptyhanded
and ate the remnants of their Castilian provisions. Discouraged
and frustrated at not finding what they had come for, they caught
fever from the climate, which was aggravated by the lack of food,
care, and shelter, and they died at such a rate the priests barely
managed to bury them. Out of 2,500 men, more than 1,000 died,
while 500 cases of illness were made worse by anguish, hunger,
and need; and from then on, this was the lot of whoever came to
the New World to find gold.

To survive a while, those who had brought clothing, tools,
and other valuables sold them to the three hundred men
[already/SLT] on the island who were half-naked, wearing a shirt
of cotton instead of linen and neither coat, cape nor trousers.
Others formed partnerships with these 300 men, buying half or a
third of their holdings, and paid them partly with clothes and
other Spanish items, owing a balance of up to 2,000 castellanos.
They did this because the three hundred owned the land and
[Indian/SLT] servant maids; thus their power was food, and their
abundance, servants and land. They were lords and kings,
although, as I said, they walked about with bare legs.

Luis de Arriaga's Plan for Spanish Settlement

At that time, the Indians were peacefully resting from the tyranny and anguish they had suffered under Francisco Roldán, all
except those who served the three hundred Spaniards, and a lot of

work they had, too! Only one province was at arms, preparing for an attack, as we shall see. A Sevillian hidalgo named Luis de Arriaga, who had come here with Columbus, sent a proposal to the Monarchs. He asked permission to bring two hundred Castilian couples in order to populate and settle four townships, and further suggested that they be given free passage as well as exemptions. Mainly, they were to be given land and terms favorable both to the settlement of such townships and to the cultivation of land. They would remain under the civil and criminal jurisdiction of the King and his successors, he exempted from the taxes raised by the King by permission of the Pope and from any other duties for a period of five years. They would have limited rights to the mining of gold, silver, copper, iron, tin, lead, quicksilver, sulphur, etc.; to seaports and anything pertaining rightfully to the Crown but found on their territories.

They should pay the Monarchs half of the gold mined by them and the Indians who accompanied them, but could not buy any from the Indians; all the brazilwood they should cut, even though cutting brazilwood was forbidden; and a third of whatever they obtained from the Indians in the way of cotton and other materials from outside the town limits, except gold and edibles; half the gold taken from the mines after deducting operational costs, plus the mining rights to mines discovered by them—and I believe this clause referred to mines found within the limits of the new towns—half of the gold and pearls from as yet undiscovered islands or the mainland, if they happened to discover them, but a fifth of everything else. Free passage applies only to persons, not to their belongings, however numerous or few.

Another privilege stipulated that no person could remain and live in such towns who had gone into exile from Castile to the Indies or who had been a Jew, a Moor, or a convert; this was to safeguard the honor of the said two hundred couples. They would have to reside five years on the island, obey the King's orders through the governor, and serve without remuneration. If any of the colonists disobeyed, if a province rebelled, or if the Indians refused to serve, they would assume the prosecution costs. If someone wished to return to Castile within this five-year period, he could do so, but he would lose all property given him by virtue of his citizenship, and said property would be disposed of according to the King's wishes.

This was the agreement the Monarchs made with Luis de Arriaga; it was to be extended to all Spaniards settling on the island. Later, Arriaga could find only forty couples and, while in

Seville, he asked that they be granted these privileges. The Monarchs consented. Back on the island, Arriaga and his forty couples found that instead of leisure and the prospect of returning wealthy, they had to work and sweat; therefore, they founded neither cities nor castles but mixed with the island population, and the rules that applied to all Spaniards applied to them. A few days later, the three hundred gold prospectors and the newcomers complained to the governor about the excessive royal dues and asked him to request that the King be satisfied with a third, instead of half, the value of the gold they extracted at such cost. The governor wrote, and the King conceded in a royal letter addressed to the governor.

At another time, they asked the King to reduce to a fourth the third they owed on cotton and other nonmetals, it was granted from Medina del Campo on December 20, 1503. Later still, finding a third on gold too onerous, the Spaniards requested a further reduction and sent a spokesman, a Sevillian named Juan de Esquivel, who negotiated a successful fifth on all metals. The decree began with "D. Ferdinand and Doña Isabela, by the grace of God, etc.," dated February 5, 1504, in Medina del Campo. I mention these trifles, of which no other historian could give such details, so that it may be seen how loath the King was to relax his hold and grant favors, however small, because poverty plagued Castile at that time and the Catholic Kings, as well as their kingdom, lacked wealth and abundance, which fact however, did not restrict their activities both in and out of Spain.

Book II, Chapter 7 (Collard). At that time, the storm that sank the fleet having subsided, the governor had good reason to decide to settle a town in La Plata Harbor, in the northern part of the island. The chief reason was that sailing to and from Castile offered less difficulties than from this harbor [Santo Domingo/SLT], La Plata being conveniently located about mid-island, ten and sixteen leagues respectively from the two important townships of Santiago and Concepción and ten to twelve leagues from the Cibao mines, considered the richest and yielding more and finer gold than the mines of San Cristóbal or any other. Moreover, many Indians lived there and only one Spanish farmer from Santiago who raised pigs and chickens. The governor sent a few citizens by ship who, once at sea, sailed to Saona, which almost touches this island, is thirty leagues from Santa Domingo and, together with a neighboring small island, forms the province of Higuey, then in a state of insurrection; these are the people about whom I said the Spaniards rejoiced when we disembarked.

Spaniards, their Dog, and the
Cacique at Saona Island

It happened that when eight men went ashore to walk and rest a while, the Indians, thinking they belonged to another crew that had done something a short time ago to which I shall presently refer, ambushed the eight men and killed them. They had legal justification which I have from good sources and relate without additions; I believe I even spare many words and leave out exaggerations about the essence of the case. There existed ample communication and friendship between the people of Saona Island and those of Santo Domingo; therefore, whether they needed it or not, the citizens here would send a caravel every now and then which the Indians would fill with bread.

One day, just before our arrival with Comendador de Lares, the caravel went out for bread, and the Indian chief, surrounded by his people, received the Spaniards as usual as if they were angels or their very own parents. They began to load the vessel with great joy. Just as Spanish civilians never take a step without girding their sword, so these always brought along dogs trained to tear Indians to pieces and of such ferocity that the Indians feared them more than the very devil. The Indians, then, were loading cassava onto a small boat that was to take it to the caravel, while their chief, staff in hand, walked to and fro in order to expedite matters and please the Christians.

One of the leashed dogs saw the chief wave a stick and walk with agitation and, since he was so well trained in attacking Indians, pulled and strained at the leash, wanting to attack. The Spaniard who held him could hardly restrain him, and he said to another man, "What if we let him loose?" Then for a laugh, he and his friend, both devils incarnate, told the dog to attack, thinking they could control him. But the dog charged like a mad horse and dragged the Spaniard behind him; he was unable to hold his grasp and let go of the leash. The dog jumped on the cacique and with his powerful jaws tore at the man's stomach, pulling out the intestines as the cacique staggered away. The Indians rushed to the unfortunate chief but he died shortly thereafter and, carrying him away for burial, they wailed and lamented their sorrow to the winds. The Spaniards returned to the caravel with their good dog and his master, then sailed to Santo Domingo, leaving such a good deed behind them.[1]

The news spread rapidly in the province of Higuey and came to the ears of Cotubano or Cotubanamá (the penultimate syllable of the first name and the ultimate of the second are pronounced long), who was the nearest and also the bravest chief around. The Indians armed themselves and resolved to take their vengeance at the first opportunity; as it happened, those eight men, all sailors I believe, going to La Plata, were the first victims. Such was the Indian rebellion, the news of which greeted us, and it was happy news because we now had a reason to get slaves.

Now, any sensible and God-fearing reader can judge for himself and without difficulty whether the Indians were right in killing eight men who themselves had not harmed them at that time, and I say, at that time, because perhaps they had harmed them before, as is likely, from what I saw from my acquaintance with some who had already been there. That time they were innocent, yet they were not killed unjustly since a nation at war with another is not obligated to discern whether an individual is innocent or guilty, unless he wears innocence on his face or manifests it right away in brief discourse.

Thus no one doubts the innocence of a child, or of a farmer busily tilling his fields, or of a people separated, by an island, from their master engaged in an unjust war, since they are ignorant of the said war or at least do not participate in it and are not responsible for it. But this case is exactly the opposite, since there was not at the time one single Spaniard on this island who did not offend or harm the Indians; consequently, the Indians had a most excellent reason to suppose that whoever came to their island from Castile came as an enemy and thus could rightfully resolve to kill him. But let God be the ultimate judge of this.

Book II, Chapter 8 (Collard). When Comendador de Lares found out how the Indians of Saona had treated those eight Christians, he determined to fight them. Indeed, like all Spaniards at that time, he seized the slightest pretext to provoke war, and in this case he added war to a previous injury since he had already tortured the Indian chief to death. The Spaniards on Saona Island knew how the Indians were bound to feel injured and bitter, and knew enough to expect revenge. But after causing them irreparable harm through insult, plunder, and murder, they [the Indians/SLT] had a legitimate reason to declare war upon them: they [the Spaniards/SLT] called it rebellion and publicized it as such, when in reality the Indian rebellion consisted of no more than a run to the woods in search of a hiding place.

The comendador notified his four townships of Santiago, Concepción, Bonao and Santo Domingo to send a contingent of soldiers, and he ordered the ablest men who had come with him to prepare for war, which they all did readily out of their greed for slaves. An all-out war was announced publicly. I believe some four hundred men assembled for it, and the same Juan de Esquivel whom we just mentioned in the preceding chapter was named cacique [captain/SLT] general, although each contingent also had its own captain.

In these sallies, it was customary to take along a good number of armed Indians from among those already conquered, and they fought strenuously, such was their fear of the Spaniards whom they accompanied and their desire to please them; and this custom was generalized later all over the Indies.

They arrived in the Higuey province—as we call the whole easternmost territory of Santo Domingo—and found the Indians ready to defend their land, if only they could have defended it as they wished. Actually, their wars are like child's play [in their preparations to defend themselves/SLT], having only naked bellies to shield them from the Spaniards' mighty steel weapons, and only bows, poisonless arrows, and stones—where stones are available—to use against the Spaniards. A Spaniard's sword and strength were such that he could cut an Indian in half, and I won't mention the horses since in one hour's time a single horseman could spear two thousand Indians. [A bit of an exaggeration/ SLT.]

The Story of the "Outstanding Exploit" of the Indian Against Two "Expert" Spanish Horsemen

It happened, then, that the Indians would resist a while in their villages and, seeing their formations scattered and their companions mangled, would flee to the woods. Naked and unarmed as they were, sometimes they performed outstanding exploits. Valdenebro and Pontevedra, two expert horsemen I knew very well, once saw an Indian in an open field, and one said to the other "Let me go and kill that man." He raced up to the Indian, who turned about and faced him; whether he shot his arrows I do not know. Valdenebro pierced him with his lance, the Indian grasped the lance with his bare hands and hoisted himself up to the horse's reins. Valdenebro drew his sword and struck the Indian with it, the Indian snapped up the sword from the Spaniard's hand. Valdenebro stabbed him with his dagger, the Indian caught the dagger from the Spaniard's hand, and Valdenebro was disarmed.

Pontevedra spurred his horse to run to his friend's rescue and speared the Indian. The Indian repeated his feat with Pontevedra's lance, sword, and dagger. The two Spaniards were disarmed; the Indian had six weapons stuck in his body and would have fought on, when one of the Spaniards dismounted and kicked him over to snatch a dagger from his body, and the Indian fell dead instantly. This exploit was much celebrated.

Once the Indians were in the woods, the next step was to form squadrons and pursue them, and whenever the Spaniards found them, they pitilessly slaughtered everyone like sheep in a corral. It was a general rule among Spaniards to be cruel—not just cruel, but extraordinarily cruel—so that harsh and bitter treatment would prevent Indians from daring to think of themselves as human beings or having a minute to think at all. So they would cut an Indian's hands and leave them dangling by a shred of skin and they would send him on saying "Go now, spread the news to your chief." They would test their swords and their manly strength on captured Indians and place bets on the slicing off of heads or the cutting of bodies in half with one blow. They burned or hanged captured chiefs; I believe they hanged the old Indian lady chief Higuanamá (the last syllable is long).

They had anchored a caravel nearby to have it ready to cross over to Saona Island. The Indians fought a while and fled but, although the region has thick forests and a number of caves, they were unable to escape from their pursuers who captured some seven hundred men, gathered them in a house and stabbed them to death. The gentleman Juan de Esquivel ordered all the corpses taken outside to line the plaza in order to count them; there were, as I said, between six hundred and seven hundred dead, which is how the Spaniards avenged the eight Christians whom the Indians had had good reason to kill but a few days earlier.

All the Indians taken alive were enslaved since this was the principal goal of Spaniards here and everywhere in the Indies, the goal to which they devoted all their thoughts and energies, their words and their good deeds. The small island of Saona was razed in this fashion, made barren when once it had been so fertile.

When the people of that kingdom understood themselves to be so injured, so persecuted and so hopelessly desperate about finding a hiding place, their chiefs sent peace messengers to the Spaniards, offering their services. Juan de Esquivel and the other captains received them with benevolence and promised not to harm them if they came out to live in Spanish settlements; but after deliberation, they agreed to have the Indians farm the King's bread in a large plantation there in exchange for their not being transported to the city of Santo Domingo and not being molested by any Spaniard.

Among those who came to make peace with the captains was an important Indian chief of renowned courage—Cotubanamá or Cotubano was his name—whose kingdom faced Saona Island and whose tall and noble bearing betrayed his noble rank. To such an outstanding person the captain general Juan de Esquivel gave his name in exchange for Cotubanamá's, and this exchange of names, making "guatiaos" of the two parties involved, was esteemed as a bond of perpetual brotherhood and confederation. Thus, the captain general and the Indian chief became "guatiaos," friends and brothers forever, and the Indians called the Captain, Cotubano, and their chief, Juan de Esquivel.

The captain had a wooden fort built in an Indian village near the sea, leaving nine Spaniards under Captain Martín de Villamán to guard it; then they all returned to their settlements with their share of slaves. While this war was being fought, the comendador removed the township of Santo Domingo to this side of the river, where it stands today. His reason was the following: all the Spanish towns in the island of Santo Domingo were on this side and he thought it more convenient to be here to avoid the delays caused by projected ferryboats to transport the inlanders coming to the city for business purposes; and I say projected ferryboats because at that time, passage to Santo Domingo was possible only by canoe. . . .

European Weapons Forbidden to the Indians

To make certain that the Indians continued to be at a disadvantage in encounters such as this destruction of Saona Island, the Catholic Sovereigns had issued these instructions concerning their securing of arms from the Spaniards:

Granada, September 16, 1501.

"Don Fernando and Doña Isabel, etc. Inasmuch as it is in the interest of Our service that none of the Indians living in the islands and Tierra Firme of the Ocean Sea carry offensive or defensive arms, and in order that there may be no noises or commotions between them and the Christians living in those islands and Tierra Firme, and so that all may live in great peace and harmony, and for other reasons that We have, We issue this order and prohibit that any Christian shall sell or trade offensive or defensive arms to the Indians, or to anyone of them. We order that the Indians shall not trade for them. The first time anyone acts to the contrary, he shall pay ten thousand maravedís, or the equivalent, to Our treasury. The second time, he shall forfeit half of all his property to Our treasury. The third time, he shall forfeit all his property to Our Treasury. . . . The persons who make the arrest shall have a share of the fines, and the judge who passes judgement shall have another fourth share. . . . We order that such sentences shall not be given or carried out, except before our governor of the islands and Tierra Firme, or his deputy. So that the above may come to the attention of everyone, and no one may claim ignorance, We order you, our governor, and other judges of the islands and Tierra Firme, that you shall have this Our letter and its contents made known to the public before a public notary, in the customary places of the islands and Tierra Firme. If, after this has been proclaimed, anyone acts to the contrary of this letter or anything in it, you shall take steps or see that action is taken against the persons and properties of those who may be found guilty, and fined . . . etc. Issued in Granada, September 16, 1501 = I, the King. = I, the Queen. = I, Gaspar, de Grycio, secretary of Our Lords, the King and the Queen, caused this to be written by Their order. (Signed by Doctor Zapata)." [Armas, Document 113]

HISTORIA DE LAS INDIAS
EXCERPTS FROM BOOK II

The Lady Anacaona

Book II, Chapter 9 (Collard). Francisco Roldán's supporters were then in the town and province of Xaragua where King Behechio and his sister Anacaona, a courageous woman who succeeded Behechio after his death, resided. These Spaniards took Indians whenever they could and forced them to build towns with the freedom to which Francisco Roldán had accustomed them.

Lady Anacaona and the many noble chieftains of the province, all very dignified, generous, and far more polite, virtuous people than the [Christian/SLT] people of this island, felt the presence of the Spaniards to be excessively onerous, pernicious, and altogether intolerable. As a result, they must have had some words with the Spaniards, either they refused to obey or their chiefs argued and threatened. The slightest resistance to the vilest and most wicked Spaniard, even to the one-time Castilian criminal, was enough to cause the rumor that the Indians were this and that and were in a state of uprising.

The comendador mayor [Ovando/SLT] decided to visit that province, either because he had had wind of this from his people there—an undisciplined bunch of savages unaccustomed to following orders except for their own vicious pleasures—or because he felt that that region was more out of control, it being more remote and famous for its distinguished people and rulers and especially celebrated for Lady Anacaona. He went with three hundred people on foot and seventy on horseback. . . .

When Queen Anacaona knew of the governor's visit, she, being prudent and courteous, sent for all her dignitaries and people of the villages to meet in Xaragua in order to greet and feast the "guamiquina" (the penult is long) of the Christians, which in her language means "the lord of the Christians." There came a marvelous crowd of people so well groomed it was a pleasure to see: I have already said how outstanding the people of this island were in matters of elegance. Anacaona and her people came in great numbers to receive the governor and his three hundred men, celebrating joyfully with songs and dances as they had done when greeting Christopher Columbus's brother, the Adelantado.

The comendador mayor was housed in a caney, a large building finely wrought and beautifully made of wood and straw—such as I described in my Apologetical History—while his men stayed in nearby houses with other Spaniards. Anacaona treated them like royal guests, having game brought from her forests and fish from the sea, cassava and whatever else they had, in addition to servants to tend their tables and horses, and beautiful dances, fiestas, and games.

The comendador mayor chose not to appreciate this very much. For shortly afterwards, he decided to perform what Spaniards always perform on arrival in the Indies, that is to say, when they come to a heavily settled area, being so outnumbered that they make sure all hearts tremble at the mere mention of the name Christians; therefore they terrorize the natives by performing a large-scale and cruel massacre. This lord-governor decided to follow the custom and to do something famous, although certainly not in the manner of Romans, much less of Christians, and I have no doubt that he was led to it by those Romans, the spawn of Francisco Roldán. One Sunday after dinner he ordered some of his men and horses out under the pretext of putting on a jousting show and kept the others inside and fully armed. Anacaona says that she and her chiefs wish to see the games, and this pleases the comendador very much. He asks them all to come inside, saying he wants to speak to them.

Now, the plan was for the horsemen to surround the house and wait for the signal inside: the comendador was to put a hand on a gold piece he wore around his neck and his men would then draw their swords, tie up the Indian princes—including Anacaona—and wait for further orders. *Ipse dixit et facta sunt omnia.* Queen Anacaona comes in, so noble and fine a lady, so gracious to the Christians and long suffering of their insults; some eighty of her people follow her; simply and unsuspectingly, they stand and wait for the comendador to speak. But the comendador does not speak; instead, he puts his hand on the jewel on his chest; his satellites draw their swords; Anacaona and her people tremble like leaves and think they will be cut up to pieces right then and there. They start to cry and ask why such evildoing; the Spaniards answer by hastening to tie them; Anacaona alone is let outside; armed men guard the door of the caney to keep anyone from leaving; they set fire to the house, burning alive all those kings who, together with the wood and straw, were soon turned into burning embers.

When the tying up began, the horsemen outside ran through the town and speared as many Indians as they could while those on foot ripped bellies open. Since a large crowd had come to a reception that proved so fatal for them, great were the ravages and cruelties done to men, old people and innocent children, and great was the number of people killed. It happened that if a Spaniard from pity or greed, snatched a child away to save him from slaughter by lifting him to his horse, someone would come from behind and pierce the child with a lance. Or again, if the boy was on foot, even though someone held him by the hand, another would slash his legs off with a sword. As for the Queen, they hanged her as a mark of honor. Those who escaped this inhuman slaughter fled to the small island of Guanabo, eight leagues from here, in small boats and canoes. To punish them, the Spaniards enslaved them, and I had one given me as a slave.

This was the exploit of the comendador mayor of Alcántara, Fray Nicolás de Ovando, and this was the way he repaid the chiefs and subjects of the Xaragua province for the reception and services they had given him and for the endless insults they had suffered under Francisco Roldán and his allies. The cause they made public was that the Indians wanted to rebel and kill the seventy Spanish horsemen. But this is ridiculous, considering that seventy horsemen are enough to raze a hundred islands and all the continent, provided it has no great river, swamps, or impossible mountain passes to cross. Ten horsemen could devastate it all, especially since these poor people are not armed and walk about naked and unprotected, without suspicion or thought of evil. If it were not so, why then hadn't they killed the forty or fifty Spaniards who had stayed there and wronged them continually and had no horses? In the two or three years they were there, they certainly could have done it. Yet these are the people they said would attack four hundred men, seventy of whom had horses, knowing they had come on thirty-odd ships, a thing never heard of before, and all those thirty ships full of Christians! The lamblike innocence of these people is clear, and the injustice and cruelty of those who uprooted and killed them is also clear.

To make it even clearer, consider the following: when in 1505 King Philip and Queen Juana succeeded Isabela, rumor spread that they were preparing to send a new governor to this island. Then the comendador mayor, fearing an investigation of this incident, arranged a "trial" for those chiefs he had burned without trial, defense, or prosecution, and for that great lady who had been hanged by the Christians. He arranged this "trial" months, perhaps a whole year, after the event, here in Santo Domingo, in Santiago, and in other parts of the island, and the witnesses were those very men who had done the killing, the archenemies of the Indians and the authors of those and similar crimes. See then, how rightful, how lawfully substantiated a trial this was.

They say that Queen Isabela had heard of it before her death and had been much aggrieved. People also said that Don Alvaro of Portugal, president of the royal council at that time, had threatened the comendador with these words: "We'll have an investigation about you the likes of which you've never seen." It seems that he had no other reason than the massacre to say this since, in truth, during the many years I was here under Lares's government, I never heard or knew of any complaints against him from the Spaniards.

What I have shown here will also serve to judge the truth of Oviedo's *History*. He is always condemning the Indians and excusing the Spaniards for the decimation they brought about in the Indies, for, in reality, he was one of them. Relating this particular case, he says the Spaniards found out about the Indian plot and secret uprising, for which reason the Indians were sentenced to death. I pray to God I may never take part in similar justice of sentence, but that all my efforts may be to the contrary. Oviedo also praises the comendador mayor for his goodness toward the Indians, among other things. He speaks like a blind man and his writing is padded in all sorts of ways. The "love" this gentleman felt for the Indians will be made much clearer as I unveil the truth in the course of my *History*.

Book II, Chapter 10 (Collard). After this pitiless deed, termed "punishment" in order to inspire terror in the poor Indians, the survivors and those Indians who had heard about it fled to the woods. Chief Guarocuyá (the last syllable is long), one of Queen Anacaona's nephews who had survived the slaughter, took to hiding with a handful of men on the Sierra of Baonuco, facing the sea. The Spaniards told the comendador mayor that Guarocuyá had rebelled—to flee from Spanish cruelties is still today termed refusal to pay allegiance to the King of Castile. And to make the punishment complete, the comendador ordered pursuit, and Guarocuyá was hanged. The news spread to the neighboring finger-shaped provinces of Guahaba to the north and Hany-guayaba to the west (the middle syllable is long in both cases), and the Indians, fearing for their lives, took their pathetic weapons and armed themselves in self-defense.

The comendador mayor named two captains experienced in the shedding of Indian blood, Diego Velázquez and Rodrigo Mexía Trillo [Trujillo/SLT], to head troops to Hanyguayaba and Guahaba, respectively, Guahaba being the beautiful region which Columbus had discovered. The two captains imposed the usual treatment and the usual punishment on both provinces: Velázquez even captured the Indian Chief and had him hanged as a mark of distinction; as for Mexía, I did not find out at the time the details of his exploits. But since Indians are not equipped to fight the Spaniards, it is likely that they lost and suffered. It seems that the Indians attacked first in an attempt to fend off the Spanish blades.

Oviedo says that the Indians of Hanyguayaba were savages who lived in caves, but this is not the case. Those Indians lived a well-organized communal existence suited to the amenity of the land which, being like a garden, does not lend itself to savagery. There were no caves either, nor *spelea* as he calls them to show off his knowledge of nominatives, but rather generous fields and orchards with villages and cultivated land—I often ate the natural products there. Oviedo calls Guacayarina a different province (this is not so) because the tip of the island has rocks jutting out to sea. Indians call these rocks "zagueyes," as in the province of Higuey;

they are large enough to accommodate a village, although Indians used them as such only when the calamitous Spaniards drove them into hiding. Whoever told Oviedo he had found Indians there meant it this way, unless of course Oviedo is inventing things, as he usually does to fill up pages. . . .

This is how the comendador mayor imitated the practice which Francisco Roldán had initiated, which Columbus had tolerated and Bobadilla had developed, by allowing his Spaniards free use of Indian labor for building and maintenance work, not only for the strictly necessary, but for all kinds of secondary chores as well, with which the Spaniard measured his status. They lorded it over the Indians as if they themselves had been the natural rulers of the land, treating Indians not like vassals or subjects but worse than slaves bought in the market place. The comendador mayor nailed this practice down, so to speak (and it had the worst results), without any authority whatever since the instructions he had received from the King specified that Indians were free men who should under no circumstances be forced to servitude.

Not only did he approve of the ways of the three hundred Spaniards we found here on arrival, which were tolerated because of the fact that the Indians greatly outnumbered the Spaniards. He also added his own Spaniards and more than doubled the burden of the Indians in places as far apart as Cabana de Hanyguayaba and Guahaba, making the burden excessive and intolerable. I wish to God the bad luck of the Indians had stopped there. It was a desirable lot compared with what was to come, as this History will show.

The Evils of the Encomienda

Book II, Chapter 11 (Collard). The comendador mayor [Governor Ovando/SLT] realized very early that the provision of flour and biscuits brought from Castile was being exhausted and that starvation, death, and illness were taking a tremendous toll amongst his people. According to the King's instructions, Indians were free men (he should have guessed it without that), and the King had given him no authority to force them to work (even God had not that power). Except for the province of Higuey which, as I have mentioned, was in a state of insurrection, the Indians were peacefully going about their work and caring for their women and children without offending anyone, serving their natural lords as well as those Spaniards who had taken their women as servants and "wives" (at least the women thought of themselves as married), despite the vexations and anguish they endured as a humble and patient people.

Thus, when the comendador mayor realized the difficulties arising from having brought more people than he could maintain—allowing too many people to emigrate from Spain has always been one of the principal reasons behind the devastation of the Indies, as we shall see—he wrote to the King explaining much too much for a man of his wisdom and conscience, supposing his conscience dictated his words. I will, however, give him the benefit of the doubt and believe that he was mistaken and blind, an evil from which very few Castilians escaped.

I say he wrote a letter, not because I saw it or because the King made it known, but because he was the only person here to whom the King gave credit before making any important change in policy. Anyway, the King was informed that making Indians free men was the cause of their fleeing the Christians as well as of their avoidance of conversation and communication with Christians, so that even when offered payment, they refused to work and preferred to roam idly, making it impossible to indoctrinate them in our holy Catholic Faith, etc.

Before going any further, it must be noted now that this freedom was really nominal: the Indians were never informed that the King had decreed their freedom. They were not avoiding the Spaniards more than before on account of his freedom but rather fled to avoid the infinite and implacable vexations, the furious and rigorous oppression, the ferocious and wild condition of the Spaniards which was frightening to all Indians, just as young birds flee when they see a hawk.

This, not freedom, was and always will be the reason why Indians flee from Spaniards to hide in the entrails and subterranean paths of the earth; for they were never given their freedom, even after their acquaintance with the Christians, and this is the honest-to-goodness truth, and the King's information was falsified evil and evil falseness. For this reason, they would choose to suffer any pain rather than converse with tigers [the Spaniards/SLT], rather than appear before them to receive payment for their servile labor, even if they had been persuasively invited to a feast and spoiled with a thousand gifts.

Did we show them any law that conformed to reason that they should be convinced and know themselves under an obligation to leave home, wife, and children and come fifty or a hundred leagues to work for Spaniards, even for wages? Did the Admiral and Adelantado fight a just war against them by any chance? And what of sending slave ships to Castile? And putting iron chains on the two major kings of this island, Caonabó, the king of Maguana, and Guarionex, the king of Vega Real, causing them to drown at sea? And the insults and tyranny of Francisco Roldán and his followers over a great part of this island? In view of this, I believe no wise and Christian man would dare affirm that the Indians were forced by natural or divine law to work the Spanish farms for wages.

The same falseness applies to the statement about indoctrination into the holy Catholic Faith, for, upon my oath, the truth is that in those days and many years later, there was no more concern for their Christianization than if they had been horses or working beasts. As for this being the cause of the Spaniards' inability to find labor for their plantations and gold mines, the Indians could ask why they were complaining. If they wanted plantations, let them work the fields, and if they wanted to get rich, let them dig the gold instead of being idle and lazy, which is something Indians were not, since they lived by the sweat of their brow and more than anyone else lived by God's second precept.

Thus, the Spaniards fell into the vice they imputed to the Indians and ought not to have required the Indians to dig for gold at the cost of intolerable labor and death. They deceived the King when they said Indians refused to help them in the mines, as if the Spaniards ever worked at anything but the beating of the unfortunate Indians to make them work faster and produce gold to satisfy their insatiable greed.

Supposing they had actually preached the Faith—if indeed, except for the King, this was anyone's intention—instead of decimating the Indians by cruel wars and causing them irreparable damage, then the Indians should have contributed something to maintain the Spaniards, not all but only a sufficient number of Spaniards, thus helping to alleviate the King's expenditures.

But this contribution should not have consisted in depriving them of their freedom, depriving natural lords of their domains, destroying and disrupting their order, their towns, their ways of life, and their government, delivering them into the hands of Spaniards who used them in mines and on plantations absolutely and universally whether they were men, women, children, old people, pregnant and nursing mothers, as if all were herds of cows, sheep, or other animals. Such a contribution should have been very modest, causing the least amount of anguish and danger for their persons, houses, and cities, in order to avoid decimation and make the Faith less onerous and less odious to them.

But, since the Spanish entry into this island was so violent, bloody, and destructive of so many people, so full of manifest injustice and wrongs that were never redressed, so scandalous to the Faith which was the final objective and reason for allowing Spaniards to reside in this land, Indians were never under an obligation, and would not be now if they were alive, to contribute a single maravedí.

I know for certain that no person who possesses a moderate understanding of the laws, natural, divine, and human, would doubt this but on the contrary would affirm and would subscribe to my statement. I wanted to write this here because these are the principles and foundation of Indian affairs, the ignorance of which caused the destruction of the Indies.

Queen Isabela's Warrant Concerning Christianization of the Indians

Book II, Chapter 12 (Collard). Now it is well to note what the Queen decreed after the King had been informed of the above. Oh, kings, how easily you are deceived by the appearance of good works and reason, and how much more incredulous and aware you ought to be when you deal with ministers and other people whom you entrust with the arduous negotiations of government! You believe everyone shares your simple and clear senses, unaware of a lie because you would not tell one, which is why you hear the truth least of all men; scholars have written about this, and it is also in the Scriptures toward the end of the Book of Esther.

So then, Queen Isabela was convinced of the truth of the reports and answered with a warrant saying she held the conversion of the Indians dear to her heart and thought it preferable to achieve indoctrination by making it possible to open relations between Indians and Spaniards who would help one another and work fields and mines together for the prosperity of the island, the islanders, and the Crown of Castile. She ordered the comendador mayor:

. . . from now on to compel and urge the Indians to relate to the Spaniards, as well as work for them in construction, extraction of gold and other metals, farming and the maintenance of Christmas [Christians/SLT], residents, and inhabitants of the island, and that the day's wages be established in accordance with the individual quality of the land, the person, and the work. Each cacique will be assigned a certain number of Indians whom he will take to work and, on holidays, to hear about the Faith in certain places designated for that purpose. In order to entice the cacique and his men to work as freemen and not as slaves, they must be given wages, they must be treated well (Christians should receive better treatment than non-Christians), allowing no one to harm or displease them in any way, etc.

These are the exact words of Queen Isabela's warrant, which I transcribe here from memory but will copy later from the warrant itself.

Surely, the intention clearly shows the Queen's concern for the well-being and conversion of the Indians, a concern She kept to the day of Her death, as I will show by copying the relevant clause from Her will. If She ordered measures contrary to their well-being, the blame falls on the erroneous and ignorant information She received from the members of the council, who should have known the law since they professed it and were paid in this capacity and not as gentlemen or caballeros.

Many years later I gave information to the members of the council who had signed the warrant, yet they favored a contrary opinion attending more to the law than to facts. The warrant, it seems, contained eight points relevant to the principal aim of the Queen, hence and by obligation, to the principal aim of the comendador mayor, namely the conversion and Christianization of the Indians.

1. ". . . the better to achieve the conversion to our holy Faith, Indians should communicate with Christians" is a phrase that presupposes that the Spaniards were Christians, which they were not. Had they been Christians, the Queen's judgment was good: The Saints recommend the proximity of Gentiles, infidels, and Christians so that Christian deeds may speak for the Christian law as pure, upright, mild, gentle, and holy, and consequently lead to the glorification of its founder Jesus Christ as well as to speedy conversion, as St. Matthew testifies in Chapter 5. However, since our Spaniards committed so many unjust and vicious deeds contrary to the law of Christ, it follows that this requirement was never fulfilled and is not being fulfilled, as our History will amply demonstrate, if Christ, for whose glory this is written, gives us time to finish it. So then, the most Christian Queen and the council were deceived in their belief that it was convenient for their conversion that Indians converse with Spaniards.

2. It is clear that when the Queen said caciques should be entrusted with a certain number of Indians to offer their services for wages, she meant only a number of Indians who could work, and not whole villages, nor older people, children, women, or

noblemen, and not all together but in shifts. The comendador should have understood, for it is obvious that, had She ordered the contrary, it would have been unjust and against natural law, in which case he was under obligation, in the name of that law, to disobey.

3. Indian men and their wives, houses, and ways of life were to be respected, which means: workers should work near enough their homes to permit them to return to their families in the evening, as they do in Castile, and nobody ought to be forced to go from one city to another; but if work should demand a prolonged absence, it should not exceed a period of one week from Saturday to Saturday, and this is unjust enough.

4. Hired workers ought to be seasonal, not permanent, as the Queen's words imply (you will pay a worker according to the "day's work"), and they ought to be persuaded slowly in order to promote willingness and good feelings and make the work less harsh, although the Queen does use the word "compel," which she did under the bad influence of those who testified against the Indians and called them idle vagabonds.

5. The Queen could not possibly have recommended that labor be of such a nature as to have Indians perish at it; hence labor was intended to be moderate, to be done on working days only, with Sundays and holidays off for rest.

6. Wages were meant to be commensurate with the type of work involved so that a man would be rewarded for his sweat and be able to provide for his family, thus finding compensation for the days absent from home and neglect of daily work of maintenance of his property.

7. Indians were to be treated kindly as free men and not as slaves; and by freedom it was clearly understood that hired men had the same privileges as free men in Castile, that is to say, they are free first to attend to the necessities of their houses, choose not to give their services for hire and to abandon their wives if these happen to be the bad kind, and to rest if they are tired and be cured if they are ill. Otherwise, what good is their freedom if, having these obligations, they are still forced to be hired? Even slaves are not compelled to it without the risk of committing a grave sin on the part of the compellor.

8. It must be understood that the Queen's warrant, based on false information, was pernicious and impossible to follow without the total destruction of the Indians. The comendador mayor should have seen that supplying Spaniards with gold was not meant to cost the Indians such oppression and captivity, and

he should not have tolerated it one single day, for it had not been the Queen's intention. But even if the Queen had ordered it, he should have disobeyed because it is manifest that, had the Queen known the quality of the land, the fragility and gentleness of the Indians, the harshness of the work, the difficulties of extracting gold, the bitter life of desolation which they lived dying, and finally, the impossibility of dying with the sacraments, she would never have written such a warrant.

And if She had lived long enough to know how the comendador mayor implemented Her warrant, and how it was pernicious to the Indians, She would have detested and abominated it. But, for the Indians' misfortune, She sent it on the twentieth of December, 1503, and died a few months later, leaving the Indians without protection and without the hope of human remedies.

Victimization of the Indians Under the Guise of Isabela's Warrant

Book II, Chapter 13 (Collard). That was the substance of Queen Isabela's warrant; now it is well to mention how the comendador mayor [Governor Ovando/SLT] executed the eight points it contained.

1. I have already said and I repeat: the truth is that in the nine years the comendador governed the island, no measures were taken for the conversion of Indians and no more was done about the matter nor any more thought given to it than if the Indians were sticks, stones, cats, or dogs. This applies not only to the comendador and those who owned Indians but also to the Franciscan friars who had come with him. These were good people but they lived religiously in their houses here and in La Vega and had no other aspiration. One thing they did was brought to my knowledge: they asked permission to have the sons of some caciques (few of them to be sure), perhaps four, and taught them to read and write and I suppose their good example taught Christian doctrine, for they were good and lived virtuously.

2. He disrupted villages and distributed Indians at his pleasure, giving fifty to one and a hundred to another, according to his preferences, and these numbers included children, old people, pregnant women and nursing mothers, families of high rank as well as common people. They called this system "Indian grants" (repartimientos) and the King had his grant and his manager in each town who worked his land and mined his part of the gold. The wording of the comendador's Indian grants read like this:

"Mr. X, I grant you fifty or a hundred Indians together with the person of the cacique X, so that you may use them in your lands and your mines and teach them our holy Catholic Faith." And this was the same as to condemn them all to an absolute servitude which killed them in the end, as we shall see. This then was the nature of their freedom.

3. The men were sent out to the mines as far as eighty leagues away while their wives remained to work the soil, not with hoes or plowshares drawn by oxen, but with their own sweat and sharpened poles that were far from equalling the equipment used for similar work in Castile. They had to make silolike heaps for cassava plants, by digging 12 square feet 4 palms deep and 10,000 or 12,000 of such hills—a giant's work—next to one another had to be made; and they had other tasks of the same magnitude of whatever nature the Spaniards saw as fittest to make more money. Thus husbands and wives were together only every eight or ten months and when they met they were so exhausted and depressed on both sides that they had no mind for marital communication and in this way they ceased to procreate.

As for the newly born, they died early because their mothers, overworked and famished, had no milk to nurse them, and for this reason, while I was in Cuba, 7,000 children died in three months. Some mothers even drowned their babies from sheer desperation, while others caused themselves to abort with certain herbs that produced stillborn children. In this way husbands died in the mines, wives died at work, and children died from lack of milk, while others had not time or energy for procreation, and in a short time, this land which was so great, so powerful and fertile, though so unfortunate, was depopulated. If this concatenation of events had occurred all over the world, the human race would have been wiped out in no time.

4. The comendador provided continuous work for them. If he imposed a limitation later I do not remember it, but this is certain: he gave them little rest and most of them worked ceaselessly. He allowed cruel Spanish brutes to supervise Indians: they were called "mineros" if the work was done in the mines and "estancieros" if it was done on plantations. They treated the Indians with such rigor and inhumanity that they seemed the very ministers of Hell, driving them day and night with beatings, kicks, lashes, and blows, and calling them no sweeter name than dogs. The Spaniards then created a special police to hunt them back because mistreatment and intolerable labor led to nothing but death, and the Indians, seeing their companions die, began escaping into the

woods. In towns and Spanish villages, the comendador appointed the most honorable caballero as inspector, with a salary of 100 Indians to serve him in addition to his normal Indian grant.

These were ordinary victimizers who were that much more cruel as they were honorable. Escapees were brought before the visitador and the accuser, that is, the supposedly pious master, who accused them of being rebellious dogs and good-for-nothings and demanded stiff punishment. The visitador then had them tied to a post and he himself, with his own hands, as the most honorable man in town, took a sailor's tarred whip as tough as iron, the kind they use in galleys, and flogged them until blood ran from their naked bodies, mere skin and bones from starvation. Then, leaving them for dead, he stopped and threatened the same punishment if they tried it again. Our own eyes have seen such inhuman conduct several times, and God is witness that whatever is said of it falls short of reality.

5. "Moderate labor" turned into labor fit only for iron men: mountains are stripped from top to bottom and bottom to top a thousand times; they dig, split rocks, move stones, and carry dirt on their backs to wash it in rivers, while those who wash gold stay in the water all the time with their backs bent so constantly it breaks them; and then water invades the mines, the most arduous task of all is to dry the mines by scooping up panfuls of water and throwing it up outside.

Finally, to have an idea of what mining gold and silver requires, consider that it was next to capital punishment among the pagans when martyrs were condemned to mine metals. The Egyptian kings used to send to the gold mines only criminals, prisoners of war, and dangerous rebels who had incurred the King's wrath, and the work was such that they were chained to prevent escape; the mines were full of workers who were driven day and night without respite, flogged and whipped, as Diodorus says in Book IV, Chapter 2. He also says they were supervised by executioners like our mineros, and mentions examples that are closer to us, that is, the very people of Spain: after the Romans had defeated Spain, they bought a great number of slaves to send to the mines (in all likelihood, many, if not all, were Spaniards), and they were an incredible source of wealth, although at the cost of anguish and calamities suffered from excessive work and only the strongest could survive the labor and the blows; otherwise death was a more desirable state, as Diodorus says.

It seems, then, that by its nature, gold is the cause of death; consequently, it is proven that the calamities I have described are not at all impossible. Would to God they were not necessary, for in truth they occur wherever the Spaniards send Indians to the mines.

Book II, Chapter 14 (Collard). At first, the Indians were forced to stay six months away at work; later, the time was extended to eight months, and this was called "a shift," at the end of which they brought all the gold for minting. The King's part was subtracted, and the rest went to individuals, but for years no one kept a single peso because they owed it all to merchants and other creditors, so that the anguish and torments endured by the Indians in mining that infernal gold was consumed entirely by God and no one prospered. During the minting period, the Indians were allowed to go home, a few days' journey on foot.

One can imagine their state when they arrived after eight months, and those who found their wives there must have cried, lamenting their condition together. How could they even rest, since they had to provide for the needs of their family when their land had gone to weeds? Of those who had worked in the mines, a bare ten percent survived to start the journey home. Many Spaniards had no scruples about making them work on Sundays and holidays, if not in the mines then on minor tasks such as building and repairing houses, carrying firewood, etc. They fed them cassava bread, which is adequate nutrition only when supplemented with meat, fish, or other more substantial food. The minero killed a pig once a week but he kept more than half for himself and had the leftover apportioned and cooked daily for thirty or forty Indians, which came to a bite of meat the size of a walnut per individual, and they dipped the cassava in this as well as in the broth. It is absolutely true that while the minero was eating the Indians were under the table, just like dogs and cats, ready to snatch a bone, suck it first, then grind it and eat it with cassava. This ration applied only to mine workers, others never tasted meat in their lives and sustained themselves exclusively on cassava and other roots.

In Cuba (I mentioned this here in case I forget it when I come to the subject of Cuba) it happened that certain Spaniards provided no food at all but instead sent their Indians every two or three days to the fields to feed on fruit that was to last for another two or three days of constant work. Once, a farmer harvested a crop worth some six hundred gold pesos, and he told that story in my presence and boasted of it.

6. The comendador arranged to have wages paid as follows, which I swear is the truth: in exchange for his life of services, an

Indian received three maravedís every two days, less one-half a maravedí in order not to exceed the yearly half gold peso, that is, two hundred and twenty-five maravedís, paid them once a year as pin money or "cacona," as Indians call it, which means bonus or reward. This sum bought a comb, a small mirror, and a string of green or blue glass beads, and many did without that consolation for they were paid much less and had no way of mitigating their misery, although in truth, they offered their labor up for nothing, caring only to fill their stomachs to appease their raging hunger and find ways to escape from their desperate lives. For this loss of body and soul, then, they received less than three maravedís for two days; many years later their wages were increased to one gold peso by the order of King Hernando, and this was no less an affront, as I will show later.

7. I believe the above clearly demonstrates that the Indians were totally deprived of their freedom and were put in the harshest, fiercest, most horrible servitude and captivity which no one who has not seen it can understand. Even beasts enjoy more freedom when they are allowed to graze in the fields. But our Spaniards gave no such opportunity to Indians and truly considered them perpetual slaves, since the Indians had not the free will to dispose of their persons but instead were disposed of according to Spanish greed and cruelty, not as men in captivity but as beasts tied to a rope to prevent free movement.

When they were allowed to go home, they often found it deserted and had no other recourse than to go out into the woods to find food and to die. When they fell ill, which was very frequently because they are a delicate people unaccustomed to such work, the Spaniards did not believe them and pitilessly called them lazy dogs, and kicked and beat them; and when illness was apparent they sent them home as useless, giving them some cassava for the twenty- to eighty-league journey. They would go then, falling into the first stream and dying there in desperation; others would hold on longer, but very few ever made it home. I sometimes came upon dead bodies on my way, and upon others who were gasping and moaning in their death agony, repeating "Hungry, hungry." And this was the freedom, and good treatment, and the Christianity that Indians received under the comendador's execution of this point of the warrant.

8. This order was difficult or impossible and not designed to bring Indians to the Faith; indeed, it was pernicious and deadly and designed to destroy all Indians. Obviously, the Queen had not intended the destruction but the edification of the Indians, and the

comendador would have done well to consider this, as well as the fact that, had the Queen been alive to see the results of Her order, She would have revoked and abominated it. It is amazing how this prudent man did not realize what a deadly pestilence his order was when, at the end of each shift, he found out how many Indians were missing and how the rest suffered. And it is amazing that he did not change or revoke it, for it was impossible that he should have remained unaware of its iniquity; and, consequently, he was not excused before God or before the King. Before God, because it is in itself evil and contrary to divine and natural law to enslave free, rational beings so harshly, especially when he could see from experience that his order was the cause of it; before the King, because he completely went against what had been told him.

To remedy the loss of lives that were being consumed in mines and plantations at the end of each shift, the Spaniards asked the comendador to replace the Indians of the island and the comendador granted their request, favoring the principal and most privileged Spaniards, leaving the others unsatisfied and making new distributions every two or three years. As I said, the Queen died shortly after sending her warrant and therefore never found out about this cruel decimation. Philip and Juana succeeded Her, but Philip died before he could appraise the situation in the Indies, and Castile was two years without the presence of a King. Thus, the decimation of these poor Indians had begun and could be kept silent, and when King Hernando came to rule Castile, they kept it from Him too.

Depopulation of the Indies Under Ovando

About eight years passed under the comendador's rule, and this disorder had time to grow; no one gave it a thought, and the multitude of people who originally lived on this island, which according to the Admiral, was infinite, as we said in Book I, was consumed at such a rate that in those eight years, ninety percent had perished. From here this sweeping plague went to San Juan, Jamaica, Cuba, and the continent, spreading destruction over the whole hemisphere, as we shall see.

Thus, from the disorder that this comendador mayor, Knight of Alcantara, established on the island by distributing Indians among Spaniards, in the way we have described, there followed, through diabolical delusion and craft, the violent and raging perdition which was to sterilize and consume the greater part of mankind in these Indies.

Book II, Chapter 42 (Collard). Miguel de Pasamonte . . . arrived here in November of 1508 with such honor that he was called officially treasurer general of all the Indies, in charge of all the treasurers on the mainland and other islands; I do not know whether this was by express order of the King or the King's secretaries. He was such a person that, contrary to the Castilian practice, his office was higher than that of the auditor. The King trusted him to the degree of acting upon his recommendations in all matters concerning the Indies.

When this treasurer arrived in 1508, there were 60,000 people living on this island [Española/SLT], including the Indians; so that from 1494 . . . to 1508, over three million people had perished from war, slavery, and the mines. Who in future generations will believe this? I myself writing it as a knowledgeable eyewitness can hardly believe it, but it is a fact born of our sins, and it will be well that in time to come we lament it.

Antonio de Herrera, "Historiographer to His Catholick Majesty," has a somewhat different view of Ovando's tenure as governor of Española:

"The Government of Nicholas de Ovando was prudent enough in relation to the improving of the King's Revenue, and generally agreeable also to the Spaniards, because he allow'd them too much liberty; but at the same time he encourag'd the Clergy to instruct the Indians, and was helpful to the Franciscan Friers in building of their Monastery at Santo Domingo. Their Majesties had, as was hinted before, given strict Orders about the Instructing of the Natives, and preserving them in full Liberty, to which Purpose, all the necessary Instructions were sent from Spain, which would be too tedious to be here inserted. The Commerce of the Indies daily increasing, and very many offering to go upon new Discoveries, and to trade, their Majesties for the better Dispatch of these Affairs, commanded an India House to be establish'd in the old Palace at Sevil, with all proper Officers, where all the Goods brought over should be lodg'd. Very many resorting for Licences to go trade and discover, after duely considering whether it would be proper for their Highnesses to keep that Affair in their own Hands, it was resolv'd, to grant Leave to all Persons that were desirous to venture upon such Enterprizes, upon such Terms as should be thought equitable, they giving sufficient Security for Performance of the same."[2]

And thus the "raging perdition" resulting from the distribution of Indians to Spaniards was allowed to spread to the remainder of the Indies, as Fray Bartolomé indicates above, and not even the innocent and beautiful people discovered in the Bahamas were allowed to escape.

HISTORIA DE LAS INDIAS, BOOK II, CHAPTERS 43 AND 44

Destruction of the Lucayo or Bahaman Indians

Book II, Chapter 43 (Collard). When the Spaniards saw how fast they were killing Indians in the mines, plantations, and other endeavors, caring only to squeeze the last effort out of them, it occurred to them to replenish the supply by importing people from other islands, and they deceived King Hernando [Ferdinand/SLT] with a crafty argument. They notified him either by letter or by a special court representative, presumably with the comendador's consent, that Lucayo or Yucayo Islands close to Cuba and Española were full of an idle people who had learned nothing and could not be Christianized there. Therefore, they asked permission to send two ships to bring them to Española where they could be converted and would work in the mines, thus being of service to the King.

The King agreed, on the blind and culpable recommendation of the council, acting as if rational beings were timber cut from trees and used for buildings or a herd of sheep or any other animals and nothing much would be lost if they died at sea. Who would not blame an error so great: natives taken by force to new lands one hundred and fifty leagues away, however good or evil the reason may have been, much less to dig gold in mines where they would surely die, for a King and foreigners they had never offended? Perhaps they sought justification by deceiving the King with a falsehood, that is, that the Lucayo Indians would be instructed in the Faith: which, even if it were true was not right—and it wasn't true, for they never intended anything of the kind nor did anything in that direction. God did not want Christianity at that cost; God takes no pleasure in a good deed, no matter its magnitude, if sin against one's fellow man is the price of it, no matter how minuscule that sin may be; and this is a fact all sinners, especially in the Indies, deceive themselves into ignoring.

In total condemnation of this lie, let it be remembered that the Apostles never expatriated anyone by force in order to convert them elsewhere, nor had the universal church ever used this method, considered pernicious and detestable. Therefore, the

King's Council was very blind and, consequently, because its members are scholars, it is guilty before God, since ignorance cannot be adduced.

The King's permission arrived, and ten or twelve residents from Concepción and Santiago gathered 10,000 or 12,000 gold pesos, bought two or three ships and fifty to sixty salaried men, and raided the Indians who lived in the Lucayos in peace and security. Those are the Lucayo Indians I spoke of at length in Book I and in my Apologetical History, so blessed among all Indians in gentleness, simplicity, humility, and other natural virtues, it seems Adam's sin left them untouched. . . .

They say that the first harvesters of Lucayo Indians, fully aware of their simplicity and gentle manners (they knew this from the report of Christopher Columbus), anchored their ships and were received as they always are before our deeds prove the contrary, that is, as angels from Heaven. The Spaniards said they came from Española, where the souls of their beloved ones were resting in joy, and that their ships would take them there if they wanted to see them, for it is a fact that all Indian nations believe in the immortality of the soul. After death, the body joins the soul in certain delightful places of pleasure and comfort; some nations even believe that the souls of sinners first undergo torment. So then, with those wicked arguments, the Spaniards deceived the Indians into climbing on board ship, and men and women left their homes with their scant belongings.

On Española, they found neither father, mother, nor loved ones but iron tools and instruments and gold mines instead, where they perished in no time; some, from despair at seeing themselves deceived, took poison; others died of starvation and hard labor, for they are a delicate people who had never imagined such type of work even existed. Later, the Spaniards used every possible wile and force to trick them into ships.

At the landing sites, usually Puerto de Plata and Puerto Real on the north shore facing the Lucayos, men, women, children and old people were thrown helterskelter into lots; the old with the young, the sick with the healthy—they often fell ill in the ships, and many died of anguish, thirst, and hunger in the hottest and stuffiest holds—without any concern for keeping man and wife, father and son together, handled like the basest animals. Thus the innocent, *sicut pecora occisionis*, were divided into groups and those who had contributed their share in the raiding expedition drew lots. When someone drew an old or sick one he protested,

"Give that old man to the devil, why should I take him? To feed and bury him? And why give me that sick dog? To cure him?"

Sometimes, it happened that Indians died on the spot either from hunger, debilitation, sickness, or the pain of a father seeing his son, or a husband seeing his wife bought and taken away. How could anyone with a human heart and human entrails witness such inhuman cruelty? Where was the principle of charity, "Thou shalt love thy neighbor as thyself," in the minds of those who, forgetting that they were Christians or human beings, performed such "humanity" upon human beings? Finally, to cover the cost and pay the salaried men, they agreed to allow the sale of allotted Indians at not more than four gold pesos per piece—they referred to them as "pieces" as if they were heads of cattle. And they thought selling and transferring so cheaply was an honorable thing to do, while in truth, had the price been higher, the Indians would have received better treatment as valuable items and would have lasted longer.

Book II, Chapter 44 (Collard). As I said, the Spaniards used many ways to draw the Lucayos from their homeland where they lived as in the Golden Age, a life of which poets and historians have sung such praise. Sometimes, especially at first, they won their trust because the Indians did not suspect them, and living off guard, received them like angels. Sometimes they raided by night and other times in the open, *aperto Marte* as they say, knifing those who, having more experience of Spaniards, defended themselves with bow and arrow, a weapon [the Lucayans/SLT] ordinarily used for fishing and not for war. They brought more than 40,000 people here in a period of four or five years, men and women, children and adults, as Pedro Martyr mentions in Chapter I of the seventh *Década*. . . .

He also mentions the fact that some killed themselves from despair, while others, who were stronger, hoped to escape and return to their land and thus endured their hopeless lives, hiding in the northern mountains closer to home and hoping to find a way to cross over. Once—and Pedro Martyr records this in the same chapter—one of these Indians built a raft from a very large tree trunk called "yauruma" in the vernacular (the penultimate syllable is long), which is a light and hollow wood, tied logs to it with "liana," which is a type of extremely strong ropelike root, placed some corn from his harvest in the hollow of the logs, and filled gourds with fresh water; then, closing both ends with leaves, he took off with another Indian and a few women of his family, all great swimmers like all the Lucayos. Fifty leagues from the coast, they unfortunately met a ship coming full speed from their place of destination; they were captured and returned to Española in tears and lamentations and perished there like the rest.

We do not know but it is believable that others made the same attempt, and if so, it was to no avail, since the Spaniards were continually raiding those islands until not one single Indian remained. They chose the rockiest and most inaccessible island to corral all the Indians taken from the neighboring islands, and there they left them in charge of a Spanish guard, after breaking their canoes to prevent escape until the ship returned for another load.

Once they had 7,000 Indians and seven Spaniards guarding them like shepherds and, the ships being delayed, they ran out of cassava, which is all the food they ever gave Indians. As two ships laden with provisions neared the coast, a terrible gale storm sank them all and the islanders died of starvation; I do not remember what I heard about the fate of those shipwrecked. Nobody thought to attribute these disasters to divine punishment for sins committed here, rather, they attributed them to chance, as if there were no Rector in Heaven to see and register such cruel injustice.

Epilogue Concerning the Spaniard and the Indian World

Thus we come full circle, and the peaceful and beautiful people of the Bahamas that Columbus described, in the days of his innocence and their happiness, were also taken into the slavery that resulted from their assignment to Spaniards in encomienda.

We return again to Dr. Toynbee's request, in my Introduction, that we "think of life in another world which was suddenly and abruptly and disastrously discovered by the pre-Columbian inhabitants of the Americas when the Old World burst upon them. Think of the disastrous effect on their life of that impact, how they were conquered, massacred, raided, robbed—their whole life was broken up."

Christopher Columbus has done us a great service by making it possible for us to see the indigenous Arawaks of the Bahamas and the Greater Antilles through his eyes, as recorded in his *Journal from Aboard Ship* at the time of discovery. The historical significance of the writings of Fray Bartolomé de las Casas arises from his continuing critical discourse against the evils that resulted from the establishment of Spanish institutions in the Indies which formed the foundation for the methods used in the conquest and the encomienda. Thus his *History* is an important key to understanding the growth of Spanish communities among the Indian peoples in the Americas.

When Las Casas wrote about the years of the Columbus viceroyalty, he used as his major sources the writings and papers of the Admiral or persons associated with his faction. Fray Bartolomé could not hide the evidences of despotism and cruelty on the part of Spaniards in his *History*. He freely confesses that, during his early years, he himself was an unresponsive witness to the injustices that surrounded him.

When the Sovereigns sent new administrators to replace Columbus, his "trading-house" approach to the acquisition of the wealth of the Indies came to an end, and the three thousand persons, including Las Casas, who came with Fray Nicolás de Ovando in 1502, represented much more than additional men and supplies, for the Crown had asked that they "newly settle" Española.

241

When Governor Ovando reported that the Indians would not associate with the Spaniards by choice, the Sovereigns responded, in March, 1503, with orders that the natives should be reduced to large settlements, where it would be possible to instruct them in the faith and familiarize them with the social practices in which the Spaniards engaged.

Ovando's suggestion that Spaniards needed the labor of the Indians and would compensate them through the payment of salaries was approved by the Sovereigns, who did not know the evils that would be perpetrated as a result. Thus the royal order of Medina del Campo, dated December 20, 1503, while recognizing that the Indians were free, at the same time allowed Spaniards to *compel* Indians to work as long as they were paid for their labor.

Thus did the system of the encomienda gradually come into being. The precedents set in Española during those early years would be followed, and enlarged upon, as Spaniards spread into the two Americas. Paradoxically, the succeeding Sovereigns continued to champion the "freedom" of the Indians, while their administrators in the Indies continued to abridge it. These administrators supervised the use made of native inhabitants by the *encomenderos*, the Spaniards who received the grants of Indians in encomienda. However moderate or well intentioned the decrees and warrants of the Sovereigns appeared to be in themselves, the burden of the Spanish law visited upon the individual Indians was of a very different character. Accordingly, as Fray Bartolomé repeatedly charged, the *actual* result of assigning Indians to Spaniards in encomienda was frequently virtual slavery, and it was experienced at its worst during the years 1492–1509 in the islands of the Caribbean.

Appendix

Concerning Good Treatment
of the Indians*

Law 1: That the provisions in the clause of the testament of the Catholic Queen [1504] concerning instruction and good treatment of the Indians be observed.

> The Catholic Queen, Doña Isabel, and the
> Governing Queen in this Recopilación.

In the testament of the Most Serene and Great Catholic Queen Doña Isabel of glorious memory, the following clause is noted: "When the Holy Apostolic See granted to Us the Islands and Continent of the Ocean Sea, that were discovered or to be discovered, Our principal intention, at the time when We petitioned the well-remembered Pope Alexander the Sixth who granted this concession to Us, was to try to persuade and attract their towns and convert them to Our Holy Catholic Faith, and to send Prelates, Priests, Clerics, and other learned and God-fearing persons to those islands and continent in order to instruct their residents and inhabitants in the Catholic Faith, to give them religious instruction, to teach them good customs, and to give all necessary attention to these things, as they are amply dealt with in the letters of the concession. I very affectionately entreat the King My Lord, and I charge and command my daughter, the Princess, and her husband, the Prince: that they shall act on these intentions and fulfill them; that this shall be their principal objective; and that they shall not allow, nor give occasion, for the Indian residents and inhabitants of those Islands and Continent, occupied or to be occupied, to receive any harm to their persons and properties. They shall, moreover, command that the inhabitants be well and justly treated, and if the inhabitants have received any harm, they shall provide remedy, and make provision for it in such a way that there

*This appendix is reprinted from S. Lyman Tyler, ed. and comp., *The Indian Cause in the Spanish Laws of the Indies* (Salt Lake City: American West Center, University of Utah, 1980), pp. 247–248.

may be no transgression with regard to anything that is forbidden or commanded in the Apostolic letters of the said concession." And We, in keeping with her Catholic and pious zeal, order and command the Viceroys, Presidents, Audiencias, Governors, and Royal Justicias, and We charge the Archbishops, Bishops, and Ecclesiastical Prelates, that they shall observe that which is provided by the laws with respect to conversion of the natives, their Christian and Catholic doctrine and instruction, and their good treatment.

Notes

INTRODUCTION

1. See *The Life of the Admiral Christopher Columbus by His Son Ferdinand*, trans. and annotated by Benjamin Keen (New Brunswick, N.J.: Rutgers University Press, 1959).
2. Martín Fernández de Navarrete, *Colección de las viajes y descubrimientos que hicieron por mar los españoles desde fines del siglo XV, con varios documentos inéditos concernientes a la marina castellana y a los establicimientos españoles en Indias*, 5 vols. (Madrid, 1825–1837).
3. Samuel Kettell, *Personal narrative of the First Voyage of Columbus to America* (Boston, 1827); Samuel Eliot Morison, ed., *Journals and other Documents on the Life and Voyages of Christopher Columbus* (New York, 1963); *The Journal of Christopher Columbus*, trans. Cecil Jane [1930], revised and annotated by L.A. Vigneras, with an appendix by R. A. Skelton (London: Hakluyt Society, 1960); *Diario de Colón* 2 vol., ed. Carlos Sanz (Madrid: Bibliotheca Americana Vetustissima, 1962).
4. Morison, *Journals*, p. 43.
5. See n. 1.

1. TWO WORLDS

1. *Life in Other Worlds*, on the occasion (March 1, 1961) of the tenth anniversary of the Samual Bronfman Foundation (New York: Joseph E. Seagram & Sons, 1961).
2. S. Lyman Tyler, ed., *Concerning the Indians Lately Discovered: The Indian Cause before the Law of Nations: Colonial Period*, Occasional Paper No. 15 (Salt Lake City, Utah: American West Center, University of Utah, 1980), p. 34.
3. In our early translations from Fray Bartolomé de las Casas, *Historia de las Indias*, we used as our text the *Edición de Agustín Millares Carlo y estudio preliminar de Lewis Hanke*, 3 vols. (Mexico City: Fondo de Cultura Economica, 1951). In some cases we have used Bartolomé de las Casas, *History of the Indies*, trans. in part and ed. Andrée Collard (New York: Harper Torchbooks, 1971). In my text, book number and chapter number from the *History*, with no name following, it is our translation. The name "Collard" appears in parentheses when the text uses Collard's translation with minor emendations. Collard also used the Millares Carlo edition (Mexico City, 1951). When we use another edition of Fray Bartolomé's *History*, we will so indicate.
4. See, for example, Juan Friede and Benjamin Keen, eds., *Bartolomé de las Casas in History: Toward an Understanding of the Man and His Work* (De Kalb, Ill., 1971).

5. Fray Bartolomé, *History*, ed. Juan Pérez de Tudela Bueso (Madrid: 1957–1961) 1:xxxix–xlvi.

6. Fray Bartolomé, *History*, 1:liv.

7. Bartolomé de las Casas, *Apologética Historia Sumaria* ed. Edmundo O'Gorman, 2 vols. (Mexico City, 1967).

8. Fray Bartolomé, *History*, 1:x.

9. Fray Bartolomé, *History*, 1:xxxixff.

10. For discussions of Fray Bartolomé's disputes with Gonzalo Fernández de Oviedo and Juan Ginés de Sepulveda, see entries under their names in indexes to Friede and Keen, *Las Casas in History* (1971), and Lewis Hanke, *All Mankind Is One* (DeKalb, Ill., 1974), along with the bibliographies in both of these works. Also see *In Defense of the Indians: The Defense of the Most Reverend Lord, Don Fray Bartolomé de las Casas, of the Order of Preachers, Late Bishop of Chiapa, Against the Persecutors and Slanderers of the Peoples of the New World Discovered Across the Seas,* trans. Stafford Poole, C.M. (Dekalb, Ill., 1974). Since the last-named work lacks an index and bibliography and depends on Hanke, above, for an introduction and analysis, it is necessary to use the contents for the sixty-three chapters to determine what is being discussed. Indexes and contents in the above-mentioned publications are also helpful with respect to topics such as *encomendero*, Indian problem, Indians, Just War, slavery, etc.

11. Samuel Eliot Morison, *Admiral of the Ocean Sea: A Life of Christopher Columbus*, 2 vols. (Boston, 1942). This work, along with Morison, *Journals* (1963), remains necessary for any study of the meeting of Indians and Spaniards. The one-volume 1942 edition is a condensation of the two-volume work without notes. Hereafter I will cite the two-volume work as Morison, *Admiral* (1942), with appropriate volume and page numbers.

12. Morison, *Journals* (1963), pp. 26–29.

13. Ibid., pp. 29–30.

2. THE EUROPEAN INVASION OF THE INDIAN WORLD: COLUMBUS'S OWN ACCOUNT

1. The reference is to the Admiral's flagship, the *Santa María*. When the *Pinta, Niña,* and *Santa María* are mentioned collectively, they are correctly called vessels. The *Niña* and *Pinta* were caravels, a particular type of vessel lacking the size, superstructure, and rigging required before they could be designated a ship. The phrase "the ship" thus indicates the *Santa María*.

2. By dividing 22½ into 90, we see that, in estimating distances at sea, a league is equivalent to 4 miles. We will observe later that distances estimated on land do not compute in the same way that they do at sea.

3. Morison uses "kinky" in place of "curly," probably thinking that Columbus was comparing the natives with the indigenous Africans.

4. Keen, *Ferdinand's Life of Columbus* (1959): "They had handsome features, spoiled somewhat by their unpleasantly broad foreheads. They were of middle stature, well formed and sturdy, with olive-colored skins that gave them the appearance of Canary Islanders or sunburned peasants" (chap. 24, p. 60).

5. Keen, *Ferdinand's Life of Columbus* (1959), speaks of the people of Guanahaní, who were "astounded and marveling at the sight of the ships, which they took for animals" (chap. 23, p. 59). Their fear of these vessels, if they felt any, apparently soon subsided.

6. The two types of boats that were carried on board the vessels were the *barca*, a launch or barge, the larger of the two, and the *batel*, the smaller of the two.

7. The phrase in Spanish is "venid a ver los bombres que vinieron del cielo," "the men who came from the sky or from heaven." Since the native people did not understand the Christian concept of heaven, and since the two groups did not understand each other's language for some time anyway, I agree with Morison that the translation should be "sky," although Columbus, charmed by his first meetings with the native islanders, may have chosen to believe that they thought he and his crew came from heaven. I recall that some Polynesians saw their first sailing ships as great birds; if so, the men in them might well have been considered to have come from the sky.

8. Arawak islanders were generally peaceful, compared with the Caribs, who were aggressive and relatively more warlike.

9. Las Casas, *History*, Book I, chapter 42, says that these are not chimneys to let out smoke but cornices on the thatch roofs. An opening was left in the roof to let out smoke.

10. Las Casas, *History*, Book I, chapter 42, explains that the large dogs are not mastiffs but are like the hounds they have in Spain except that these and the small dogs do not bark.

11. Morrison suggests that, in the text which he used, *gueste* should have been *sueste*; in the Sanz text it is *oueste*, or "west."

12. Columbus writes continually about the beauty of these islands. Some readers will be interested in Samuel Eliot Morison and Mauricio Obregón, *The Caribbean as Columbus Saw It* (Boston, 1964). The book is generously illustrated with black-and-white photographs. The text tells us how a particular view may have looked to Columbus in 1492 and refers to the photographs and to other illustrations.

13. Fray Bartolomé, *History* says: "The Indians of the island Española call it an Iguana" (Book I, chap. 43). He compares it in appearance and behavior to a crocodile. Gonzalo Fernández de Oviedo, *Natural History of the West Indies*, which first appeared in Toledo in 1526 (trans. Sterling A. Stoudemire [Chapel Hill: University of North Carolina Press, 1959]) says: "The animal has four feet, long paws, well developed claws as long as those of a bird, but weak and useless in capturing prey. The animal is better to eat than to see" (p. 18).

14. Columbus's comments about Asian places reflect his reading of the travels of Marco Polo.

15. *Marcantes*, translated by Morison as "sailors." See *Marchante*, in Academy Dictionary, for references to *Mercante*, "merchant," and *mercantil*, or "mercantile."

16. It is unclear whether the ship's boat is being carried on the poop deck or is being towed astern.

3. THE DISCOVERY OF CUBA, CALLED JUANA OR CIPANGO

1. Carl Ortwin Sauer, *The Early Spanish Main* (Berkeley: 1966), p. 69.

2. Morison, *Journals* (1963), p. 183.

3. Irving Rouse, "The Arawak," in *Handbook of South American Indians,* ed. Julian H. Steward (New York, 1963), 4:530.

4. Morison, *Admiral* (1942), 1:306.

5. See also Robert K. Heimann, *Tobacco and Americans* (New York, 1960), especially the first chapter, titled "Certain Dried Leaves," pp. 6–21, with its illustrated discussion of early observations by Europeans of the Indians' use of tobacco. The second chapter, "Spanish Gold," continues the chronological presentation.

6. It is well known how the Spaniards treated the Jews and Moslems, and the Sovereigns had decreed that all ships bearing Jews should leave Spanish ports by August 2, 1492, the day before Columbus departed from Palos, with his three vessels.

7. Morison, *Journals* (1963), p. 93, n. 2, suggests that Babeque is probably Great Inagua Island. Fray Bartolomé (*History*, Book I, chap. 47) says that the island or land called Babeque or Bohío is believed to be the island Española.

8. Rouse, "The Arawak," pp. 542–43.

4. ESPAÑOLA AND GUACANAGARI

1. Sauer, *Early Spanish Main* (1966), p. 53, suggests that the Admiral sometimes confused the yam or sweet potato with the casssava, which we know as manioc, the island's most important staple.

2. Sanz, *Diario* (1962), in the entry for this date, reads *pan de ajes y gonza avellanada y de cinco o seis maneras frutas.* Three different translators have rendered *gonza avellanada* as "nutty colored, or nutty tasting, quince or chufa, and shriveled." Both Morison and Vigneras in their notes carefully explain their choice of "quince" and "chufa," respectively. I am still not certain about this.

3. Fray Bartolomé, *History* (Tudela edition, Madrid, 1957–61).

5. INTERLUDE

1. Keen, *Ferdinand's Life of Columbus* (1959), chap. 62, pp. 150–169 ("The Relation of Fray Ramón Pane").
2. Silvio Zavala, *New Viewpoints of the Spanish Colonization of America* (Philadelphia, 1943), pp. 6–7.
3. For a discussion of the rights of Indians in relation to Europeans, see "The European Legal Theorists Vitoria, Grotius, Vattel and the Indians of the Americas," in Tyler, *Concerning the Indians Lately Discovered*, pp. 11–29.
4. Frances G. Davenport, editor, *European Treaties bearing on the History of the United States and its Dependencies to 1648*, Doc. 7, "The Bull Inter Caetera (Alexander VI), May 4, 1493" (Washington, D.C., 1917), pp. 77–78.
5. Fray Bartolomé, *History* (Tudela edition, Madrid, 1957–61).
6. Morison, *Admiral* (1942), 2:206–207.
7. Morison, *Journals* (1963), pp. 209–212.
8. Troy S. Floyd, *The Columbus Dynasty in the Caribbean, 1492–1526* (Albuquerque, 1973), p. 23.

6. HOME FROM THE SEA, THEN BACK TO ESPAÑOLA

1. Concerning the Collard material, see Chapter 1, n. 3.
2. For another account of what was found and what happened at Navidad, see Keen, *Ferdinand's Life of Columbus* (1959), chaps. 49 and 50, pp. 117–121.

7. DISCOVERY OF CIBAO, SOUTH CUBA, AND JAMAICA

1. For a map of "Isabela and Cibao," and the route followed to them, see Keen, *Ferdinand's Life of Columbus* (1959), chap. 42, p. 125.
2. I observed earlier that there was a difference between the sea league and the land league as used by Columbus in his estimated distances. Morison, *Admiral* (1492), 1:26–262, n. 28, suggests that four Roman miles were equivalent to the sea league and three Roman miles to the land league.
3. Sauer, *Early Spanish Main* (1966), chapter 4, "Española under Columbus." Sauer, a geographer, includes maps showing particular regions of the island in detail and locating places mentioned in Fray Bartolomé's *History*.
4. Morison, *Admiral* (1942), 2:124–125, and n. 13, p. 127, says that a dog was let loose against the Indians here. Juan Fonseca, who represented the Crown in equipping the fleet for the second voyage, sent along "a pack of twenty purebread mastiffs and greyhounds. These dogs, and the others that followed, were to lay a bloody trail across the islands

and mainland of the new found world." (John Grier Varner and Jeannette Johnson Varner, *Dogs of the Conquest* [Norman, Okla., 1983], pp. 4–5). This is said to have been "the first occasion on which dogs were used against the nations of the New World and predates their formal use in pitched battle on the Vega Real" (ibid.).

8. THE SUBJUGATION OF ESPAÑOLA: A BITTER HARVEST

1. Varner and Varner, *Dogs of the Conquest* (1983), pp. 5–11, gives further information concerning the use made of these dogs on this occasion.
2. Sauer, *Early Spanish Main* (1966), pp. 85, 86, and n. 20.
3. Antonio Rumeo de Armas, *La politica indigenista de Isabel la Católica* (Valladolid, 1969). I refer to section of numbered documents that begins on p. 151.
4. Armas, *La politica indigenista de Isabel la Católica*, chap. 13, pp. 10–11.
5. Ibid., p. 12.

9. THE INDIANS DURING THE FINAL YEARS UNDER CHRISTOPHER COLUMBUS, 1495–1500

1. Antonio de Herrera y Tordesillas, *General History of the vast Continent and Islands of America, Commonly Call'd the West-Indies, etc., to 1531*, first published in Madrid, 1720, translated into English by John Stevens and published in 6 volumes (London, 1740). I am using the AMS reprint (New York, 1973).
2. Armas, *Politica Indigenista de Isabel la Católica* (1969), chap. 14, pp. 137–138.

10. GOVERNOR NICOLÁS DE OVANDO AND THE INDIANS, 1501–1509

1. The Spanish reaction to this action at Saona, and later in the province of Higuey, is also reported in Varner and Varner, *Dogs of the Conquest* (1983), pp. 16 and 17–19.
2. Herrera, *General History* (1740), 1:279.

Index

251